House of MYSTERY

SAFE AS HOUSES

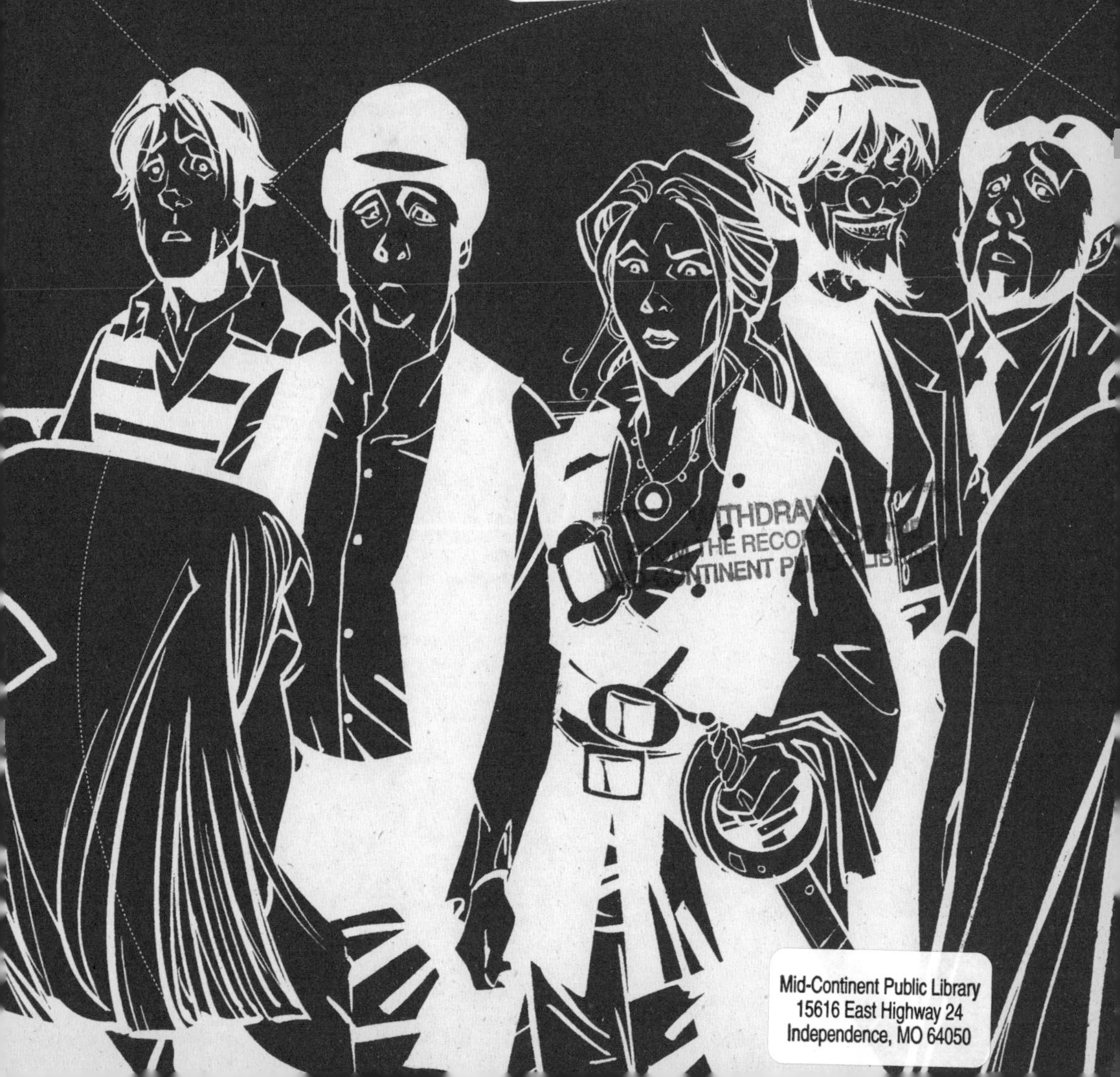

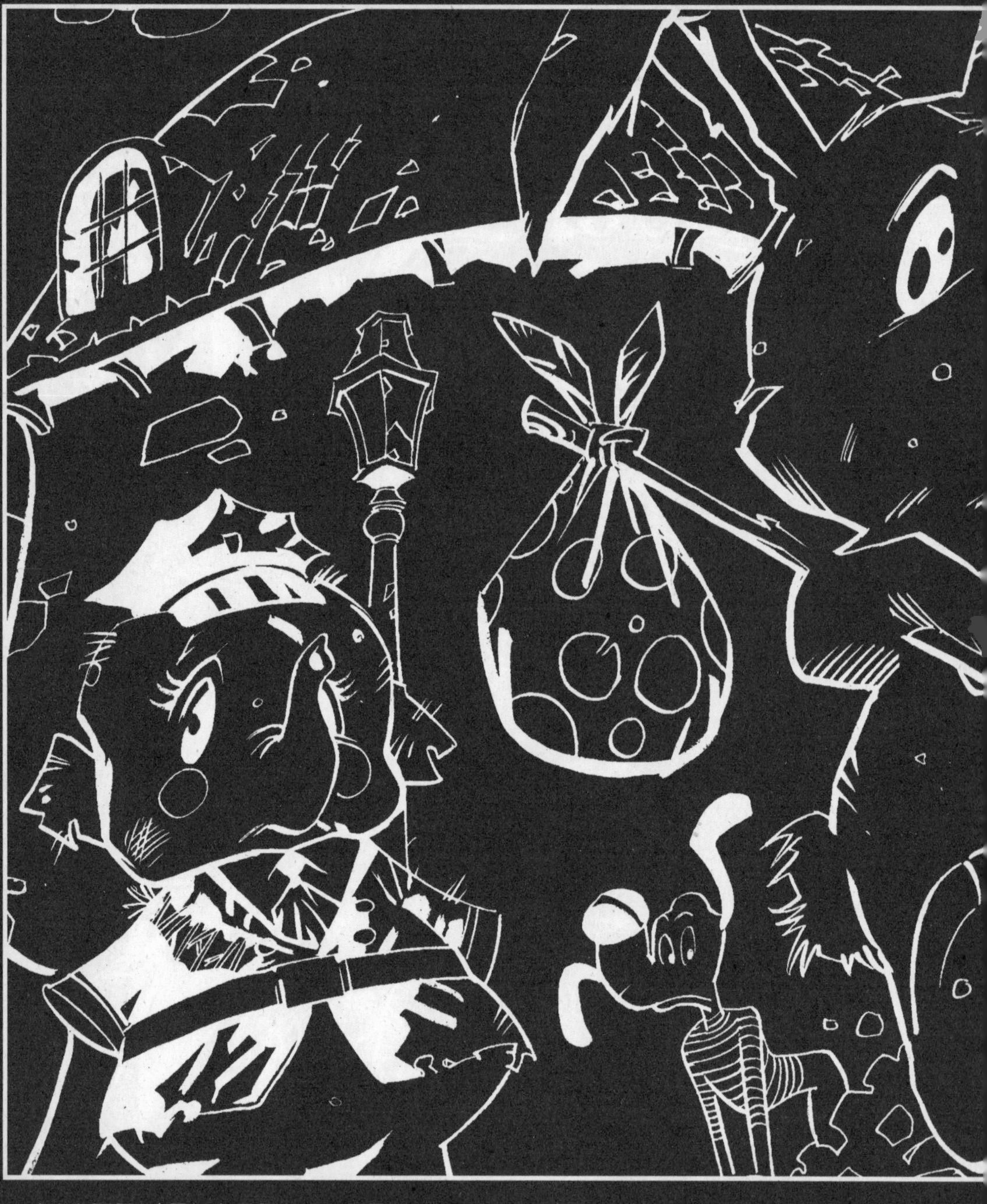

MATTHEW STURGES WRITER
LUCA ROSSI • WERTHER DELL'EDERA
JOSÉ MARZÁN JR. ARTISTS
LEE LOUGHRIDGE COLORIST
TODD KLEIN LETTERER
ESAO ANDREWS COVER ART AND ORIGINAL SERIES COVERS
MATTHEW STURGES SHORT STORY WRITER
CRISTIANO CUCINA • BRENDAN McCARTHY • PHIL NOTO
ESAO ANDREWS • CARINE BRANCOWITZ SHORT STORY ARTISTS

House of MYSTERY

SAFE AS HOUSES

ANGELA RUFINO SHELLY BOND   EDITORS-ORIGINAL SERIES
IAN SATTLER   DIRECTOR EDITORIAL, SPECIAL PROJECTS AND ARCHIVAL EDITIONS
SCOTT NYBAKKEN   EDITOR
ROBBIN BROSTERMAN   DESIGN DIRECTOR-BOOKS

KAREN BERGER   SENIOR VP-EXECUTIVE EDITOR, VERTIGO
BOB HARRAS   VP-EDITOR IN CHIEF

DIANE NELSON   PRESIDENT
DAN DIDIO AND JIM LEE   CO-PUBLISHERS
GEOFF JOHNS   CHIEF CREATIVE OFFICER
JOHN ROOD   EXECUTIVE VP-SALES, MARKETING AND BUSINESS DEVELOPMENT
AMY GENKINS   SENIOR VP, BUSINESS AND LEGAL AFFAIRS
NAIRI GARDINER   SENIOR VP-FINANCE
JEFF BOISON   VP-PUBLISHING OPERATIONS
MARK CHIARELLO   VP-ART DIRECTION AND DESIGN
JOHN CUNNINGHAM   VP-MARKETING
TERRI CUNNINGHAM   VP-TALENT RELATIONS AND SERVICES
ALISON GILL   SENIOR VP-MANUFACTURING AND OPERATIONS
DAVID HYDE   VP-PUBLICITY
HANK KANALZ   SENIOR VP-DIGITAL
JAY KOGAN   VP-BUSINESS AND LEGAL AFFAIRS, PUBLISHING
JACK MAHAN   VP-BUSINESS AFFAIRS, TALENT
NICK NAPOLITANO   VP-MANUFACTURING ADMINISTRATION
RON PERAZZA   VP-ONLINE
SUE POHJA   VP-BOOK SALES
COURTNEY SIMMONS   SENIOR VP-PUBLICITY
BOB WAYNE   SENIOR VP, SALES

HOUSE OF MYSTERY: SAFE AS HOUSES

DC COMICS
1700 BROADWAY, NEW YORK, NY 10019
A WARNER BROS. ENTERTAINMENT COMPANY.
PRINTED IN THE USA. FIRST PRINTING.
ISBN: 978-1-4012-3154-5.

SUSTAINABLE
FORESTRY
INITIATIVE

Certified Fiber Sourcing

Fiber used in this product line meets the
sourcing requirements of the SFI program.
www.sfiprogram.org SGS-SFICOC-0130

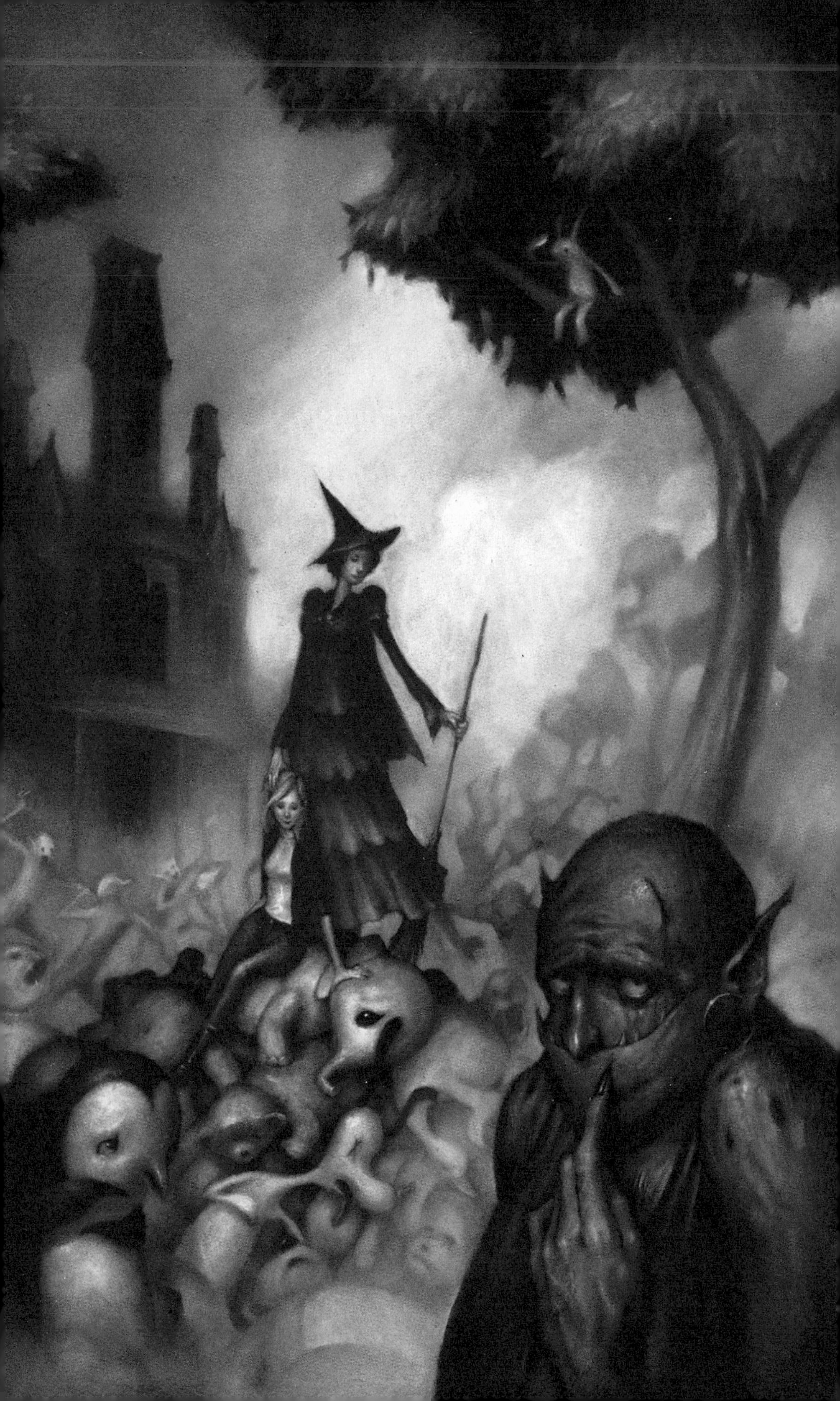

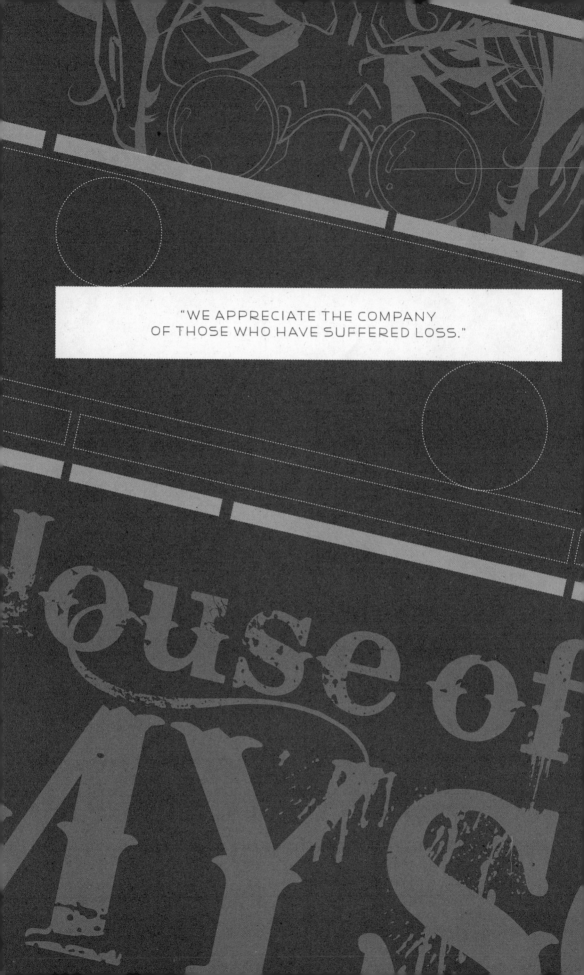

"WE APPRECIATE THE COMPANY
OF THOSE WHO HAVE SUFFERED LOSS."

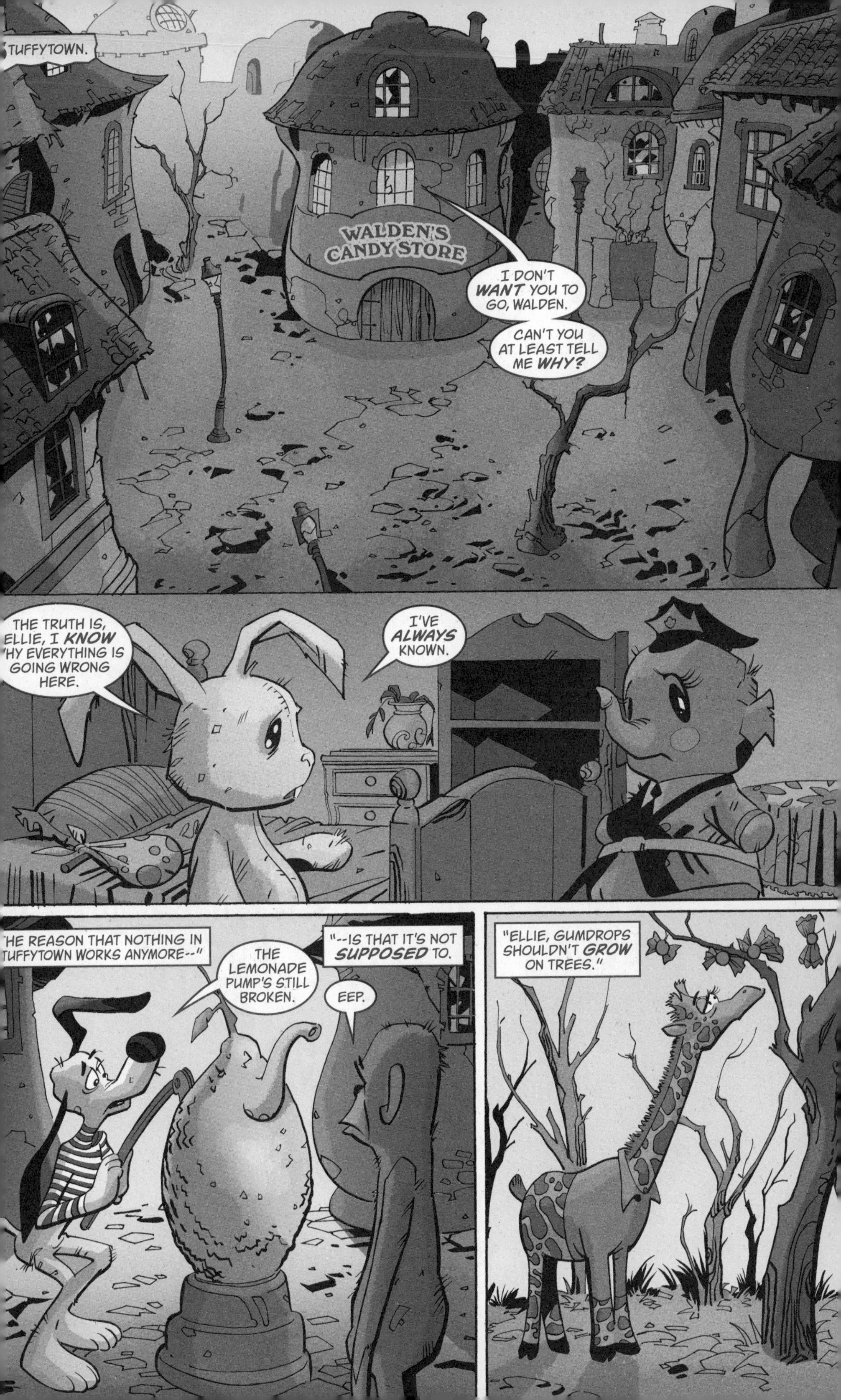

TUFFYTOWN.
WALDEN'S CANDY STORE
I DON'T *WANT* YOU TO GO, WALDEN.
CAN'T YOU AT LEAST TELL ME *WHY?*
THE TRUTH IS, ELLIE, I *KNOW* WHY EVERYTHING IS GOING WRONG HERE.
I'VE *ALWAYS* KNOWN.
"THE REASON THAT NOTHING IN TUFFYTOWN WORKS ANYMORE--"
THE LEMONADE PUMP'S STILL BROKEN.
"--IS THAT IT'S NOT *SUPPOSED* TO.
EEP.
"ELLIE, GUMDROPS SHOULDN'T *GROW* ON TREES."

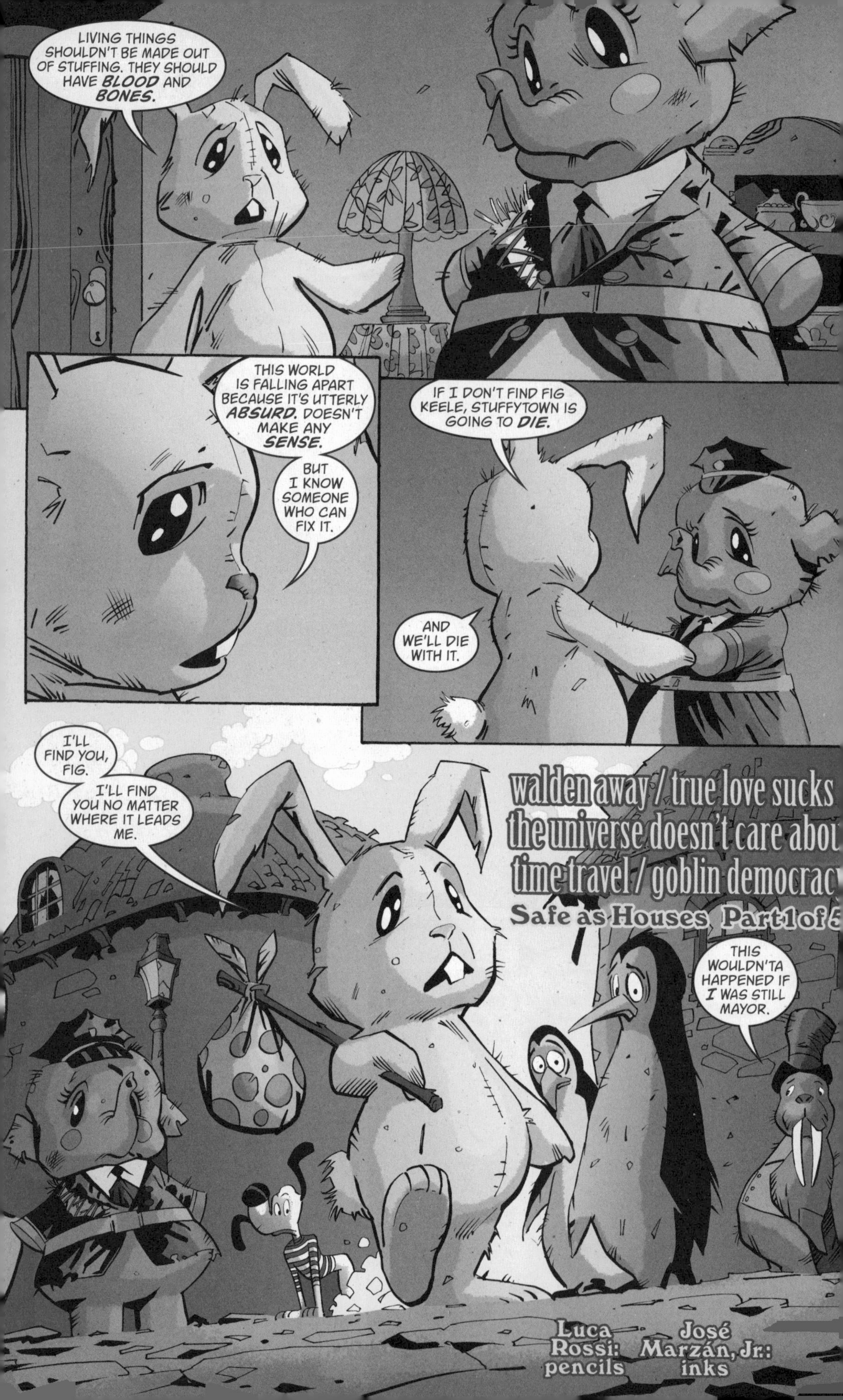
LIVING THINGS SHOULDN'T BE MADE OUT OF STUFFING. THEY SHOULD HAVE BLOOD AND BONES.
THIS WORLD IS FALLING APART BECAUSE IT'S UTTERLY ABSURD. DOESN'T MAKE ANY SENSE.
BUT I KNOW SOMEONE WHO CAN FIX IT.
IF I DON'T FIND FIG KEELE, STUFFYTOWN IS GOING TO DIE.
AND WE'LL DIE WITH IT.
I'LL FIND YOU, FIG.
I'LL FIND YOU NO MATTER WHERE IT LEADS ME.
walden away / true love sucks
the universe doesn't care abou
time travel / goblin democrac
Safe as Houses Part 1 of 5
THIS WOULDN'TA HAPPENED IF I WAS STILL MAYOR.
Luca Rossi: pencils
José Marzán, Jr.: inks

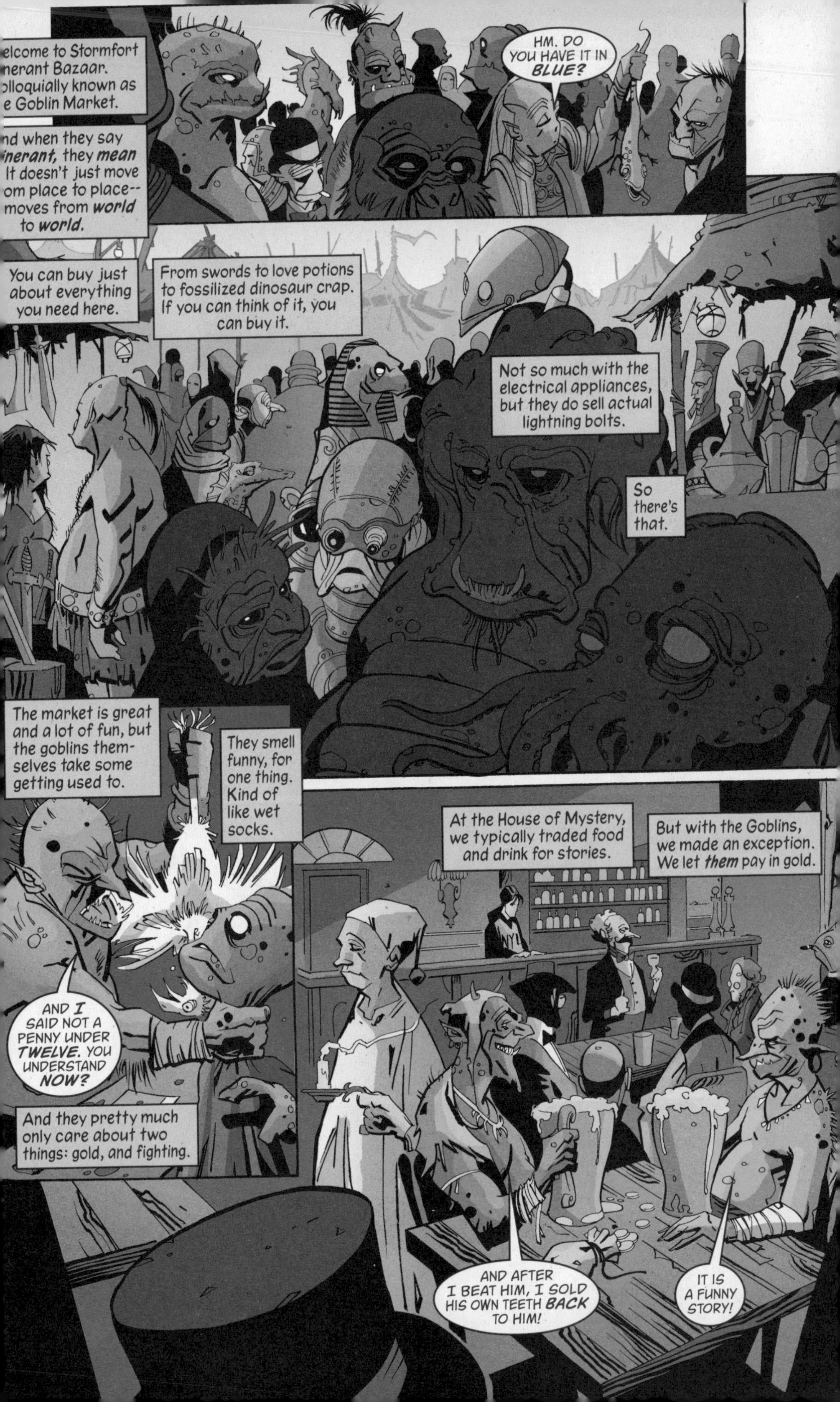
elcome to Stormfort
nerant Bazaar.
olloquially known as
e Goblin Market.
nd when they say
inerant, they mean
It doesn't just move
om place to place--
moves from world
to world.
HM. DO
YOU HAVE IT IN
BLUE?
You can buy just
about everything
you need here.
From swords to love potions
to fossilized dinosaur crap.
If you can think of it, you
can buy it.
Not so much with the
electrical appliances,
but they do sell actual
lightning bolts.
So
there's
that.
The market is great
and a lot of fun, but
the goblins them-
selves take some
getting used to.
They smell
funny, for
one thing.
Kind of
like wet
socks.
AND I
SAID NOT A
PENNY UNDER
TWELVE. YOU
UNDERSTAND
NOW?
And they pretty much
only care about two
things: gold, and fighting.
At the House of Mystery,
we typically traded food
and drink for stories.
But with the Goblins,
we made an exception.
We let them pay in gold.
AND AFTER
I BEAT HIM, I SOLD
HIS OWN TEETH BACK
TO HIM!
IT IS
A FUNNY
STORY!

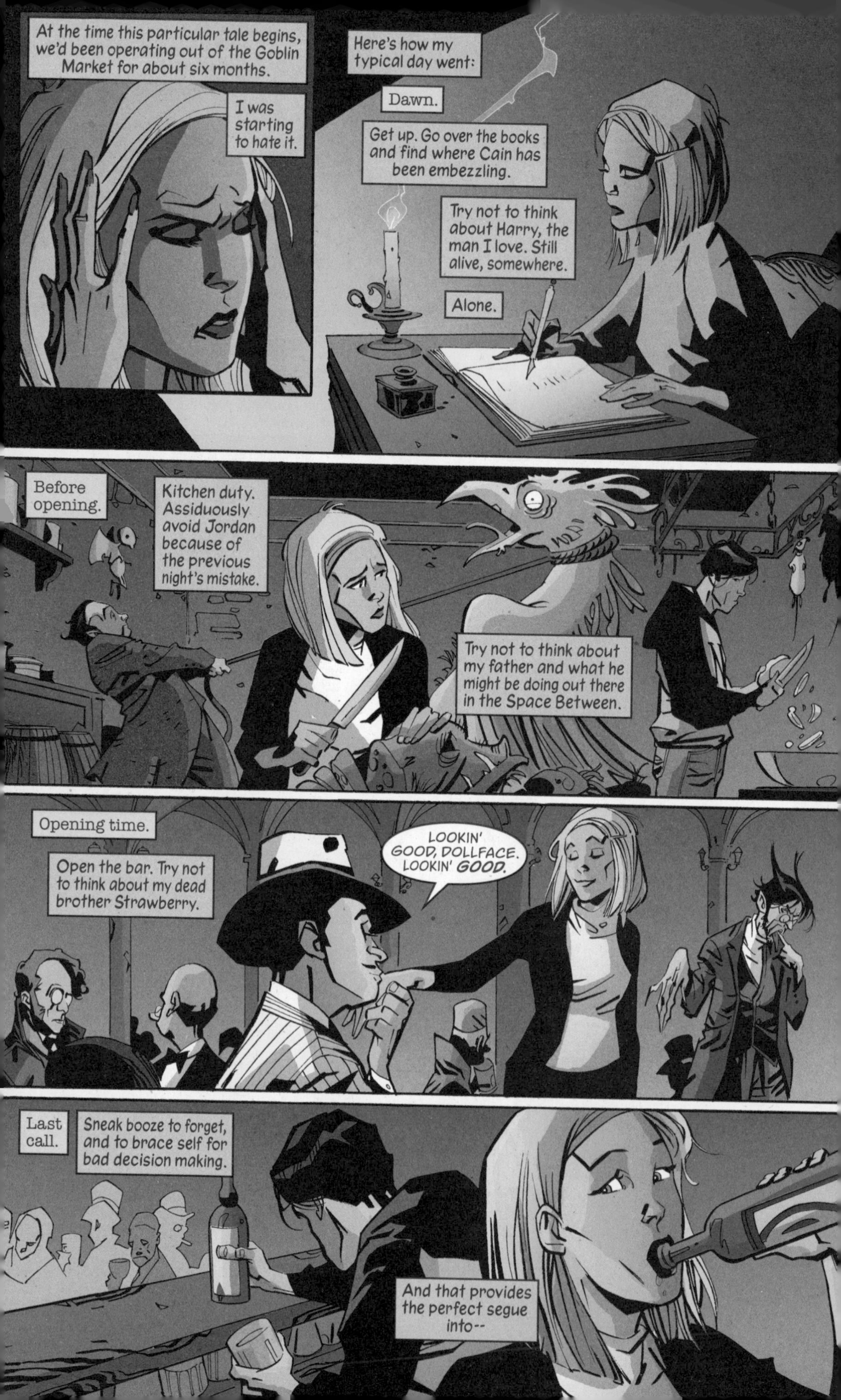

At the time this particular tale begins, we'd been operating out of the Goblin Market for about six months.
I was starting to hate it.
Here's how my typical day went:
Dawn.
Get up. Go over the books and find where Cain has been embezzling.
Try not to think about Harry, the man I love. Still alive, somewhere.
Alone.
Before opening.
Kitchen duty. Assiduously avoid Jordan because of the previous night's mistake.
Try not to think about my father and what he might be doing out there in the Space Between.
Opening time.
Open the bar. Try not to think about my dead brother Strawberry.
LOOKIN' GOOD, DOLLFACE. LOOKIN' GOOD.
Last call.
Sneak booze to forget, and to brace self for bad decision making.
And that provides the perfect segue into--

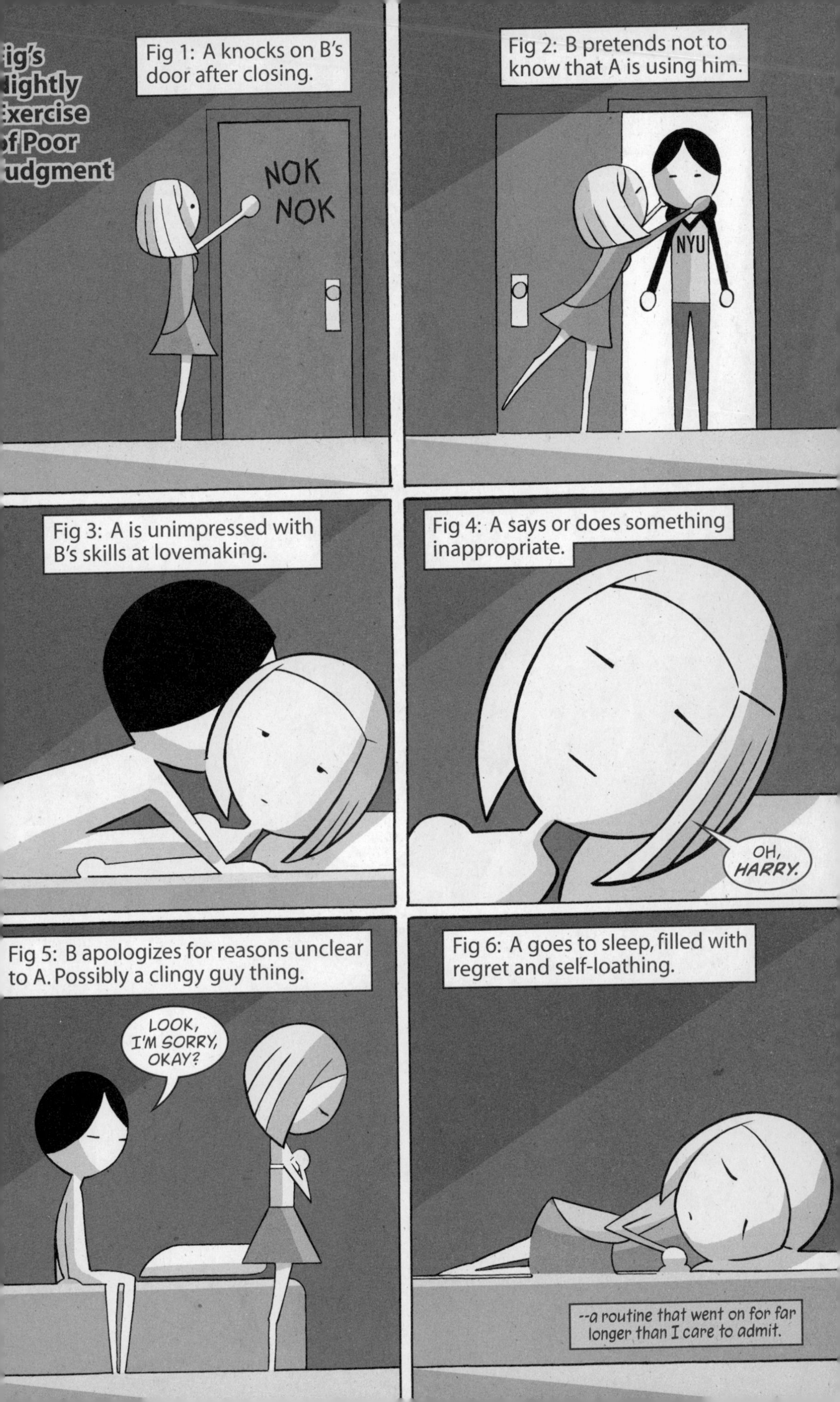

ig's
lightly
xercise
f Poor
udgment
Fig 1: A knocks on B's door after closing.
NOK NOK
Fig 2: B pretends not to know that A is using him.
NYU
Fig 3: A is unimpressed with B's skills at lovemaking.
Fig 4: A says or does something inappropriate.
OH, HARRY.
Fig 5: B apologizes for reasons unclear to A. Possibly a clingy guy thing.
LOOK, I'M SORRY, OKAY?
Fig 6: A goes to sleep, filled with regret and self-loathing.
--a routine that went on for far longer than I care to admit.

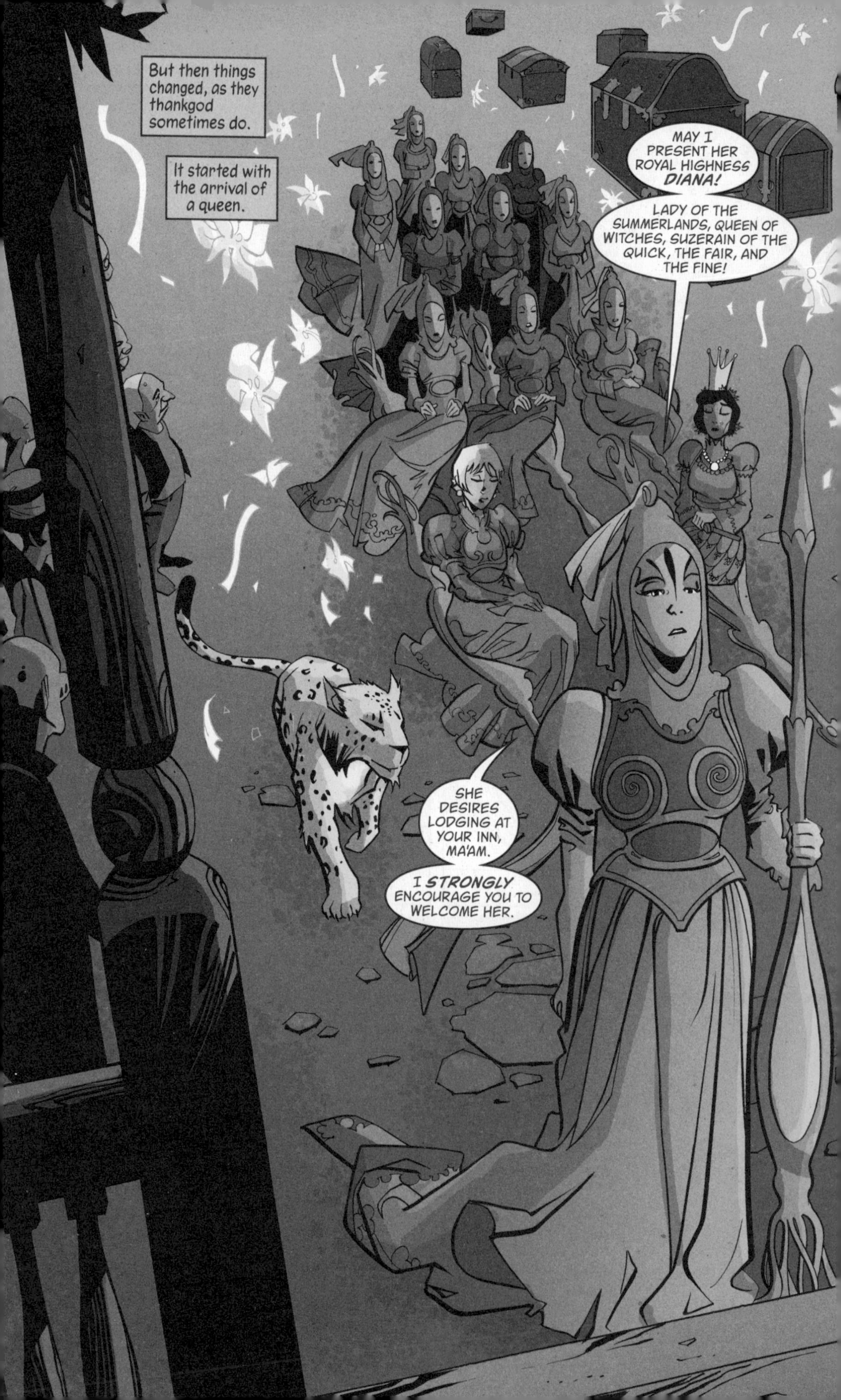

But then things changed, as they thankgod sometimes do.
It started with the arrival of a queen.
MAY I PRESENT HER ROYAL HIGHNESS DIANA!
LADY OF THE SUMMERLANDS, QUEEN OF WITCHES, SUZERAIN OF THE QUICK, THE FAIR, AND THE FINE!
SHE DESIRES LODGING AT YOUR INN, MA'AM.
I STRONGLY ENCOURAGE YOU TO WELCOME HER.

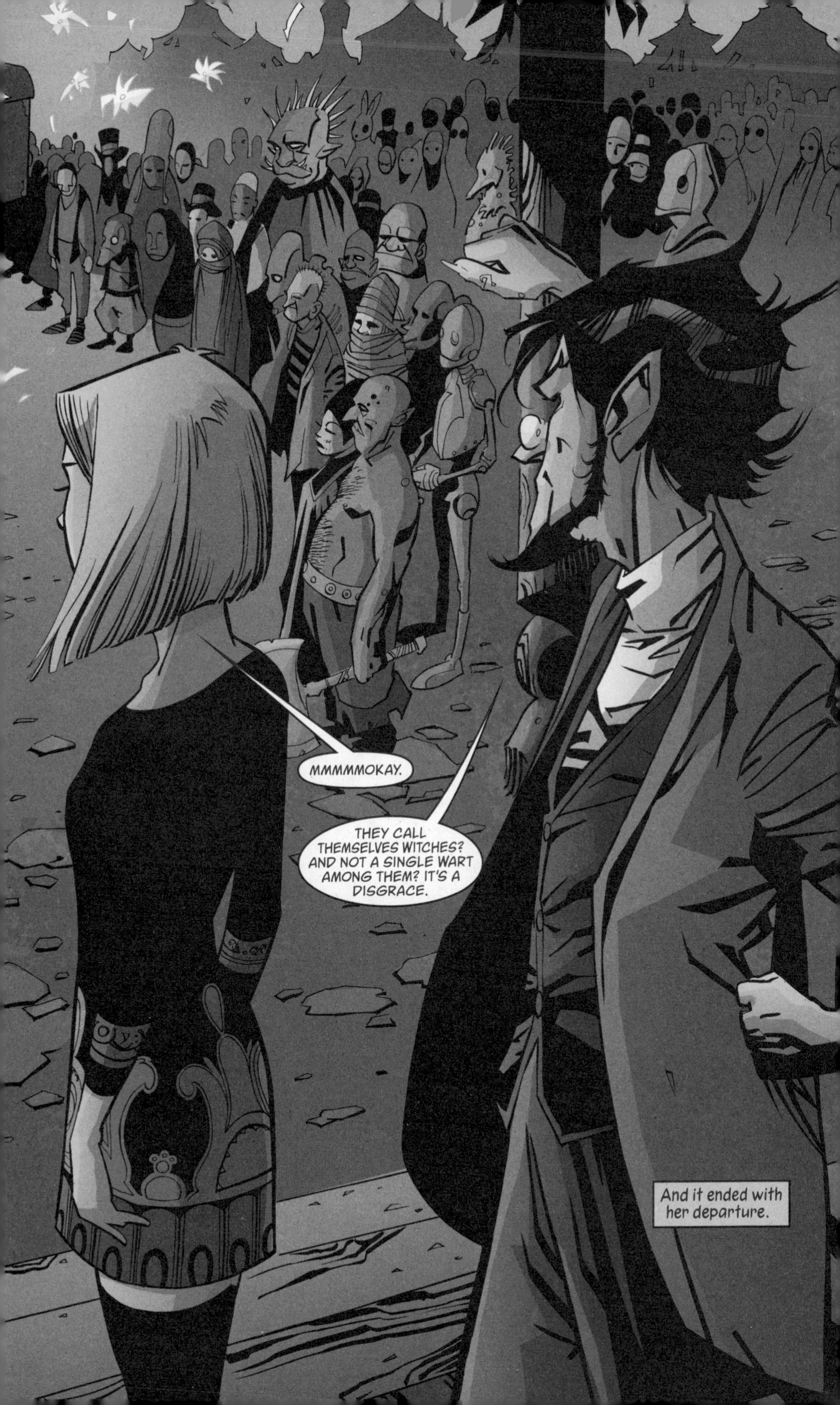

MMMMMOKAY.
THEY CALL THEMSELVES WITCHES? AND NOT A SINGLE WART AMONG THEM? IT'S A DISGRACE.
And it ended with her departure.

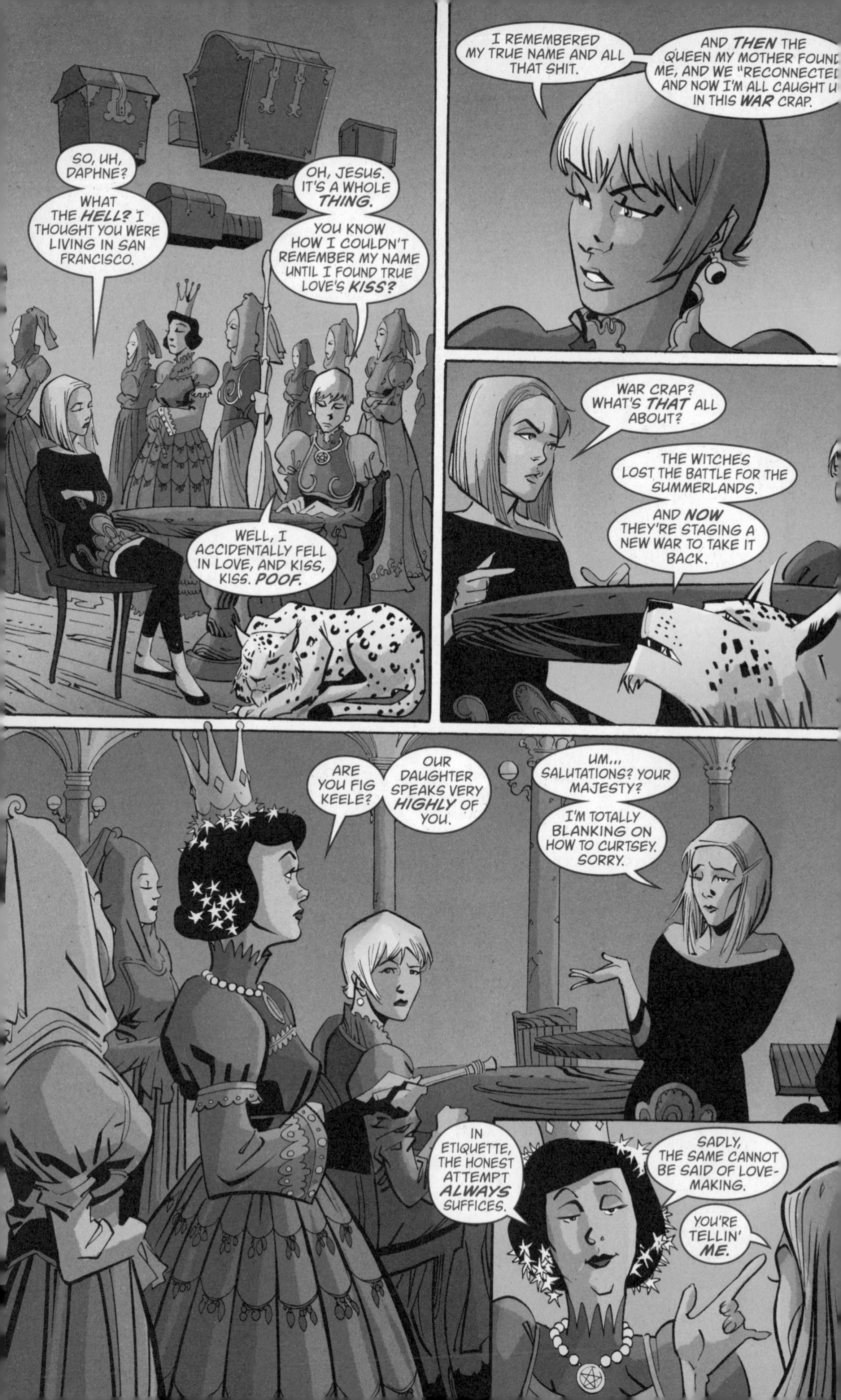
SO, UH, DAPHNE?
WHAT THE HELL? I THOUGHT YOU WERE LIVING IN SAN FRANCISCO.
OH, JESUS. IT'S A WHOLE THING.
YOU KNOW HOW I COULDN'T REMEMBER MY NAME UNTIL I FOUND TRUE LOVE'S KISS?
WELL, I ACCIDENTALLY FELL IN LOVE, AND KISS, KISS. POOF.
I REMEMBERED MY TRUE NAME AND ALL THAT SHIT.
AND THEN THE QUEEN MY MOTHER FOUND ME, AND WE "RECONNECTED," AND NOW I'M ALL CAUGHT UP IN THIS WAR CRAP.
WAR CRAP? WHAT'S THAT ALL ABOUT?
THE WITCHES LOST THE BATTLE FOR THE SUMMERLANDS.
AND NOW THEY'RE STAGING A NEW WAR TO TAKE IT BACK.
ARE YOU FIG KEELE?
OUR DAUGHTER SPEAKS VERY HIGHLY OF YOU.
UM... SALUTATIONS? YOUR MAJESTY?
I'M TOTALLY BLANKING ON HOW TO CURTSEY. SORRY.
IN ETIQUETTE, THE HONEST ATTEMPT ALWAYS SUFFICES.
SADLY, THE SAME CANNOT BE SAID OF LOVE-MAKING.
YOU'RE TELLIN' ME.

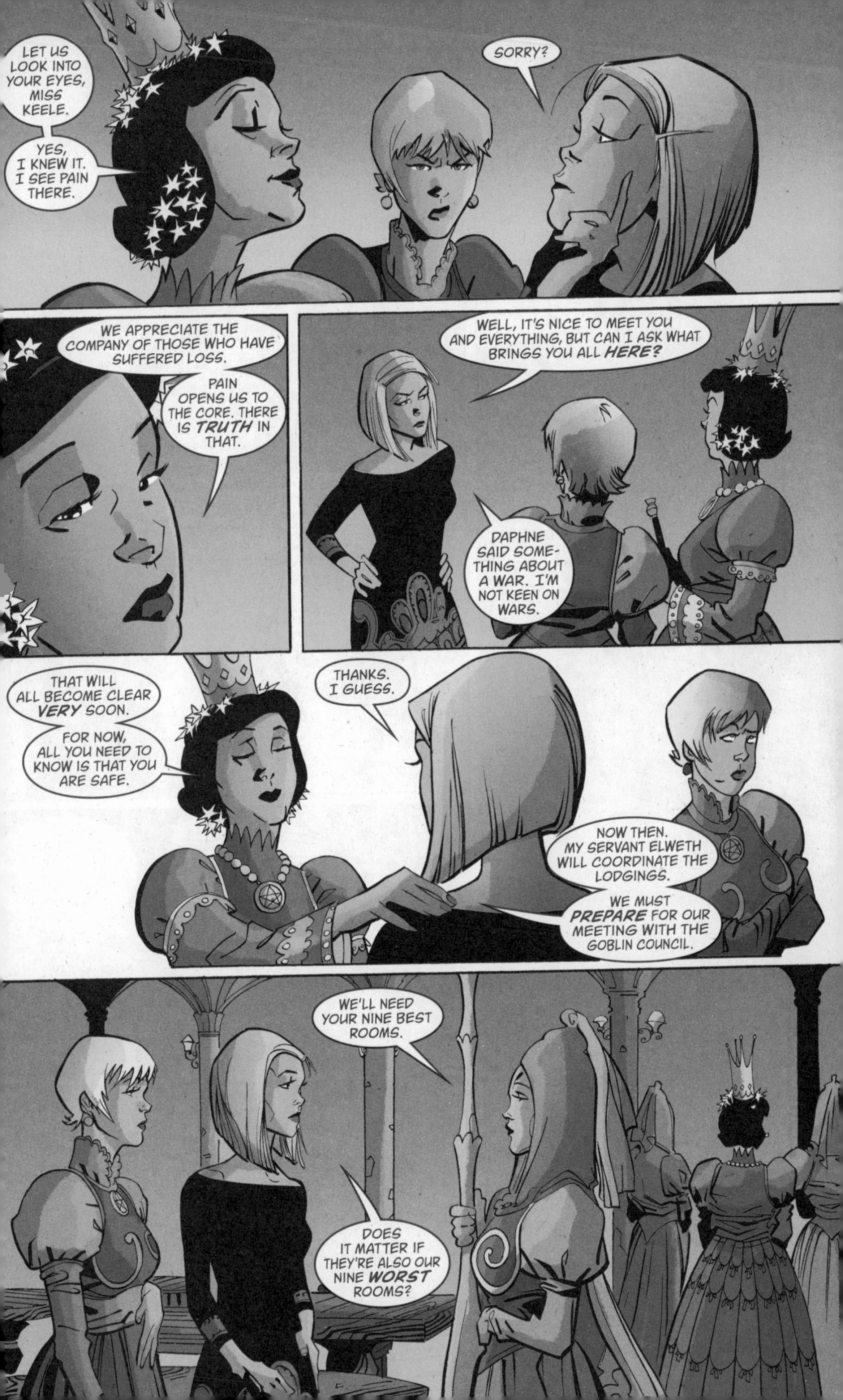
LET US LOOK INTO YOUR EYES, MISS KEELE.
YES, I KNEW IT. I SEE PAIN THERE.
SORRY?
WE APPRECIATE THE COMPANY OF THOSE WHO HAVE SUFFERED LOSS.
PAIN OPENS US TO THE CORE. THERE IS TRUTH IN THAT.
WELL, IT'S NICE TO MEET YOU AND EVERYTHING, BUT CAN I ASK WHAT BRINGS YOU ALL HERE?
DAPHNE SAID SOME-THING ABOUT A WAR. I'M NOT KEEN ON WARS.
THAT WILL ALL BECOME CLEAR VERY SOON.
FOR NOW, ALL YOU NEED TO KNOW IS THAT YOU ARE SAFE.
THANKS. I GUESS.
NOW THEN. MY SERVANT ELWETH WILL COORDINATE THE LODGINGS.
WE MUST PREPARE FOR OUR MEETING WITH THE GOBLIN COUNCIL.
WE'LL NEED YOUR NINE BEST ROOMS.
DOES IT MATTER IF THEY'RE ALSO OUR NINE WORST ROOMS?

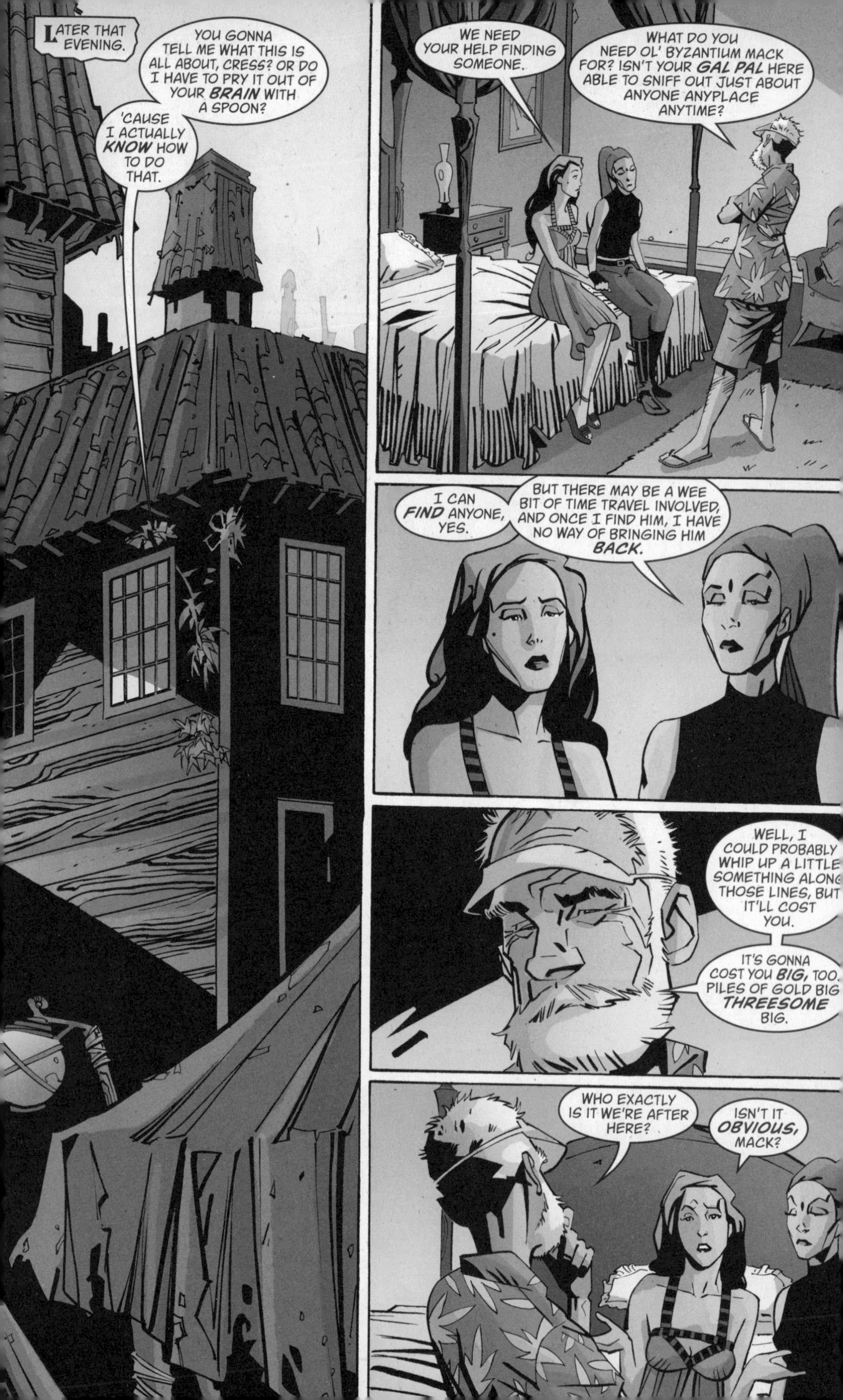
LATER THAT EVENING.
YOU GONNA TELL ME WHAT THIS IS ALL ABOUT, CRESS? OR DO I HAVE TO PRY IT OUT OF YOUR BRAIN WITH A SPOON?
'CAUSE I ACTUALLY KNOW HOW TO DO THAT.
WE NEED YOUR HELP FINDING SOMEONE.
WHAT DO YOU NEED OL' BYZANTIUM MACK FOR? ISN'T YOUR GAL PAL HERE ABLE TO SNIFF OUT JUST ABOUT ANYONE ANYPLACE ANYTIME?
I CAN FIND ANYONE, YES.
BUT THERE MAY BE A WEE BIT OF TIME TRAVEL INVOLVED, AND ONCE I FIND HIM, I HAVE NO WAY OF BRINGING HIM BACK.
WELL, I COULD PROBABLY WHIP UP A LITTLE SOMETHING ALONG THOSE LINES, BUT IT'LL COST YOU.
IT'S GONNA COST YOU BIG, TOO. PILES OF GOLD BIG THREESOME BIG.
WHO EXACTLY IS IT WE'RE AFTER HERE?
ISN'T IT OBVIOUS, MACK?

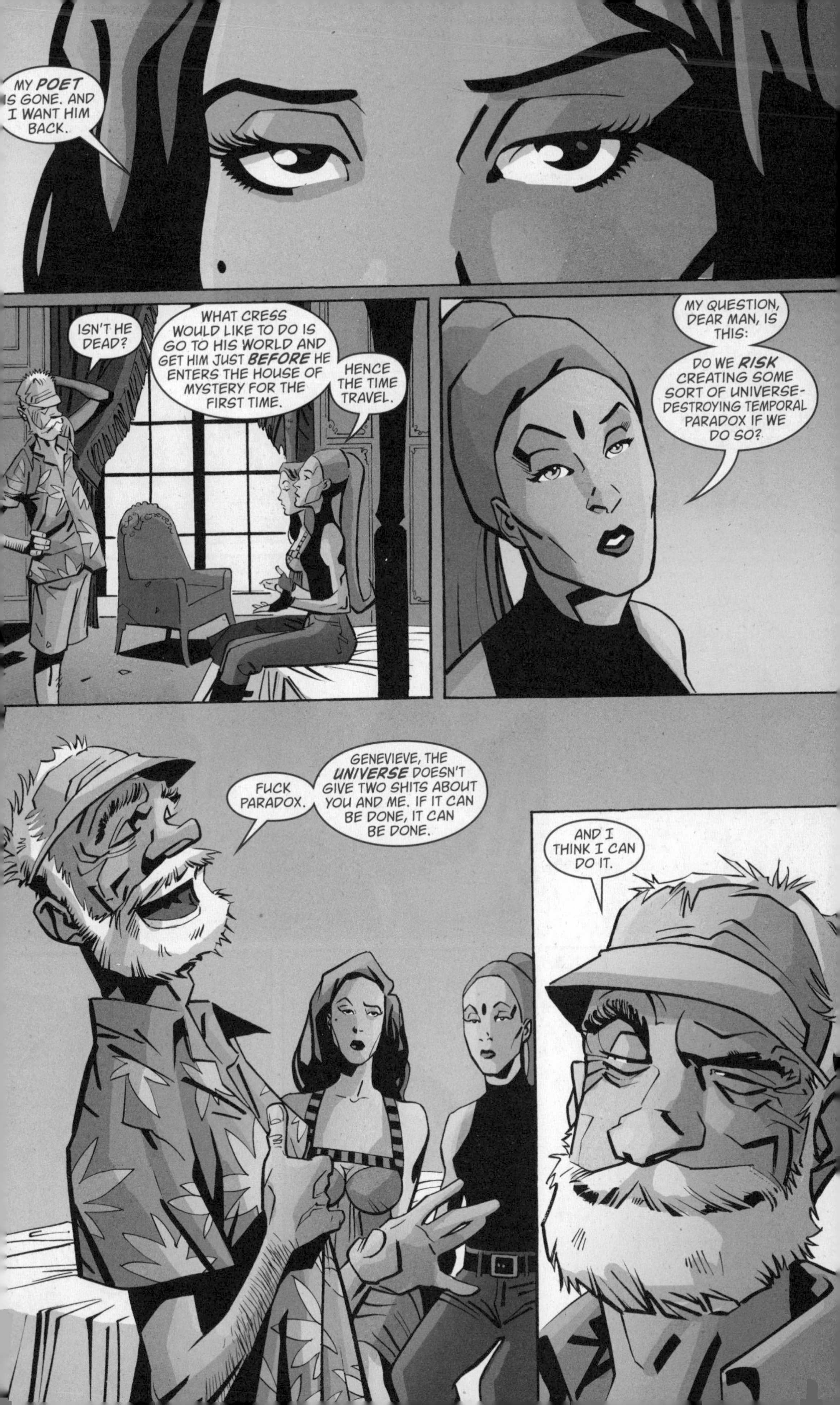

MY POET IS GONE. AND I WANT HIM BACK.
ISN'T HE DEAD?
WHAT CRESS WOULD LIKE TO DO IS GO TO HIS WORLD AND GET HIM JUST BEFORE HE ENTERS THE HOUSE OF MYSTERY FOR THE FIRST TIME.
HENCE THE TIME TRAVEL.
MY QUESTION, DEAR MAN, IS THIS:
DO WE RISK CREATING SOME SORT OF UNIVERSE-DESTROYING TEMPORAL PARADOX IF WE DO SO?
FUCK PARADOX.
GENEVIEVE, THE UNIVERSE DOESN'T GIVE TWO SHITS ABOUT YOU AND ME. IF IT CAN BE DONE, IT CAN BE DONE.
AND I THINK I CAN DO IT.

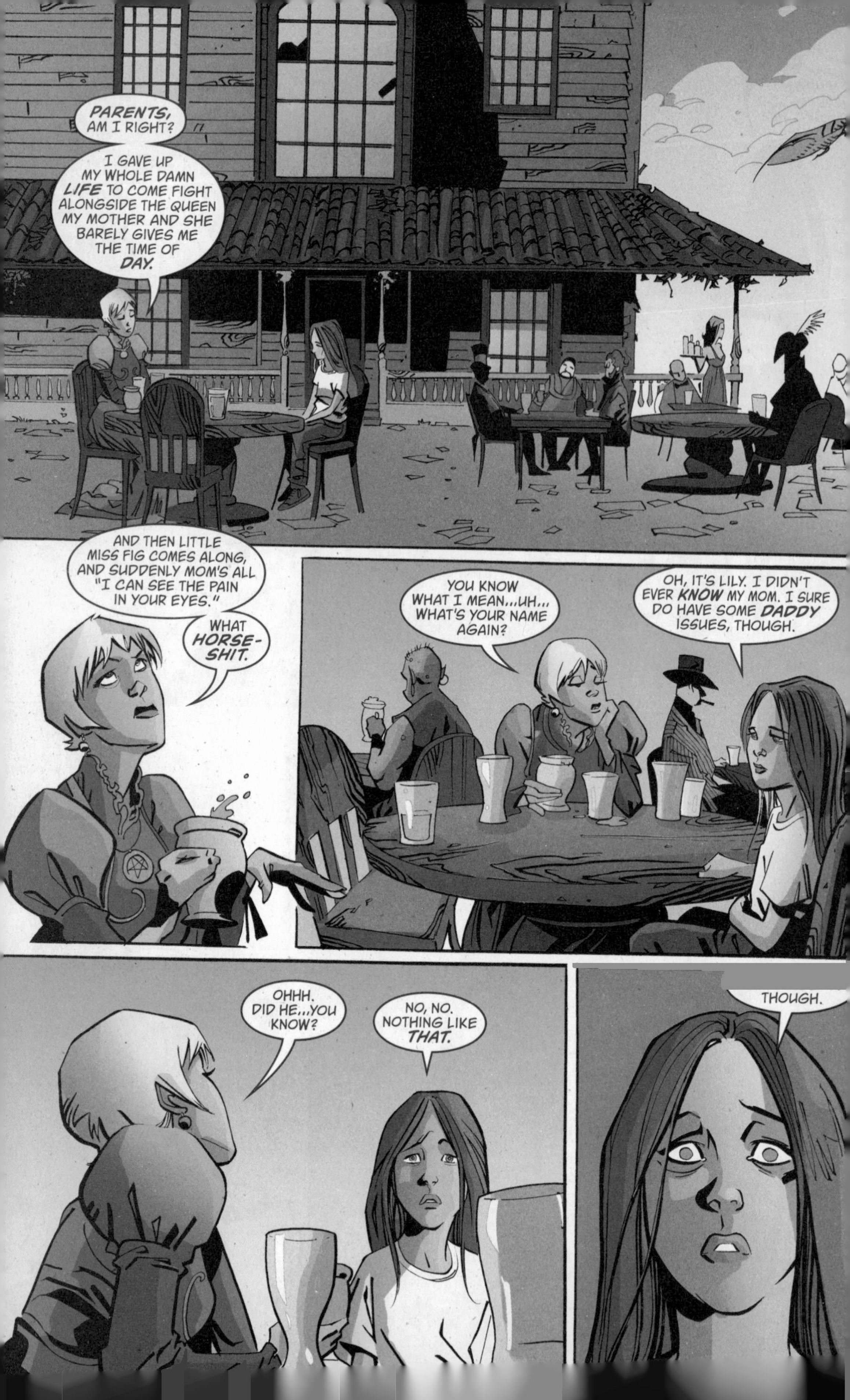
PARENTS, AM I RIGHT?
I GAVE UP MY WHOLE DAMN LIFE TO COME FIGHT ALONGSIDE THE QUEEN MY MOTHER AND SHE BARELY GIVES ME THE TIME OF DAY.
AND THEN LITTLE MISS FIG COMES ALONG, AND SUDDENLY MOM'S ALL "I CAN SEE THE PAIN IN YOUR EYES."
WHAT HORSE-SHIT.
YOU KNOW WHAT I MEAN...UH... WHAT'S YOUR NAME AGAIN?
OH, IT'S LILY. I DIDN'T EVER KNOW MY MOM. I SURE DO HAVE SOME DADDY ISSUES, THOUGH.
OHHH. DID HE...YOU KNOW?
NO, NO. NOTHING LIKE THAT.
THOUGH.

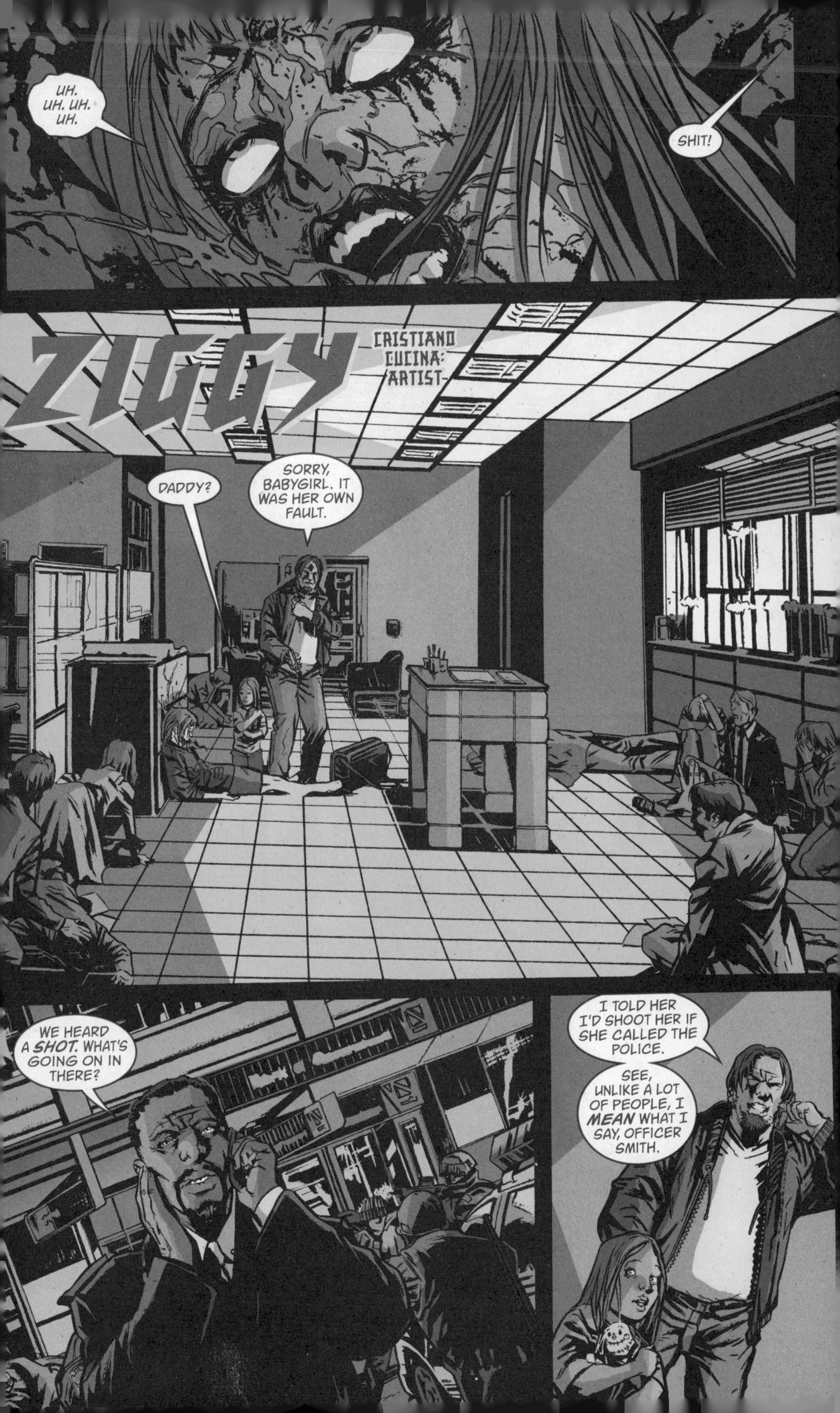
UH. UH. UH. UH.
SHIT!
ZIGGY
CRISTIANO CUCINA: ARTIST
DADDY?
SORRY, BABYGIRL. IT WAS HER OWN FAULT.
WE HEARD A SHOT. WHAT'S GOING ON IN THERE?
I TOLD HER I'D SHOOT HER IF SHE CALLED THE POLICE.
SEE, UNLIKE A LOT OF PEOPLE, I MEAN WHAT I SAY, OFFICER SMITH.

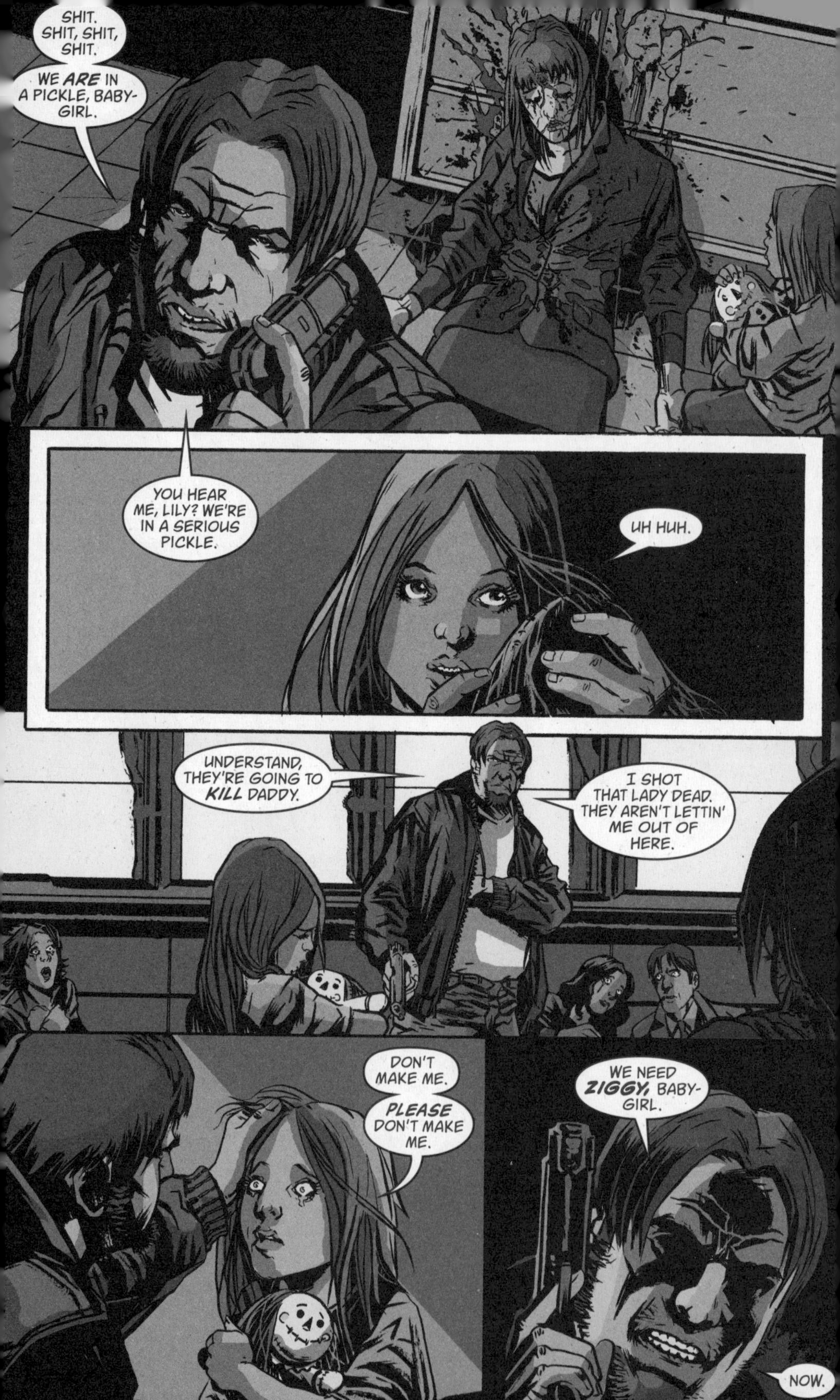
SHIT. SHIT, SHIT, SHIT.
WE ARE IN A PICKLE, BABY-GIRL.
YOU HEAR ME, LILY? WE'RE IN A SERIOUS PICKLE.
UH HUH.
UNDERSTAND, THEY'RE GOING TO KILL DADDY.
I SHOT THAT LADY DEAD. THEY AREN'T LETTIN' ME OUT OF HERE.
DON'T MAKE ME.
PLEASE DON'T MAKE ME.
WE NEED ZIGGY, BABY-GIRL.
NOW.

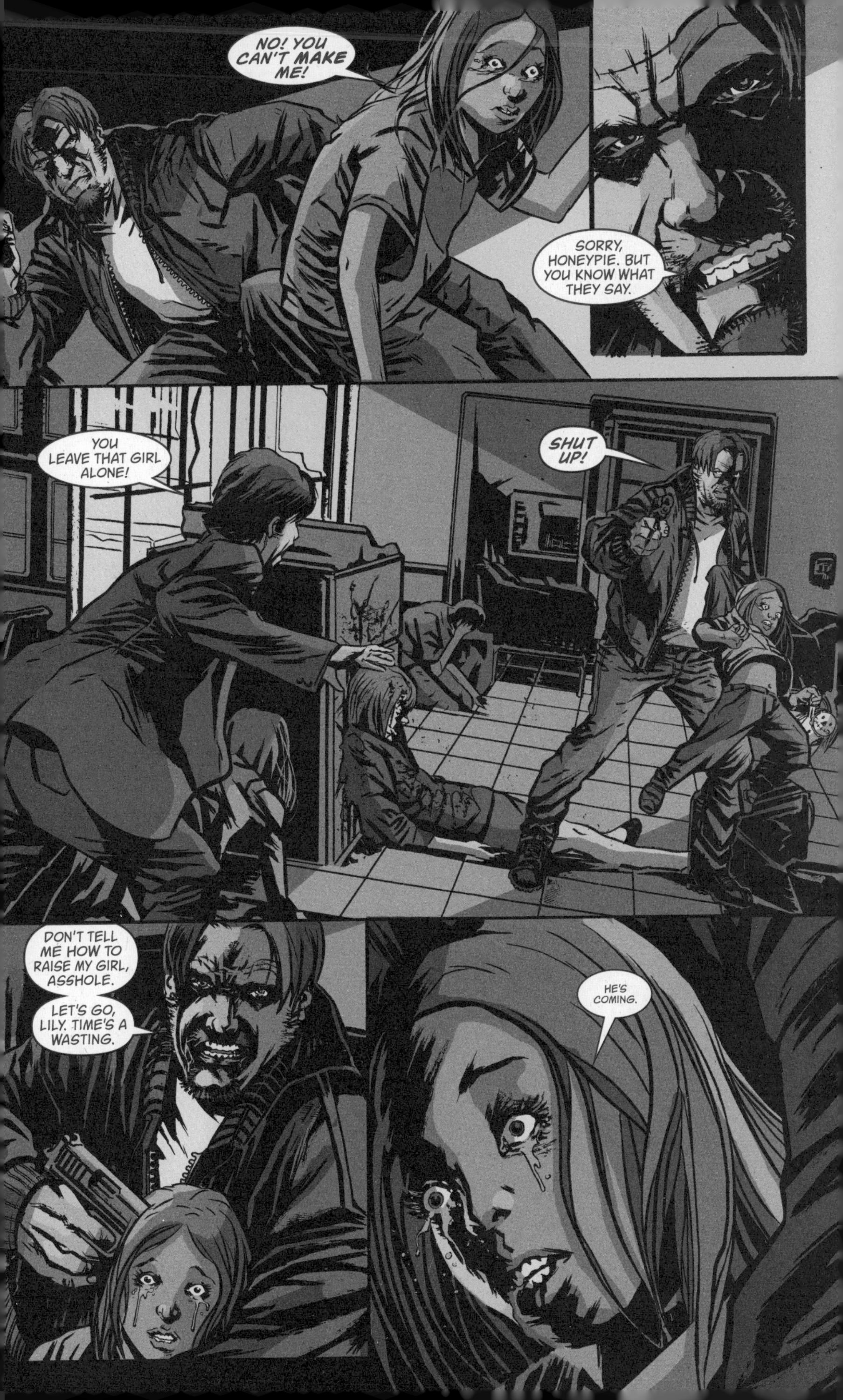
NO! YOU CAN'T MAKE ME!
SORRY, HONEYPIE. BUT YOU KNOW WHAT THEY SAY.
YOU LEAVE THAT GIRL ALONE!
SHUT UP!
DON'T TELL ME HOW TO RAISE MY GIRL, ASSHOLE.
LET'S GO, LILY. TIME'S A WASTING.
HE'S COMING.

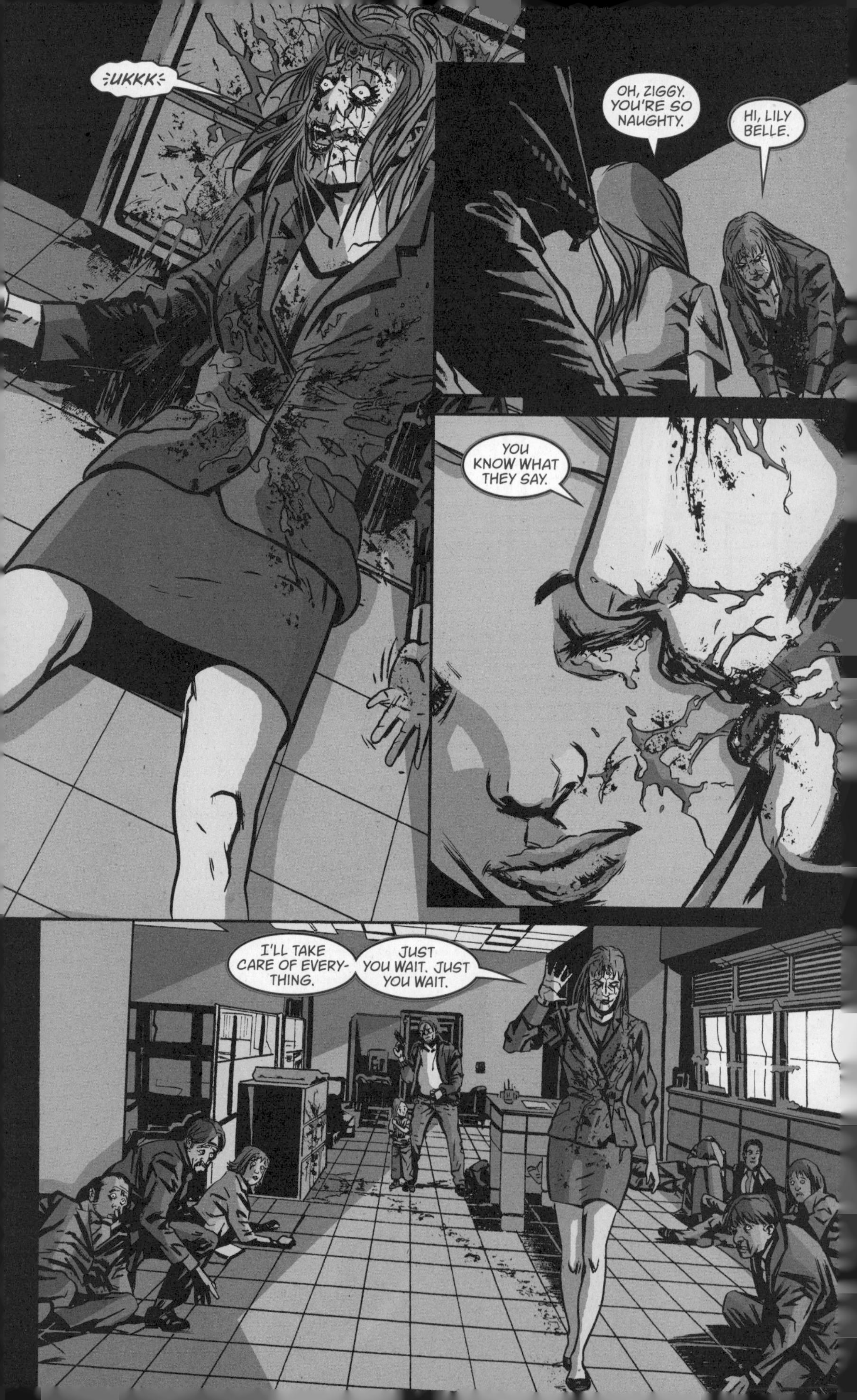
UKKK
OH, ZIGGY. YOU'RE SO NAUGHTY.
HI, LILY BELLE.
YOU KNOW WHAT THEY SAY.
I'LL TAKE CARE OF EVERY-THING.
JUST YOU WAIT. JUST YOU WAIT.

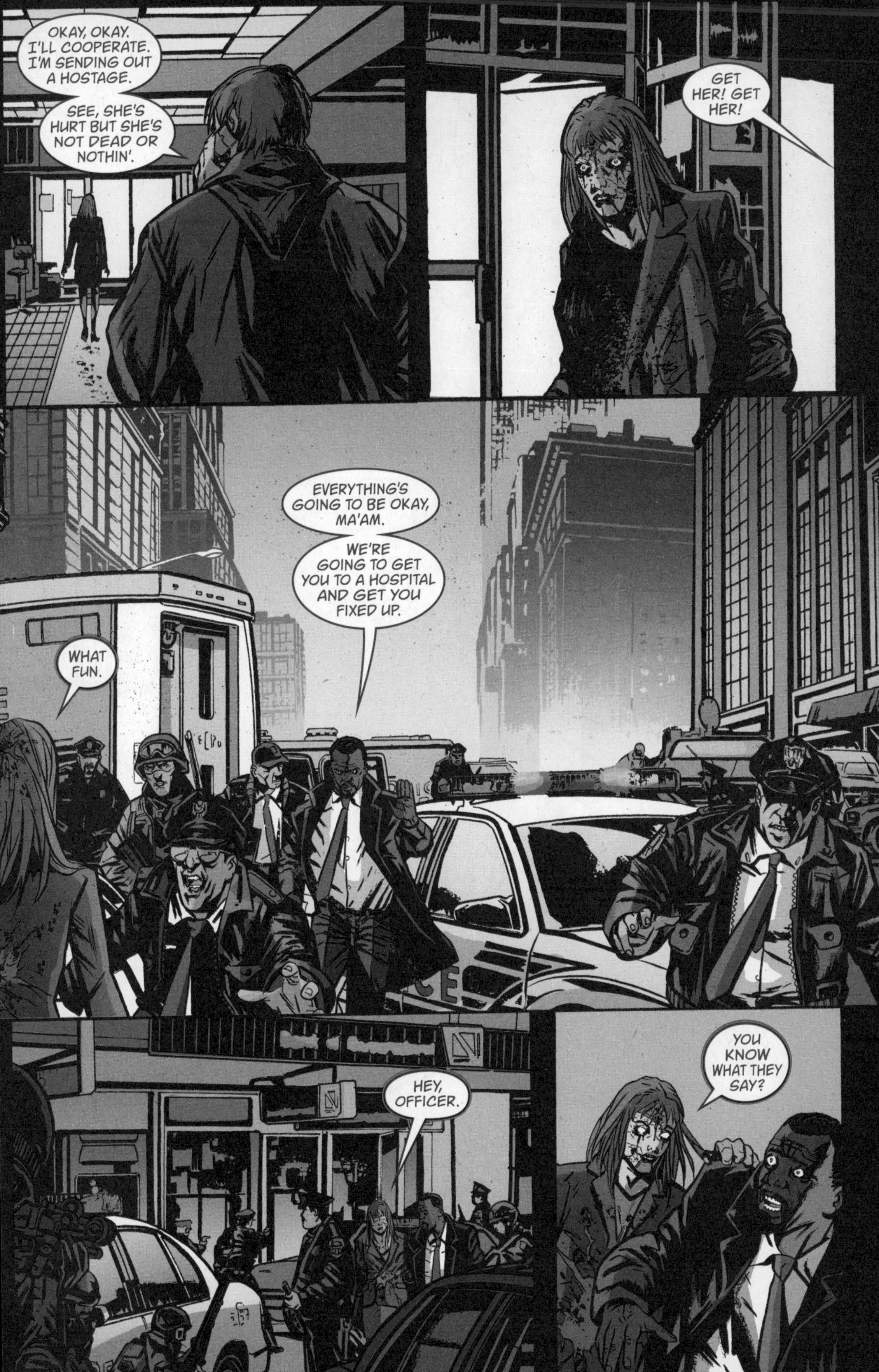

OKAY, OKAY. I'LL COOPERATE. I'M SENDING OUT A HOSTAGE.
SEE, SHE'S HURT BUT SHE'S NOT DEAD OR NOTHIN'.
GET HER! GET HER!
EVERYTHING'S GOING TO BE OKAY, MA'AM.
WE'RE GOING TO GET YOU TO A HOSPITAL AND GET YOU FIXED UP.
WHAT FUN.
HEY, OFFICER.
YOU KNOW WHAT THEY SAY?

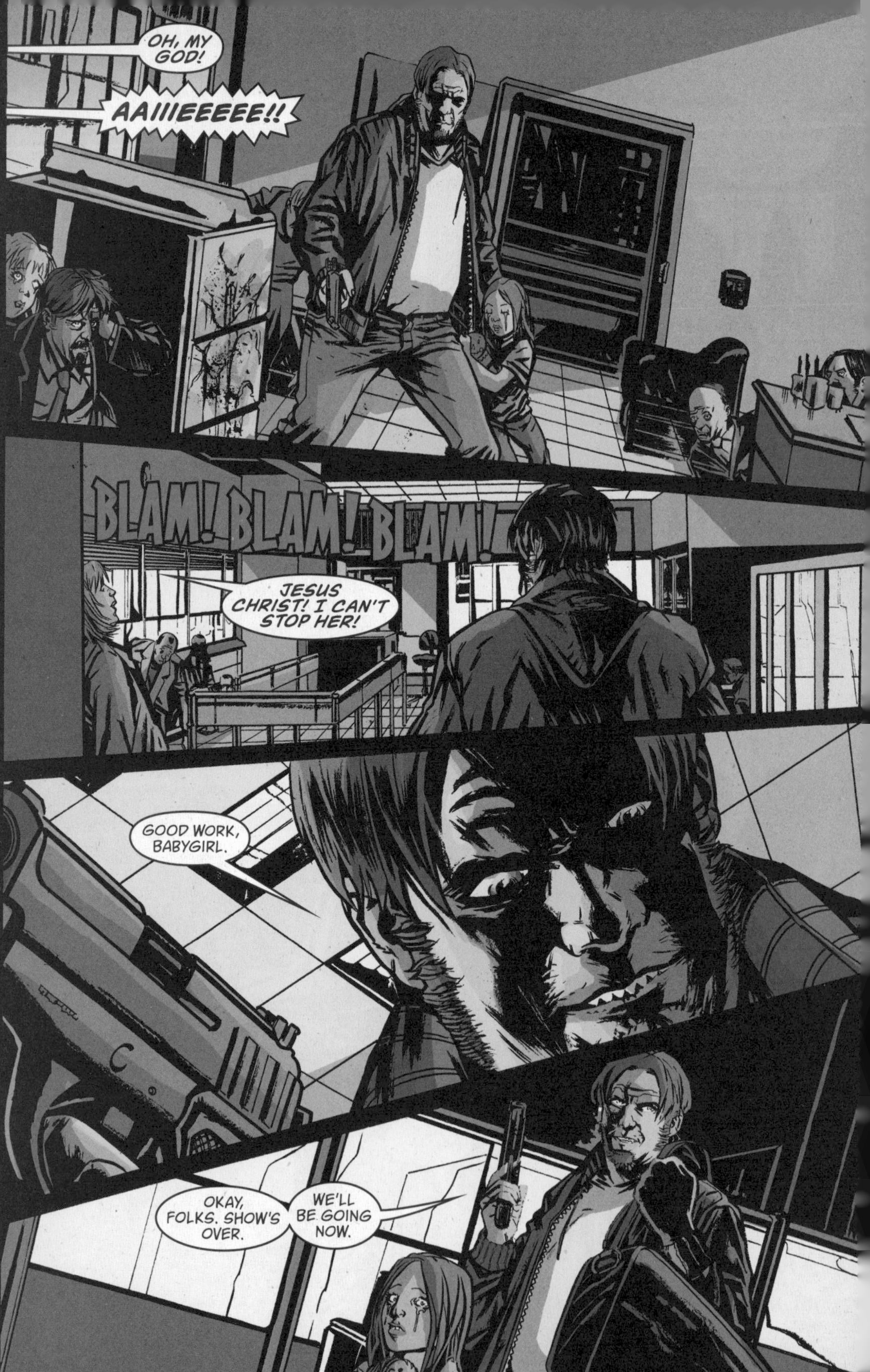
OH, MY GOD!
AAIIIEEEEE!!
BLAM! BLAM! BLAM!
JESUS CHRIST! I CAN'T STOP HER!
GOOD WORK, BABYGIRL.
OKAY, FOLKS. SHOW'S OVER.
WE'LL BE GOING NOW.

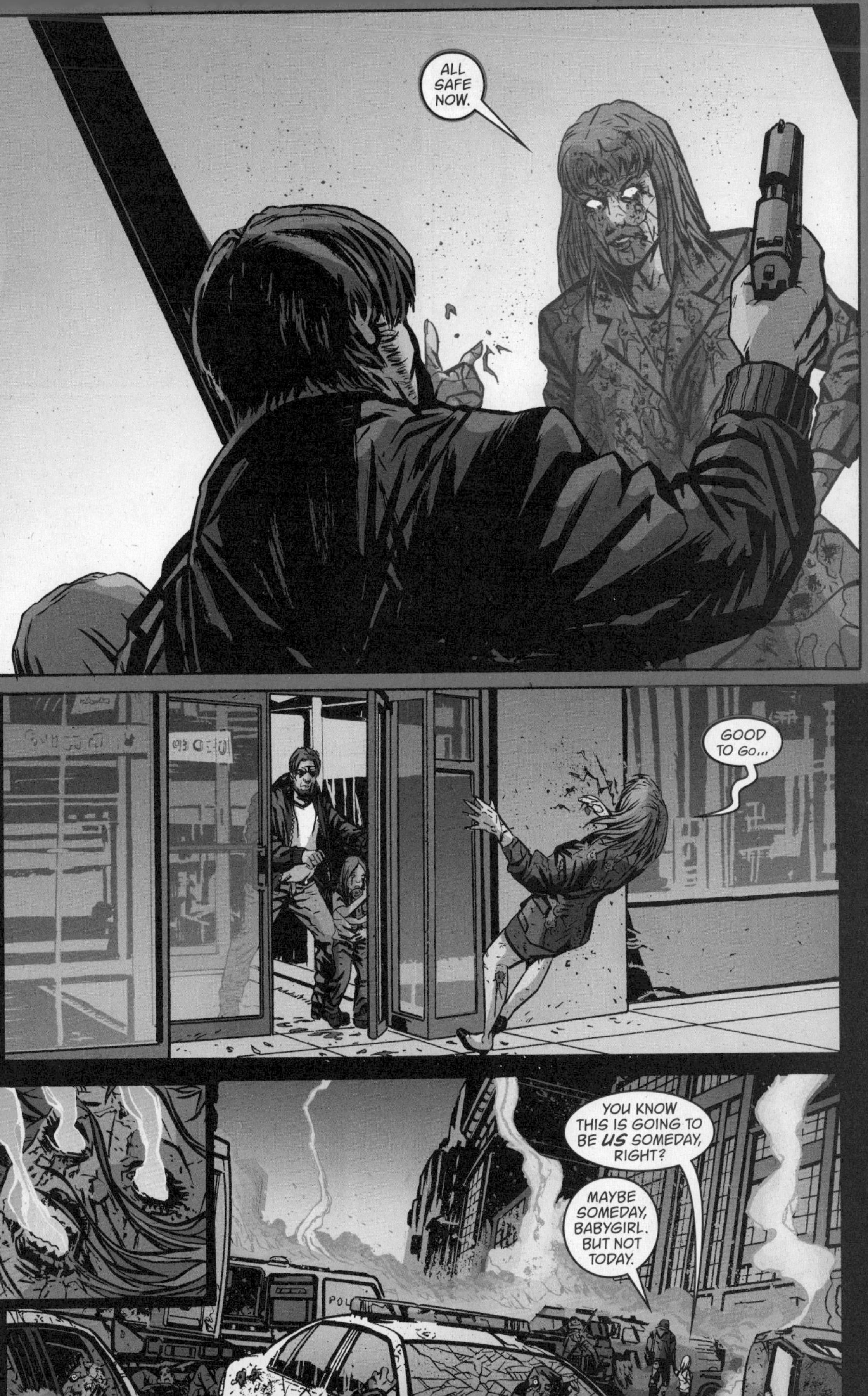
ALL SAFE NOW.
GOOD TO GO...
YOU KNOW THIS IS GOING TO BE *US* SOMEDAY, RIGHT?
MAYBE SOMEDAY, BABYGIRL. BUT NOT TODAY.

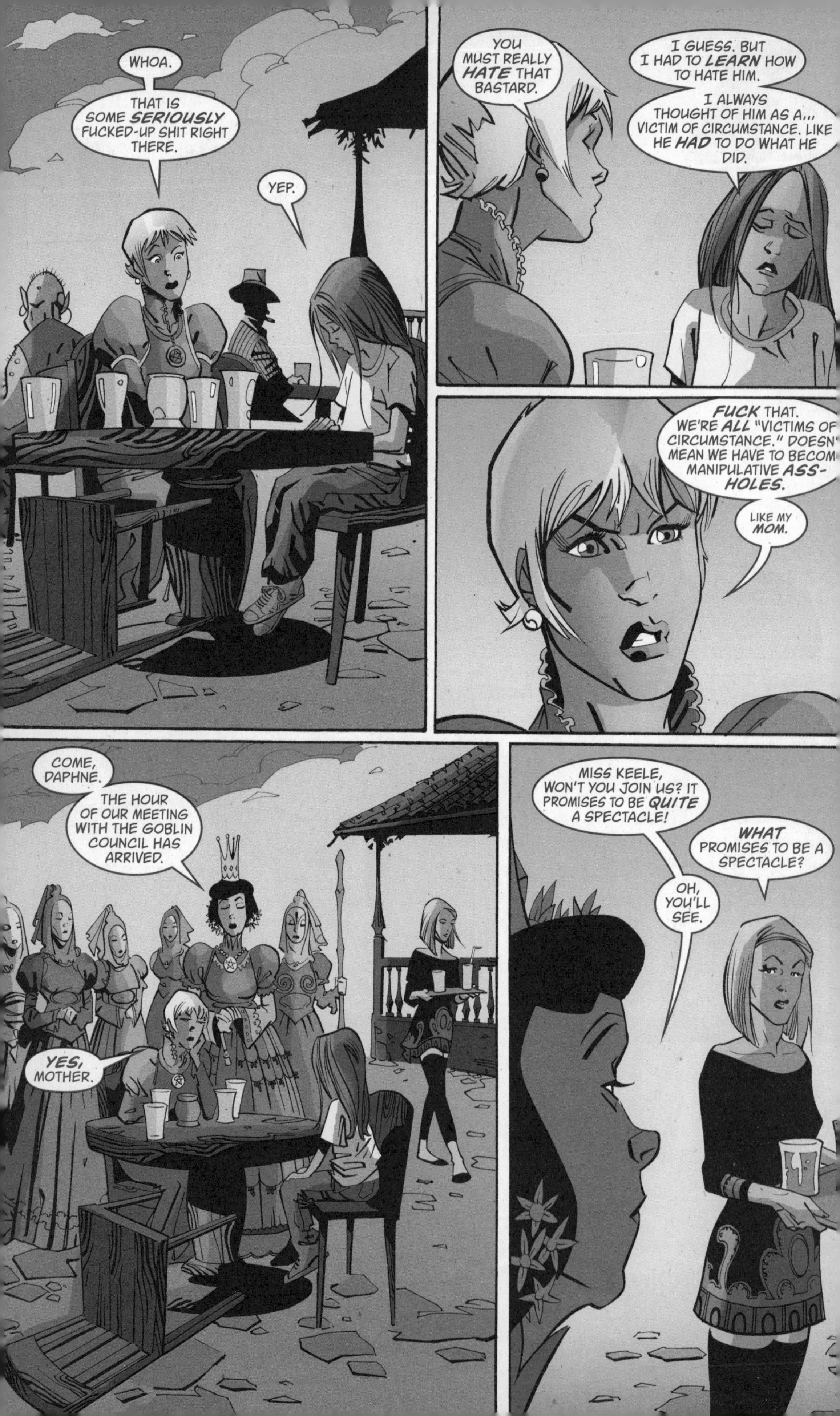
WHOA.
THAT IS SOME SERIOUSLY FUCKED-UP SHIT RIGHT THERE.
YEP.
YOU MUST REALLY HATE THAT BASTARD.
I GUESS. BUT I HAD TO LEARN HOW TO HATE HIM.
I ALWAYS THOUGHT OF HIM AS A... VICTIM OF CIRCUMSTANCE. LIKE HE HAD TO DO WHAT HE DID.
FUCK THAT. WE'RE ALL "VICTIMS OF CIRCUMSTANCE." DOESN' MEAN WE HAVE TO BECOM MANIPULATIVE ASS-HOLES.
LIKE MY MOM.
COME, DAPHNE.
THE HOUR OF OUR MEETING WITH THE GOBLIN COUNCIL HAS ARRIVED.
YES, MOTHER.
MISS KEELE, WON'T YOU JOIN US? IT PROMISES TO BE QUITE A SPECTACLE!
WHAT PROMISES TO BE A SPECTACLE?
OH, YOU'LL SEE.

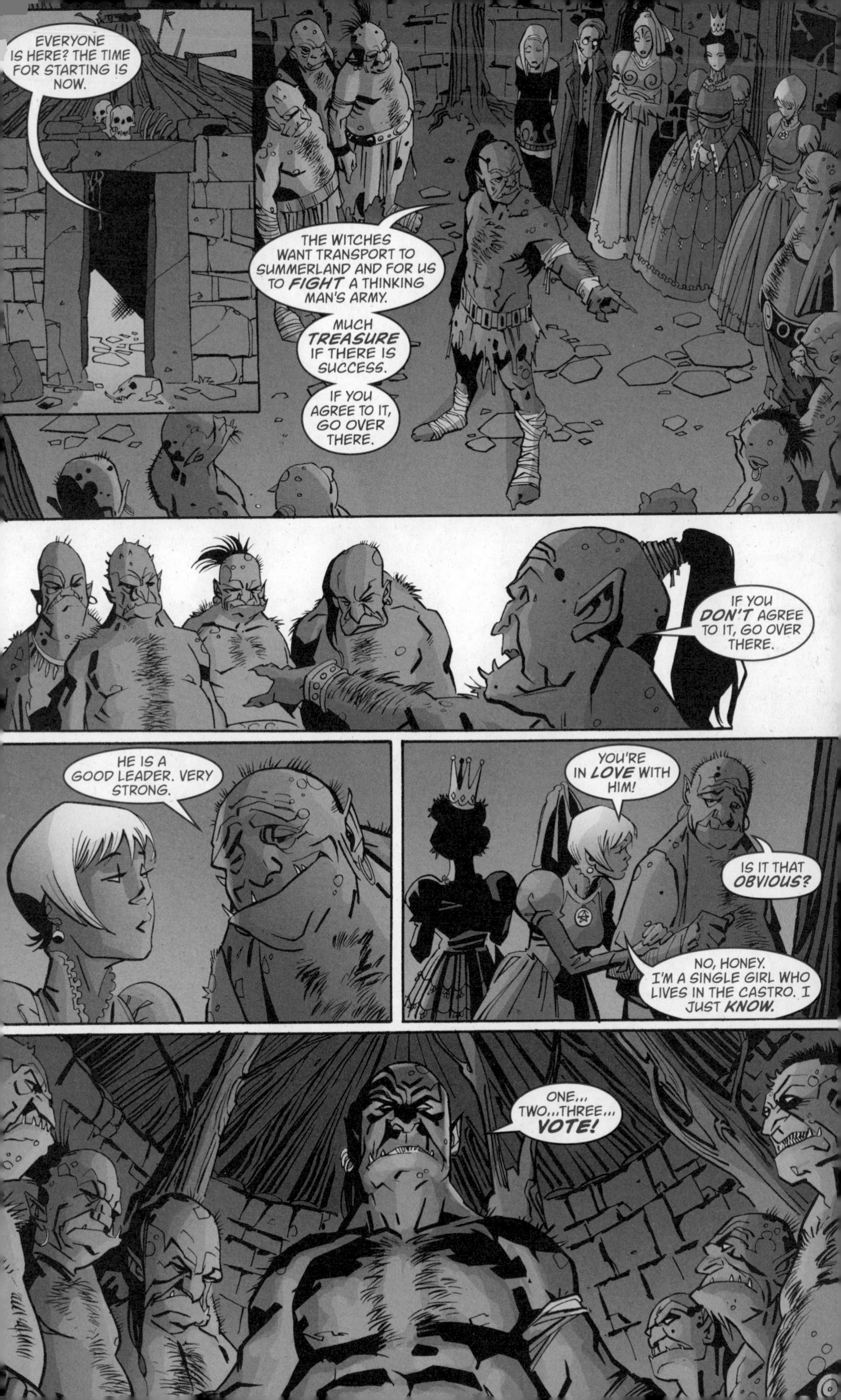
EVERYONE IS HERE? THE TIME FOR STARTING IS NOW.
THE WITCHES WANT TRANSPORT TO SUMMERLAND AND FOR US TO FIGHT A THINKING MAN'S ARMY.
MUCH TREASURE IF THERE IS SUCCESS.
IF YOU AGREE TO IT, GO OVER THERE.
IF YOU DON'T AGREE TO IT, GO OVER THERE.
HE IS A GOOD LEADER. VERY STRONG.
YOU'RE IN LOVE WITH HIM!
IS IT THAT OBVIOUS?
NO, HONEY. I'M A SINGLE GIRL WHO LIVES IN THE CASTRO. I JUST KNOW.
ONE... TWO...THREE... VOTE!

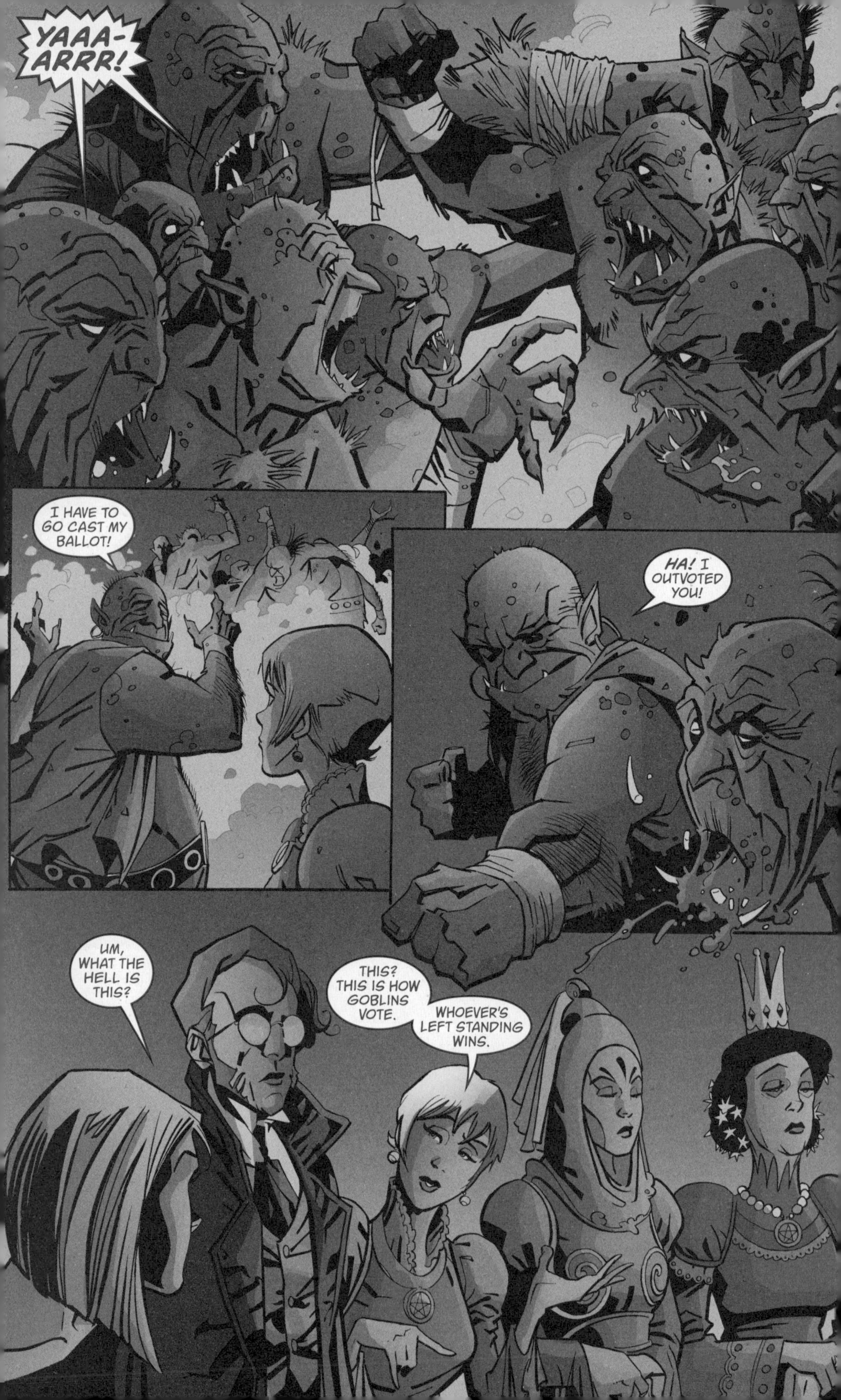
YAAA-ARRR!
I HAVE TO GO CAST MY BALLOT!
HA! I OUTVOTED YOU!
UM, WHAT THE HELL IS THIS?
THIS? THIS IS HOW GOBLINS VOTE.
WHOEVER'S LEFT STANDING WINS.

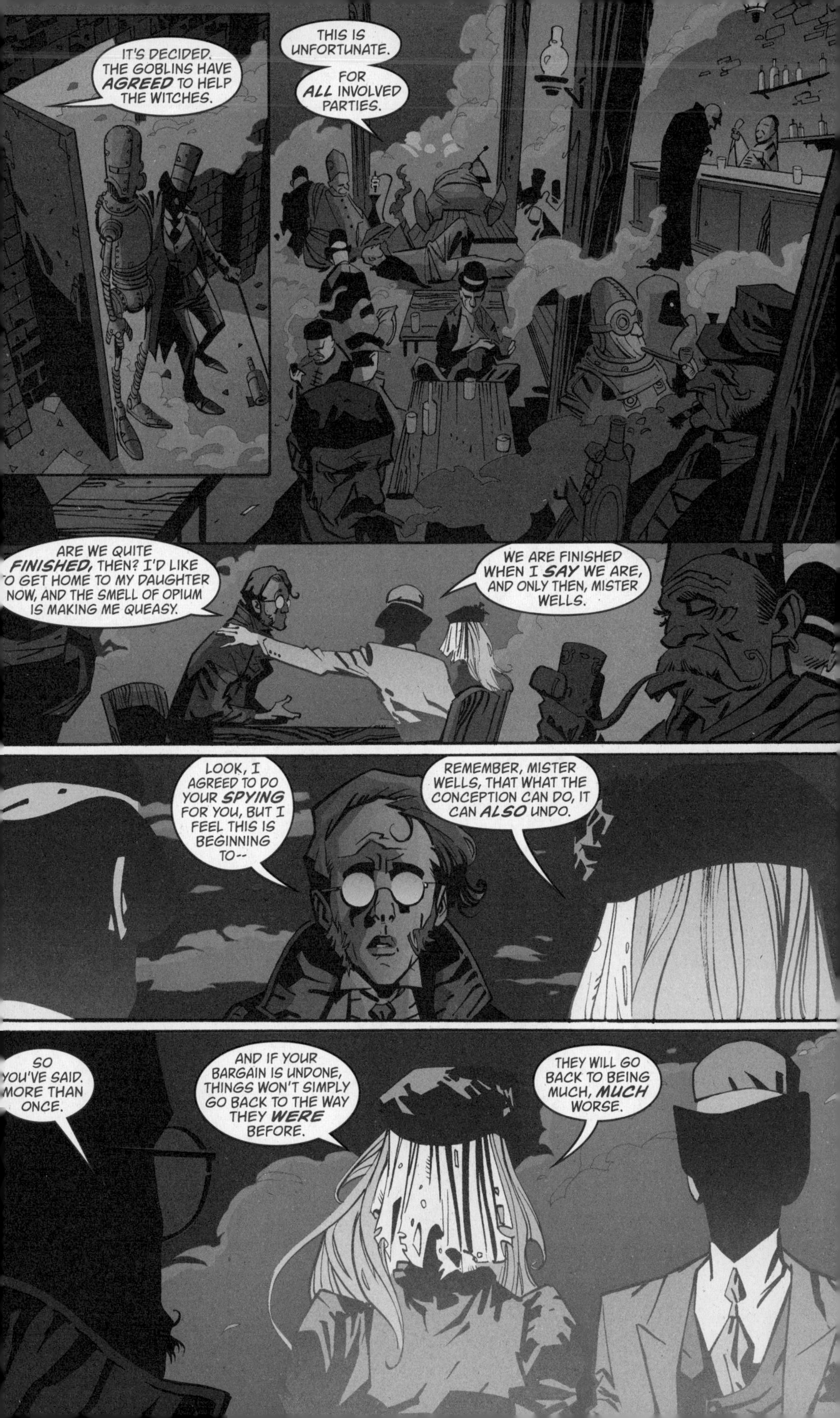
IT'S DECIDED. THE GOBLINS HAVE AGREED TO HELP THE WITCHES.
THIS IS UNFORTUNATE.
FOR ALL INVOLVED PARTIES.
ARE WE QUITE FINISHED, THEN? I'D LIKE TO GET HOME TO MY DAUGHTER NOW, AND THE SMELL OF OPIUM IS MAKING ME QUEASY.
WE ARE FINISHED WHEN I SAY WE ARE, AND ONLY THEN, MISTER WELLS.
LOOK, I AGREED TO DO YOUR SPYING FOR YOU, BUT I FEEL THIS IS BEGINNING TO--
REMEMBER, MISTER WELLS, THAT WHAT THE CONCEPTION CAN DO, IT CAN ALSO UNDO.
SO YOU'VE SAID. MORE THAN ONCE.
AND IF YOUR BARGAIN IS UNDONE, THINGS WON'T SIMPLY GO BACK TO THE WAY THEY WERE BEFORE.
THEY WILL GO BACK TO BEING MUCH, MUCH WORSE.

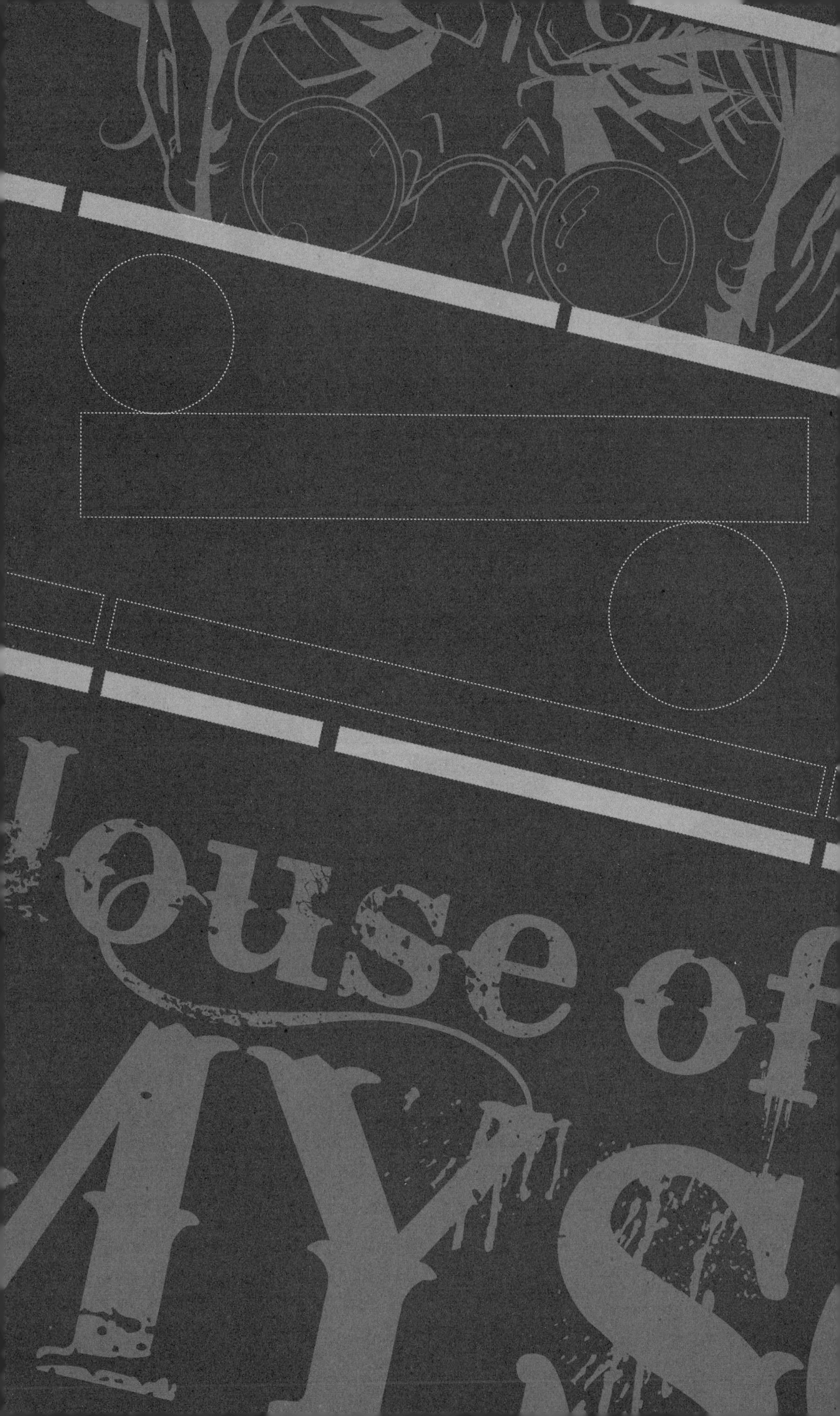

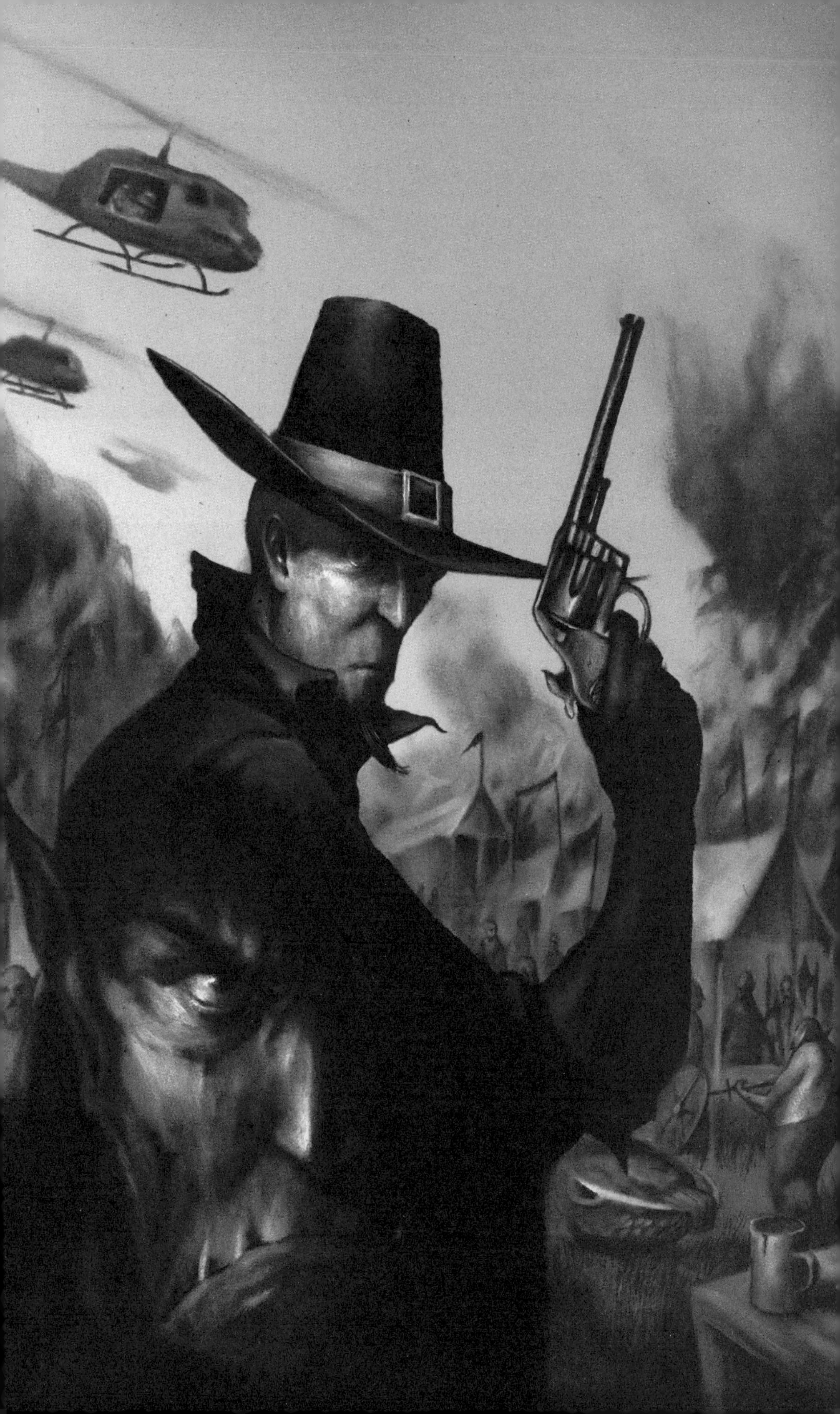

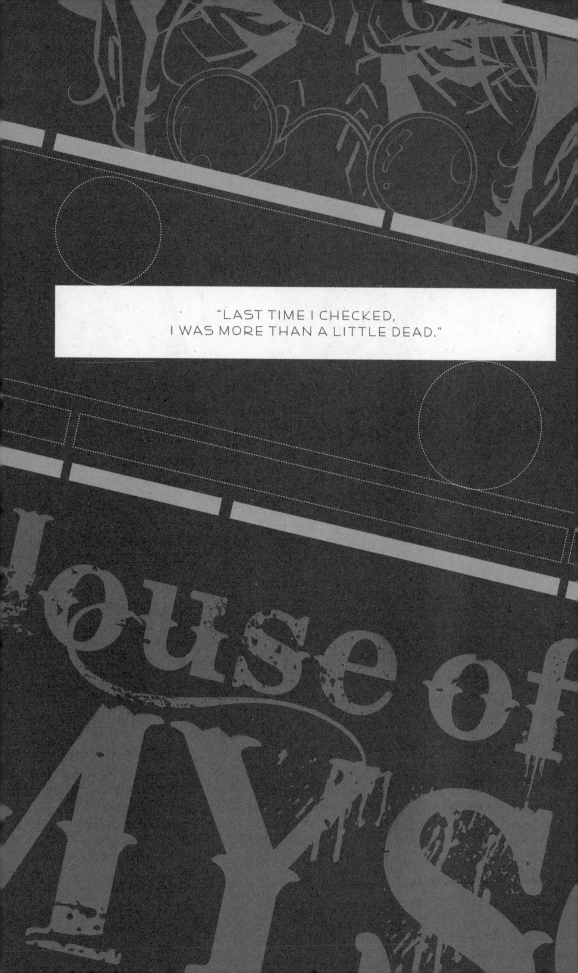

"LAST TIME I CHECKED,
I WAS MORE THAN A LITTLE DEAD."

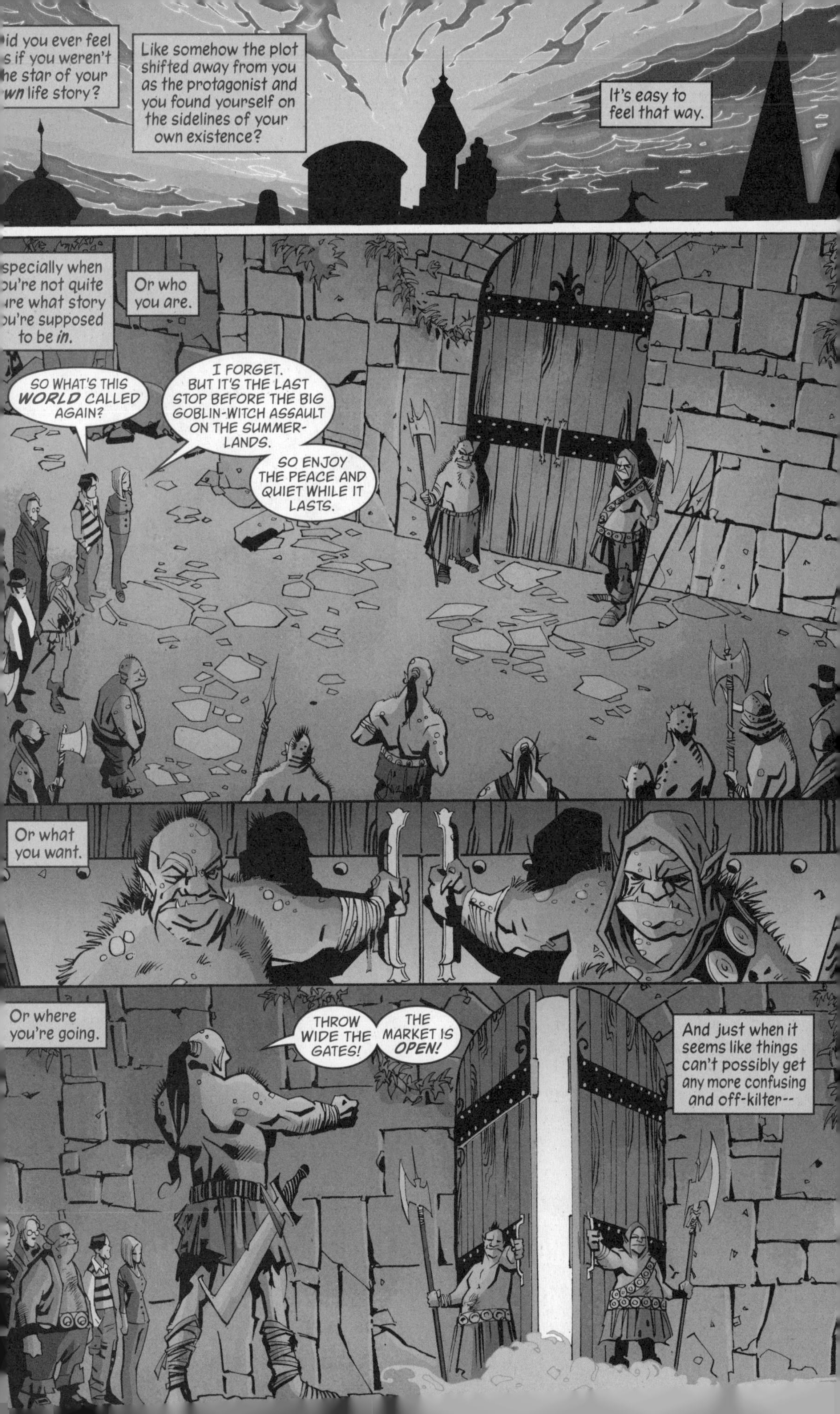

id you ever feel s if you weren't he star of your wn life story?
Like somehow the plot shifted away from you as the protagonist and you found yourself on the sidelines of your own existence?
It's easy to feel that way.
specially when u're not quite re what story u're supposed to be *in*.
Or who you are.
SO WHAT'S THIS ***WORLD*** CALLED AGAIN?
I FORGET. BUT IT'S THE LAST STOP BEFORE THE BIG GOBLIN-WITCH ASSAULT ON THE SUMMER-LANDS.
SO ENJOY THE PEACE AND QUIET WHILE IT LASTS.
Or what you want.
Or where you're going.
THROW WIDE THE GATES!
THE MARKET IS ***OPEN!***
And just when it seems like things can't possibly get any more confusing and off-kilter--

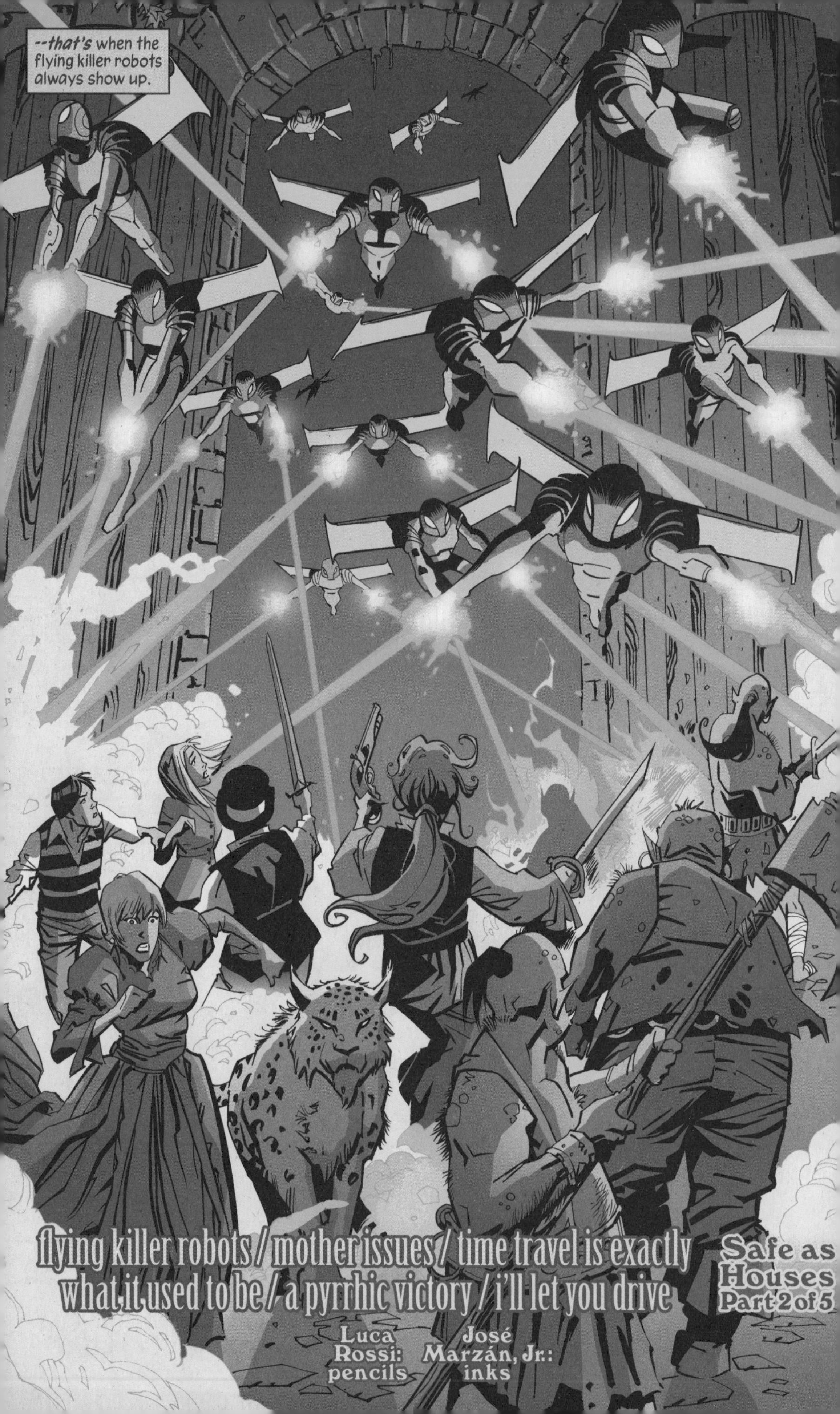
--that's when the flying killer robots always show up.
flying killer robots / mother issues / time travel is exactly what it used to be / a pyrrhic victory / i'll let you drive
Safe as Houses Part 2 of 5
Luca Rossi: pencils
José Marzán, Jr.: inks

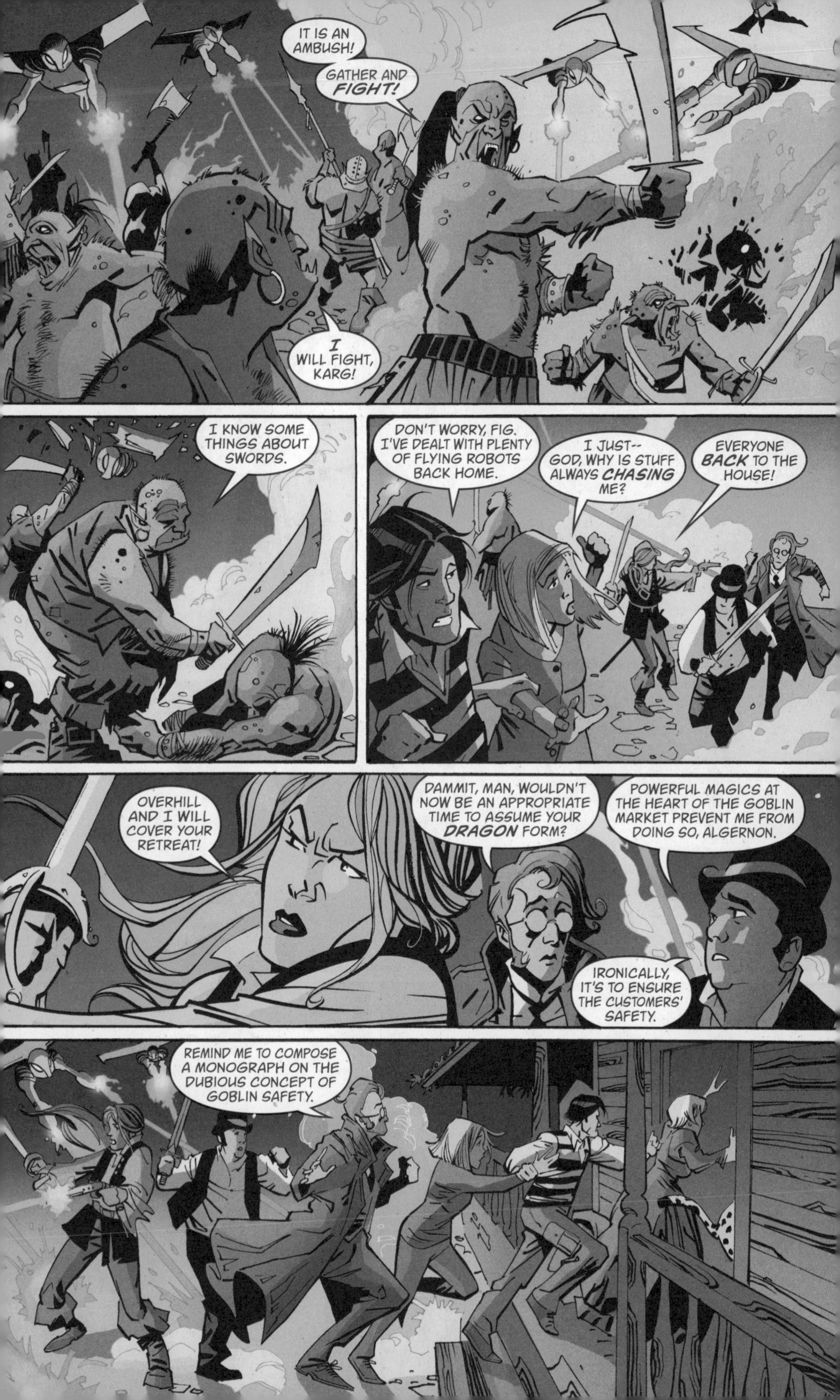

IT IS AN AMBUSH!
GATHER AND FIGHT!
I WILL FIGHT, KARG!
I KNOW SOME THINGS ABOUT SWORDS.
DON'T WORRY, FIG. I'VE DEALT WITH PLENTY OF FLYING ROBOTS BACK HOME.
I JUST-- GOD, WHY IS STUFF ALWAYS CHASING ME?
EVERYONE BACK TO THE HOUSE!
OVERHILL AND I WILL COVER YOUR RETREAT!
DAMMIT, MAN, WOULDN'T NOW BE AN APPROPRIATE TIME TO ASSUME YOUR DRAGON FORM?
POWERFUL MAGICS AT THE HEART OF THE GOBLIN MARKET PREVENT ME FROM DOING SO, ALGERNON.
IRONICALLY, IT'S TO ENSURE THE CUSTOMERS' SAFETY.
REMIND ME TO COMPOSE A MONOGRAPH ON THE DUBIOUS CONCEPT OF GOBLIN SAFETY.

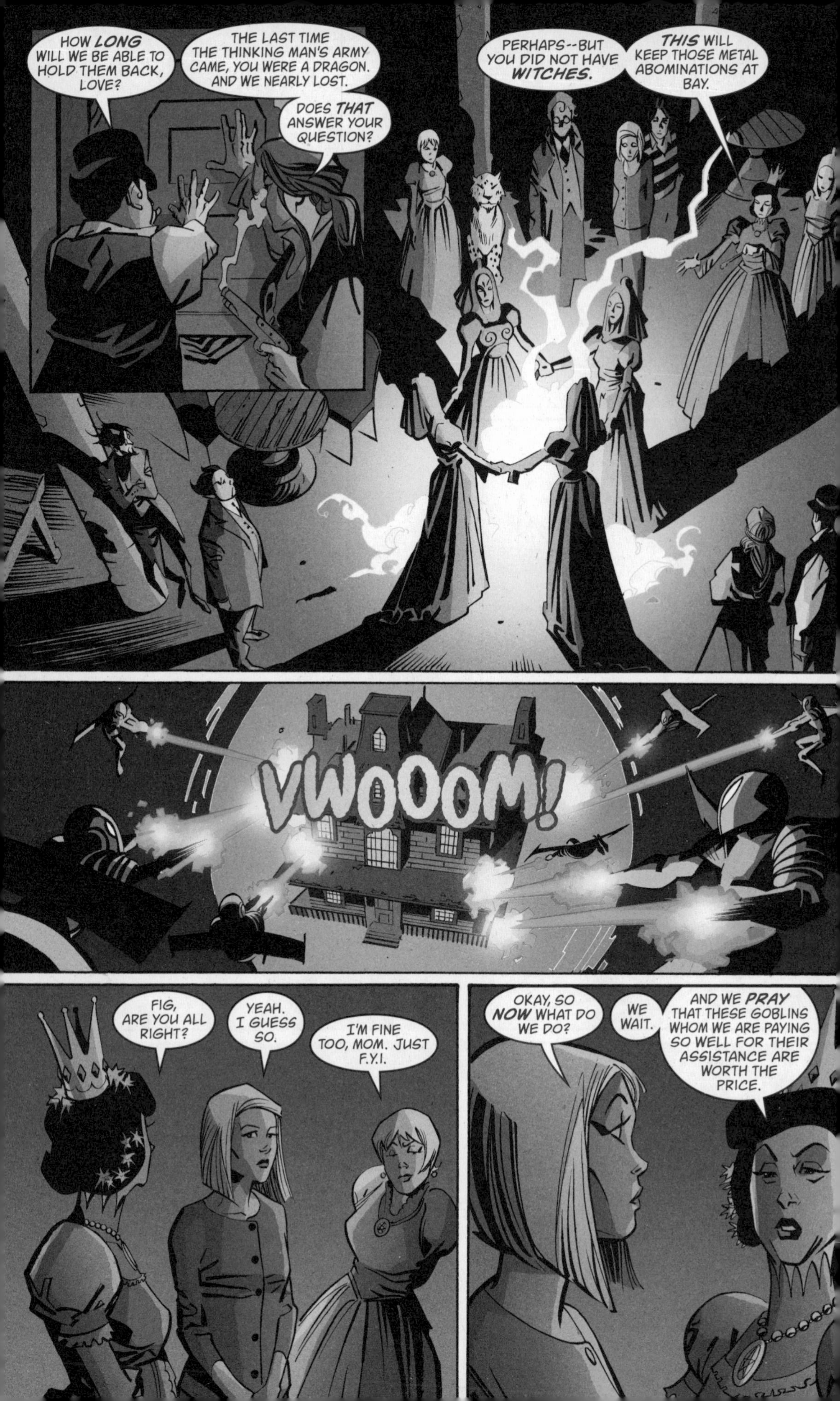
HOW LONG WILL WE BE ABLE TO HOLD THEM BACK, LOVE?
THE LAST TIME THE THINKING MAN'S ARMY CAME, YOU WERE A DRAGON. AND WE NEARLY LOST.
DOES THAT ANSWER YOUR QUESTION?
PERHAPS--BUT YOU DID NOT HAVE WITCHES.
THIS WILL KEEP THOSE METAL ABOMINATIONS AT BAY.
VWOOOM!
FIG, ARE YOU ALL RIGHT?
YEAH. I GUESS SO.
I'M FINE TOO, MOM. JUST F.Y.I.
OKAY, SO NOW WHAT DO WE DO?
WE WAIT.
AND WE PRAY THAT THESE GOBLINS WHOM WE ARE PAYING SO WELL FOR THEIR ASSISTANCE ARE WORTH THE PRICE.

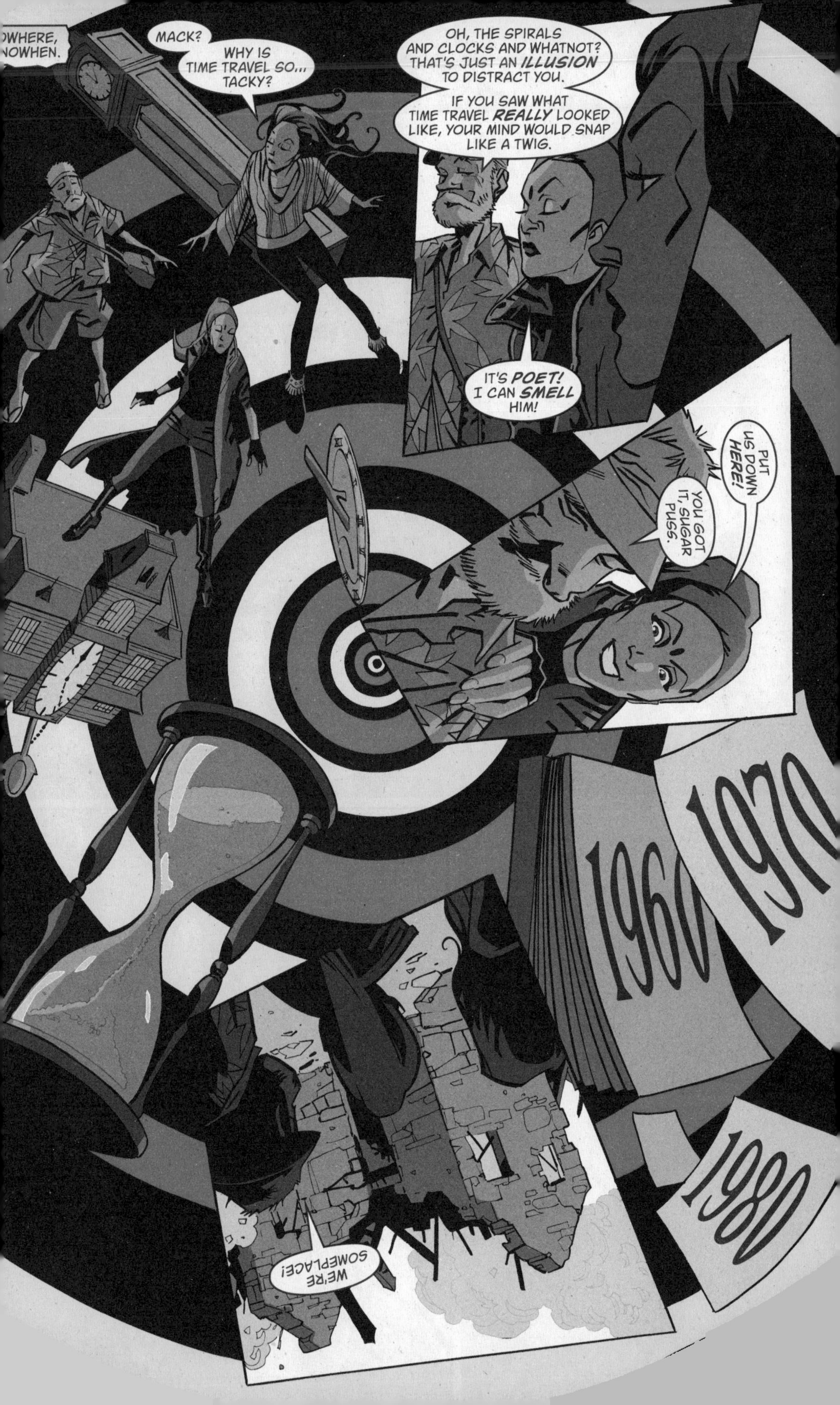
OWHERE,
NOWHEN.
MACK?
WHY IS TIME TRAVEL SO... TACKY?
OH, THE SPIRALS AND CLOCKS AND WHATNOT? THAT'S JUST AN ILLUSION TO DISTRACT YOU.
IF YOU SAW WHAT TIME TRAVEL REALLY LOOKED LIKE, YOUR MIND WOULD SNAP LIKE A TWIG.
IT'S POET! I CAN SMELL HIM!
PUT US DOWN HERE!
YOU GOT IT, SUGAR PUSS.
1960
1970
1980
WE'RE SOMEPLACE!

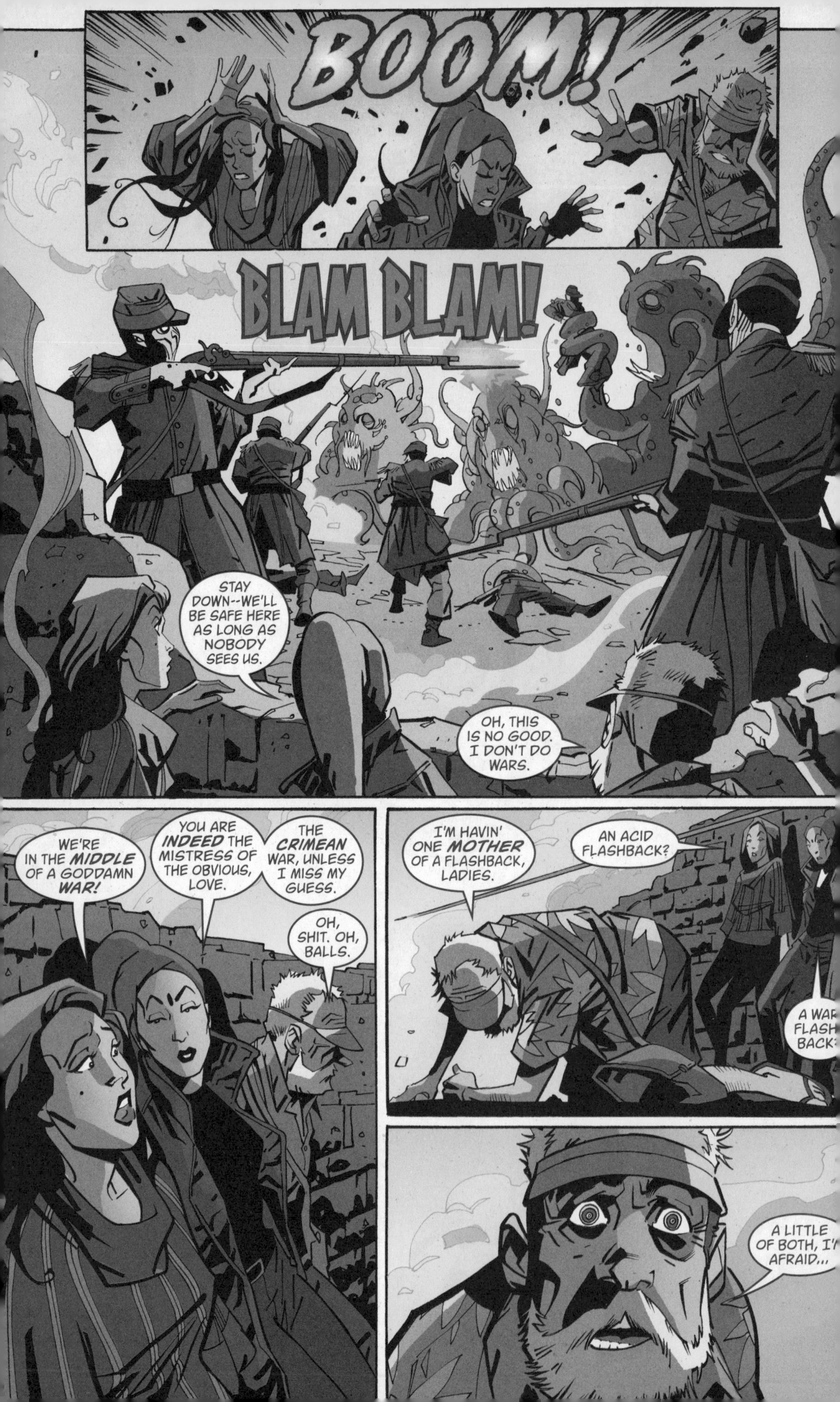
BOOM!
BLAM BLAM!
STAY DOWN--WE'LL BE SAFE HERE AS LONG AS NOBODY SEES US.
OH, THIS IS NO GOOD. I DON'T DO WARS.
WE'RE IN THE MIDDLE OF A GODDAMN WAR!
YOU ARE INDEED THE MISTRESS OF THE OBVIOUS, LOVE.
THE CRIMEAN WAR, UNLESS I MISS MY GUESS.
OH, SHIT. OH, BALLS.
I'M HAVIN' ONE MOTHER OF A FLASHBACK, LADIES.
AN ACID FLASHBACK?
A WAR FLASHBACK?
A LITTLE OF BOTH, I'M AFRAID...

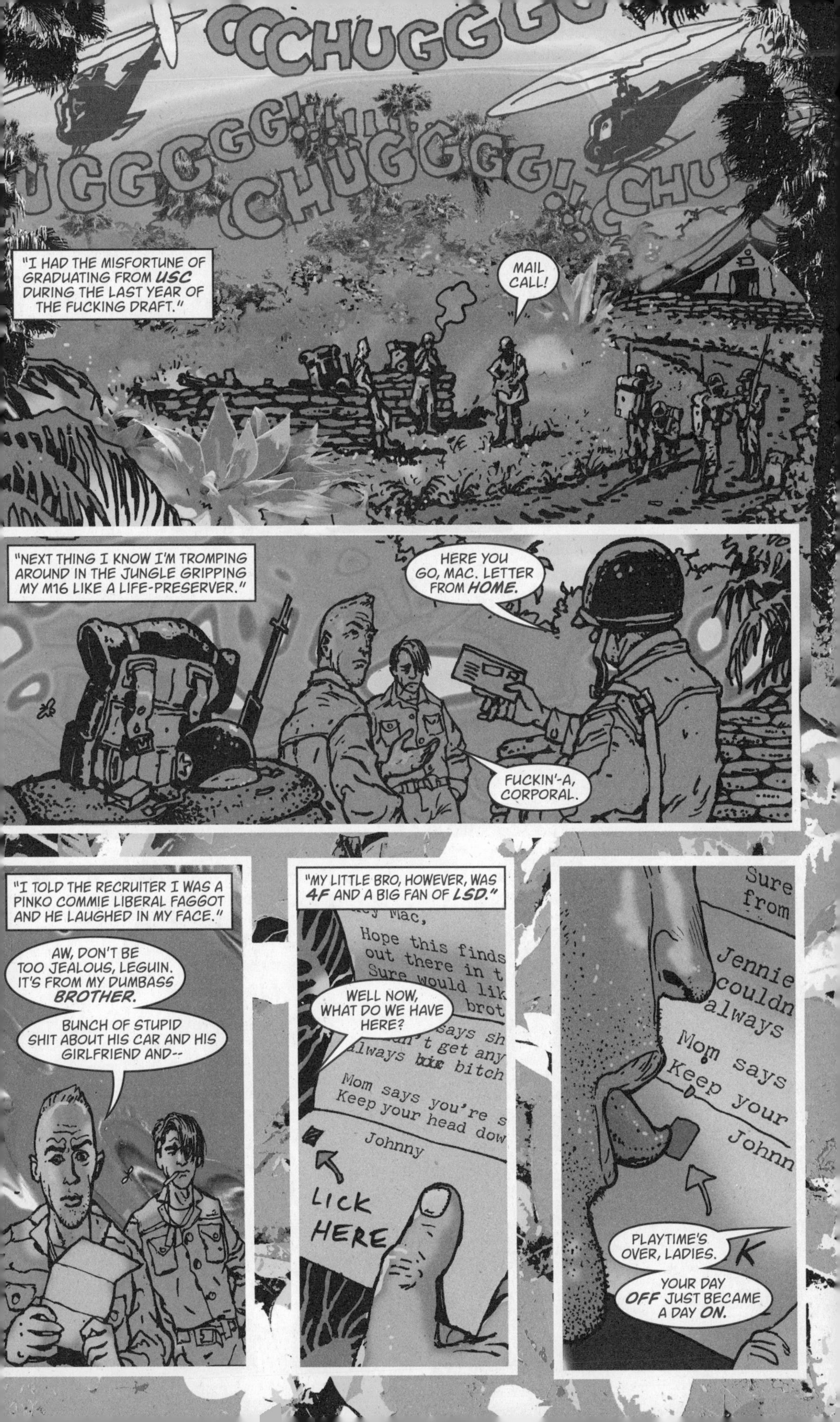

CCCHUGGG
UGGGGGG!!!!
CHUGGGGG!!
CHU
"I HAD THE MISFORTUNE OF GRADUATING FROM USC DURING THE LAST YEAR OF THE FUCKING DRAFT."
MAIL CALL!
"NEXT THING I KNOW I'M TROMPING AROUND IN THE JUNGLE GRIPPING MY M16 LIKE A LIFE-PRESERVER."
HERE YOU GO, MAC. LETTER FROM HOME.
FUCKIN'-A, CORPORAL.
"I TOLD THE RECRUITER I WAS A PINKO COMMIE LIBERAL FAGGOT AND HE LAUGHED IN MY FACE."
AW, DON'T BE TOO JEALOUS, LEGUIN. IT'S FROM MY DUMBASS BROTHER.
BUNCH OF STUPID SHIT ABOUT HIS CAR AND HIS GIRLFRIEND AND--
"MY LITTLE BRO, HOWEVER, WAS 4F AND A BIG FAN OF LSD."
Hope this finds
out there in t
Sure would lik
brot
WELL NOW, WHAT DO WE HAVE HERE?
always bitch
Mom says you're s
Keep your head dow
Johnny
LICK HERE
Sure
from
Jennie
couldn
always
Mom says
Keep your
Johnn
PLAYTIME'S OVER, LADIES.
YOUR DAY OFF JUST BECAME A DAY ON.

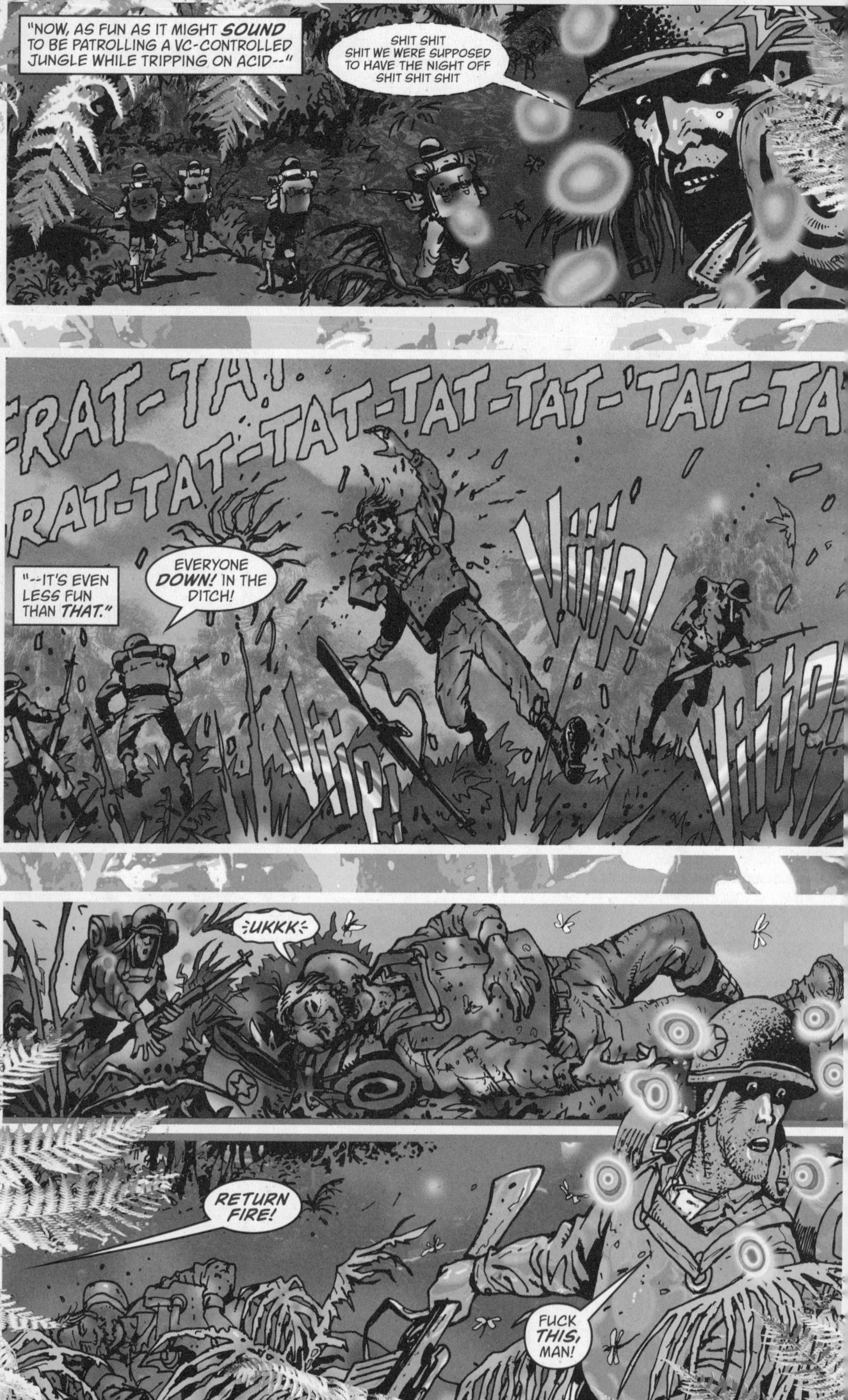
"NOW, AS FUN AS IT MIGHT SOUND TO BE PATROLLING A VC-CONTROLLED JUNGLE WHILE TRIPPING ON ACID--"
SHIT SHIT SHIT WE WERE SUPPOSED TO HAVE THE NIGHT OFF SHIT SHIT SHIT
RAT-TAT!
RAT-TAT-TAT-TAT-TAT-'TAT-TAT
"--IT'S EVEN LESS FUN THAN THAT."
EVERYONE DOWN! IN THE DITCH!
Viiip!
Viiip!
Viiip!
UKKK
RETURN FIRE!
FUCK THIS, MAN!

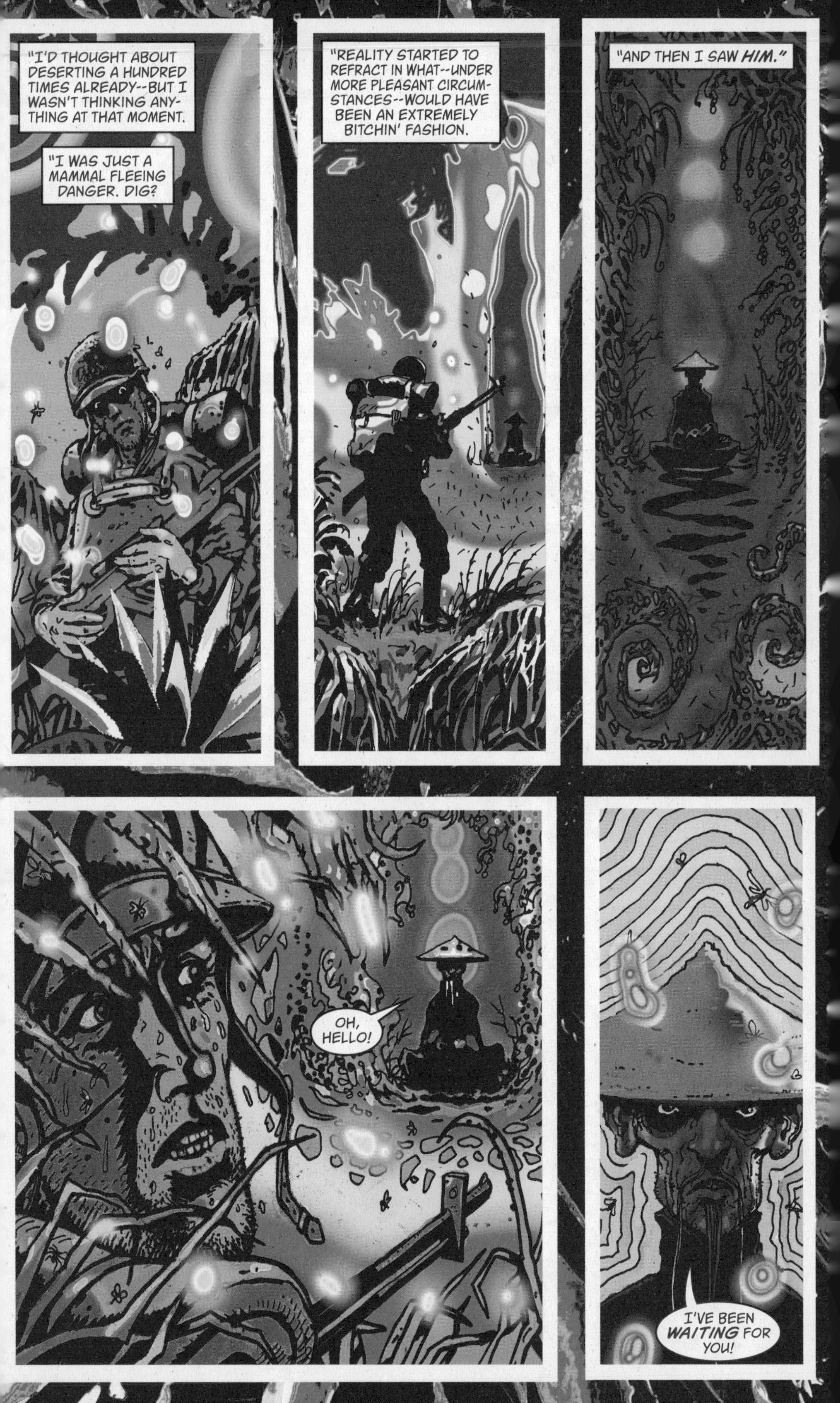
"I'D THOUGHT ABOUT DESERTING A HUNDRED TIMES ALREADY--BUT I WASN'T THINKING ANYTHING AT THAT MOMENT.
"I WAS JUST A MAMMAL FLEEING DANGER. DIG?
"REALITY STARTED TO REFRACT IN WHAT--UNDER MORE PLEASANT CIRCUMSTANCES--WOULD HAVE BEEN AN EXTREMELY BITCHIN' FASHION.
"AND THEN I SAW HIM."
OH, HELLO!
I'VE BEEN WAITING FOR YOU!

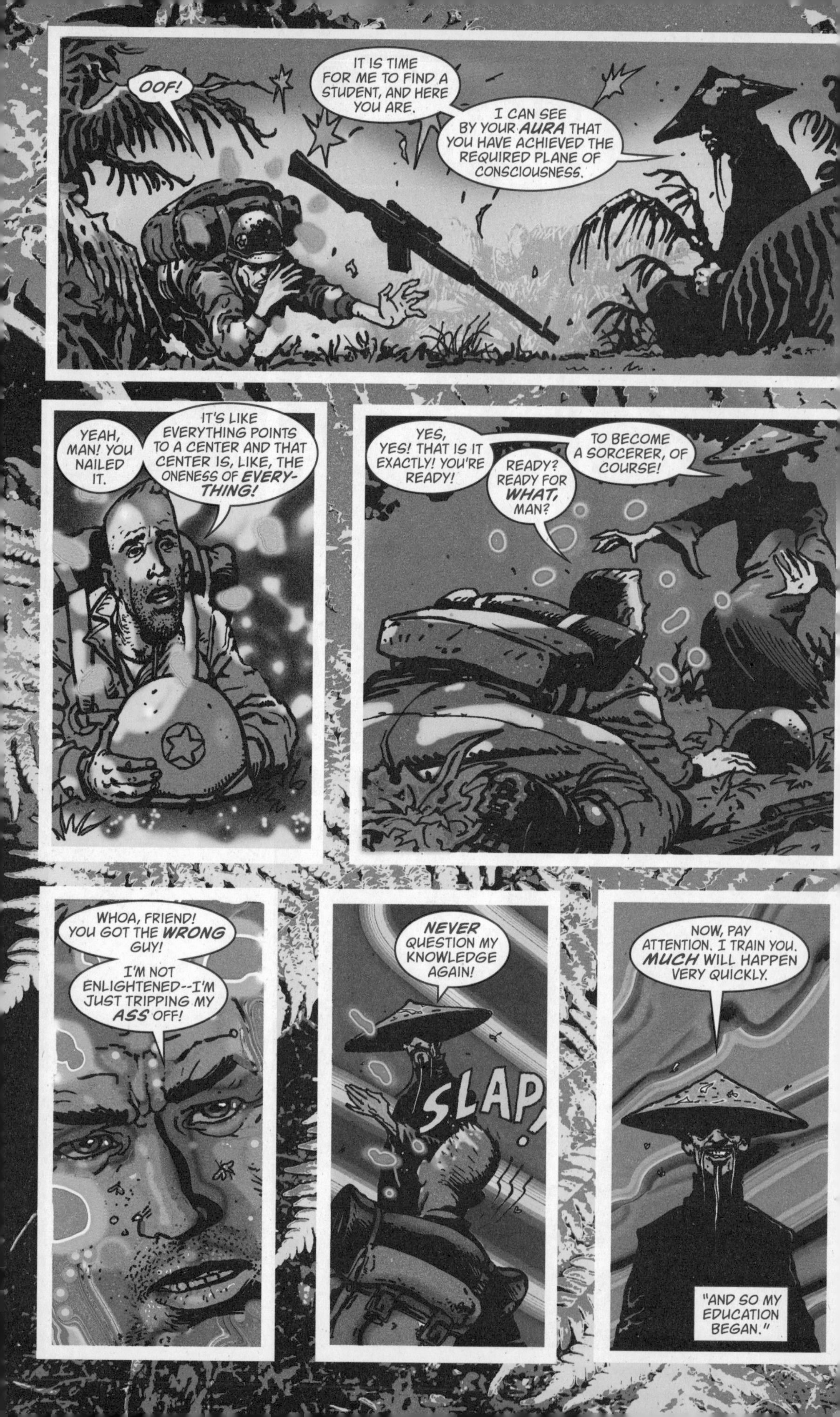
OOF!
IT IS TIME FOR ME TO FIND A STUDENT, AND HERE YOU ARE.
I CAN SEE BY YOUR AURA THAT YOU HAVE ACHIEVED THE REQUIRED PLANE OF CONSCIOUSNESS.
YEAH, MAN! YOU NAILED IT.
IT'S LIKE EVERYTHING POINTS TO A CENTER AND THAT CENTER IS, LIKE, THE ONENESS OF EVERY-THING!
YES, YES! THAT IS IT EXACTLY! YOU'RE READY!
READY? READY FOR WHAT, MAN?
TO BECOME A SORCERER, OF COURSE!
WHOA, FRIEND! YOU GOT THE WRONG GUY!
I'M NOT ENLIGHTENED--I'M JUST TRIPPING MY ASS OFF!
NEVER QUESTION MY KNOWLEDGE AGAIN!
SLAP!
NOW, PAY ATTENTION. I TRAIN YOU. MUCH WILL HAPPEN VERY QUICKLY.
"AND SO MY EDUCATION BEGAN."

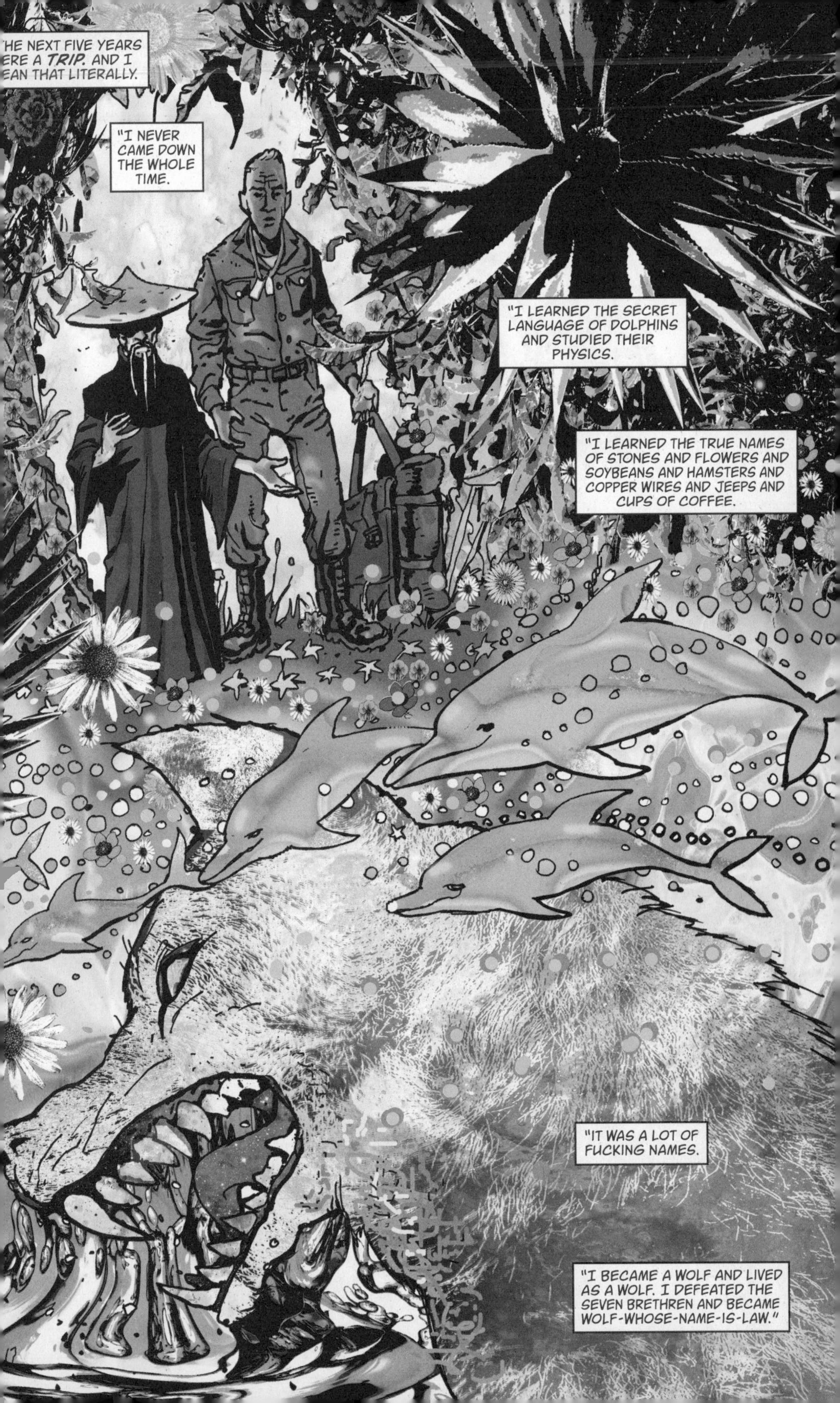

HE NEXT FIVE YEARS ERE A TRIP. AND I EAN THAT LITERALLY.
"I NEVER CAME DOWN THE WHOLE TIME.
"I LEARNED THE SECRET LANGUAGE OF DOLPHINS AND STUDIED THEIR PHYSICS.
"I LEARNED THE TRUE NAMES OF STONES AND FLOWERS AND SOYBEANS AND HAMSTERS AND COPPER WIRES AND JEEPS AND CUPS OF COFFEE.
"IT WAS A LOT OF FUCKING NAMES.
"I BECAME A WOLF AND LIVED AS A WOLF. I DEFEATED THE SEVEN BRETHREN AND BECAME WOLF-WHOSE-NAME-IS-LAW."

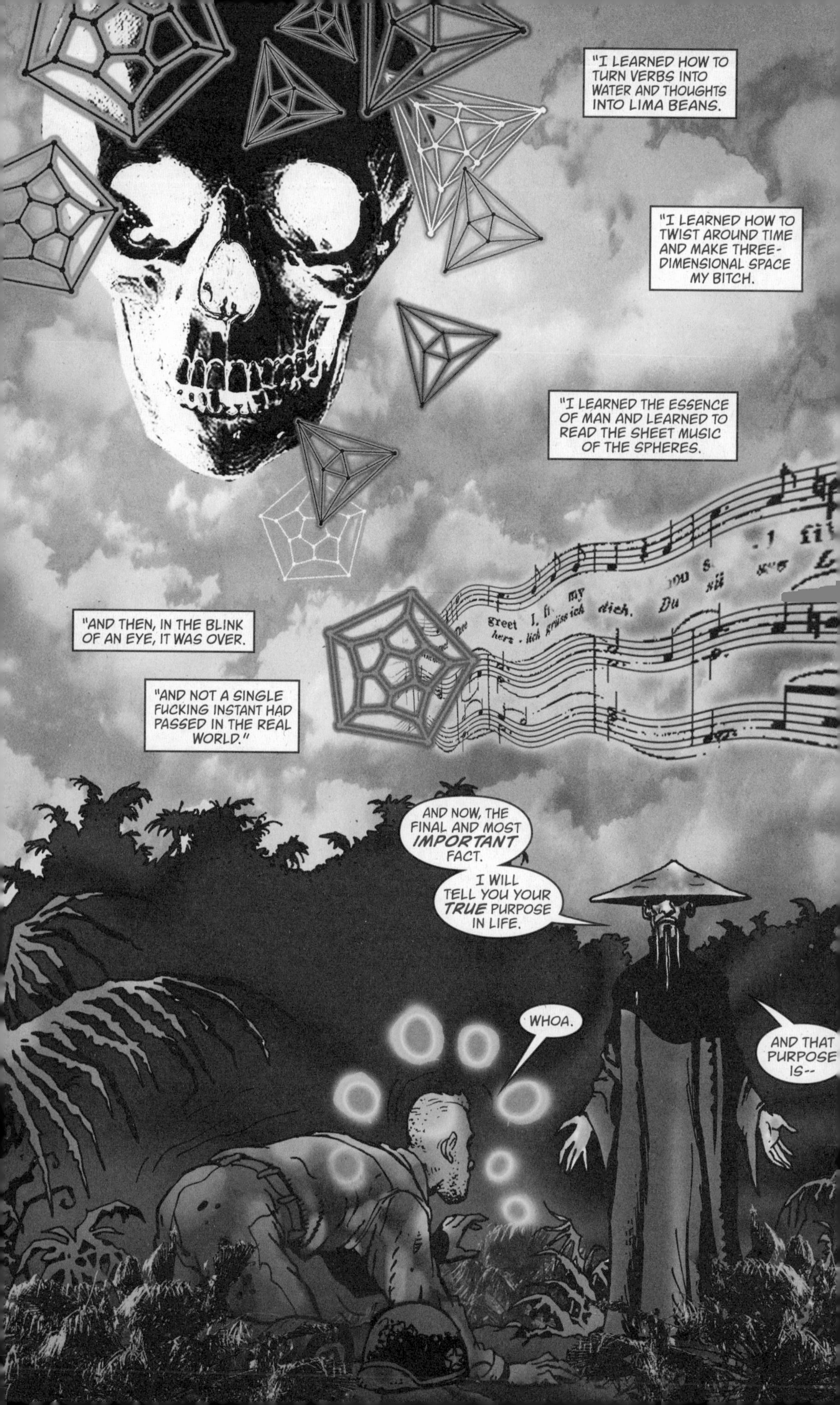
"I LEARNED HOW TO TURN VERBS INTO WATER AND THOUGHTS INTO LIMA BEANS.
"I LEARNED HOW TO TWIST AROUND TIME AND MAKE THREE-DIMENSIONAL SPACE MY BITCH.
"I LEARNED THE ESSENCE OF MAN AND LEARNED TO READ THE SHEET MUSIC OF THE SPHERES.
"AND THEN, IN THE BLINK OF AN EYE, IT WAS OVER.
"AND NOT A SINGLE FUCKING INSTANT HAD PASSED IN THE REAL WORLD."
AND NOW, THE FINAL AND MOST IMPORTANT FACT.
I WILL TELL YOU YOUR TRUE PURPOSE IN LIFE.
WHOA.
AND THAT PURPOSE IS--

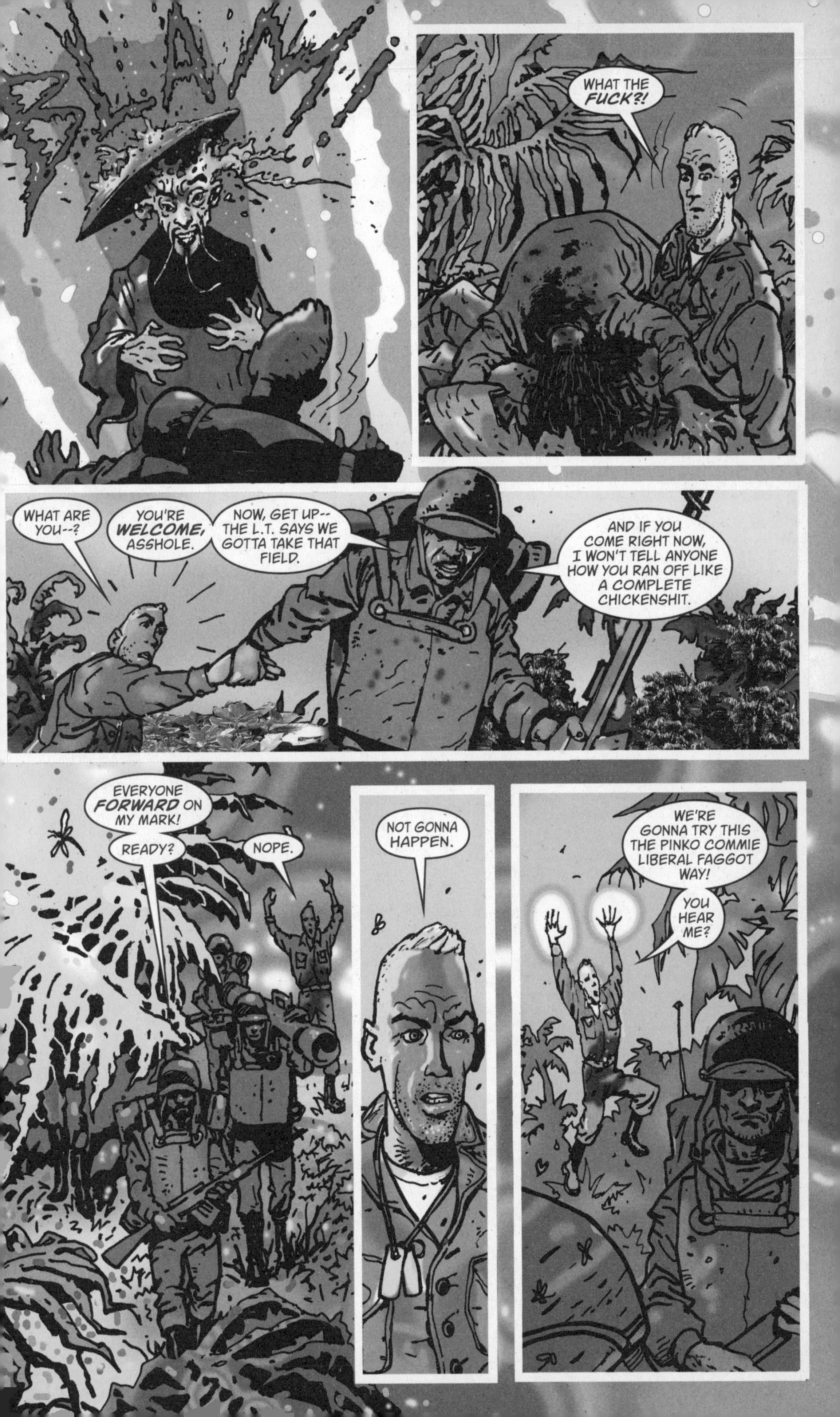
BLAM!!
WHAT THE FUCK?!
WHAT ARE YOU--?
YOU'RE WELCOME, ASSHOLE.
NOW, GET UP-- THE L.T. SAYS WE GOTTA TAKE THAT FIELD.
AND IF YOU COME RIGHT NOW, I WON'T TELL ANYONE HOW YOU RAN OFF LIKE A COMPLETE CHICKENSHIT.
EVERYONE FORWARD ON MY MARK!
READY?
NOPE.
NOT GONNA HAPPEN.
WE'RE GONNA TRY THIS THE PINKO COMMIE LIBERAL FAGGOT WAY!
YOU HEAR ME?

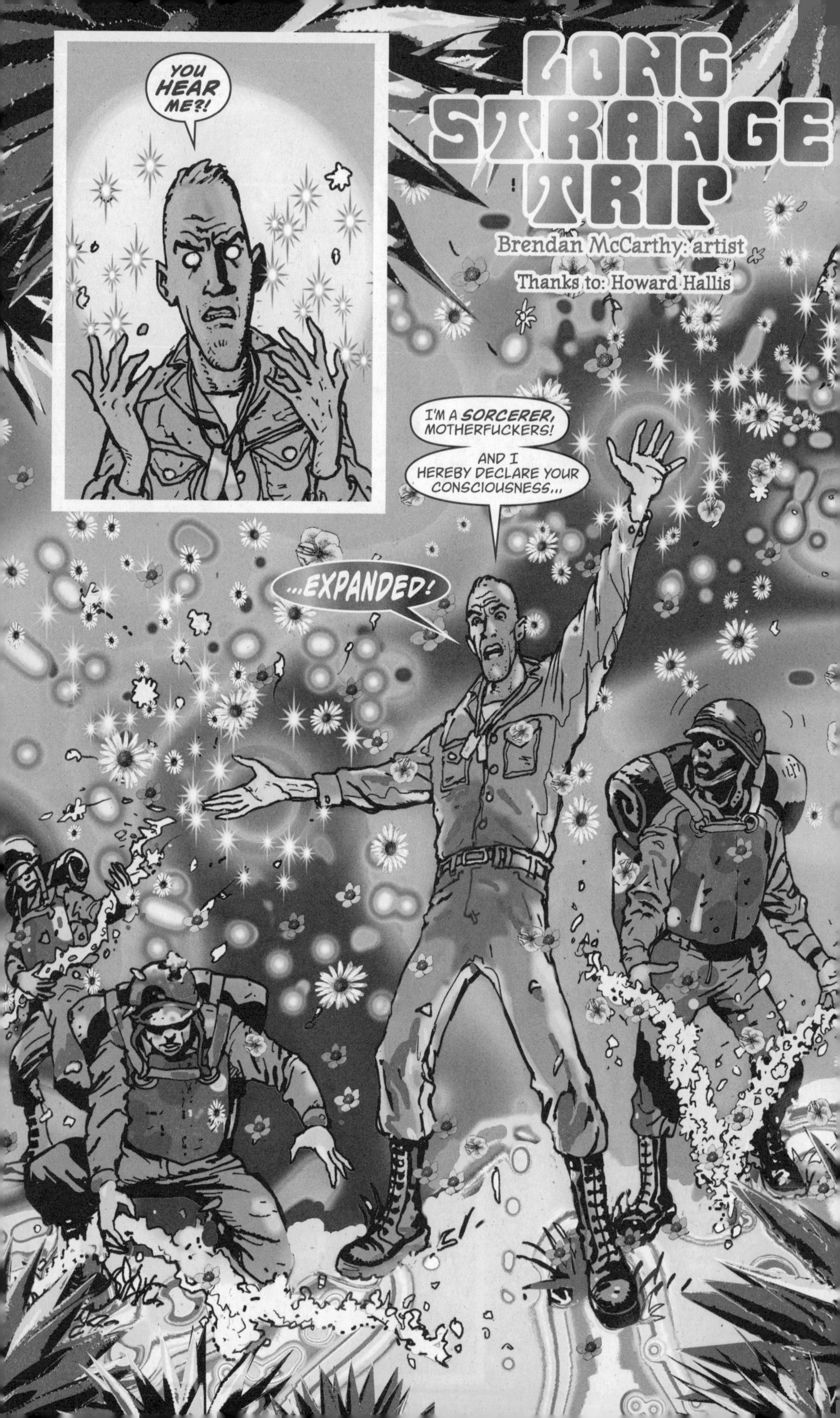

LONG STRANGE TRIP
Brendan McCarthy: artist
Thanks to: Howard Hallis
YOU HEAR ME?!
I'M A SORCERER, MOTHERFUCKERS!
AND I HEREBY DECLARE YOUR CONSCIOUSNESS...
...EXPANDED!

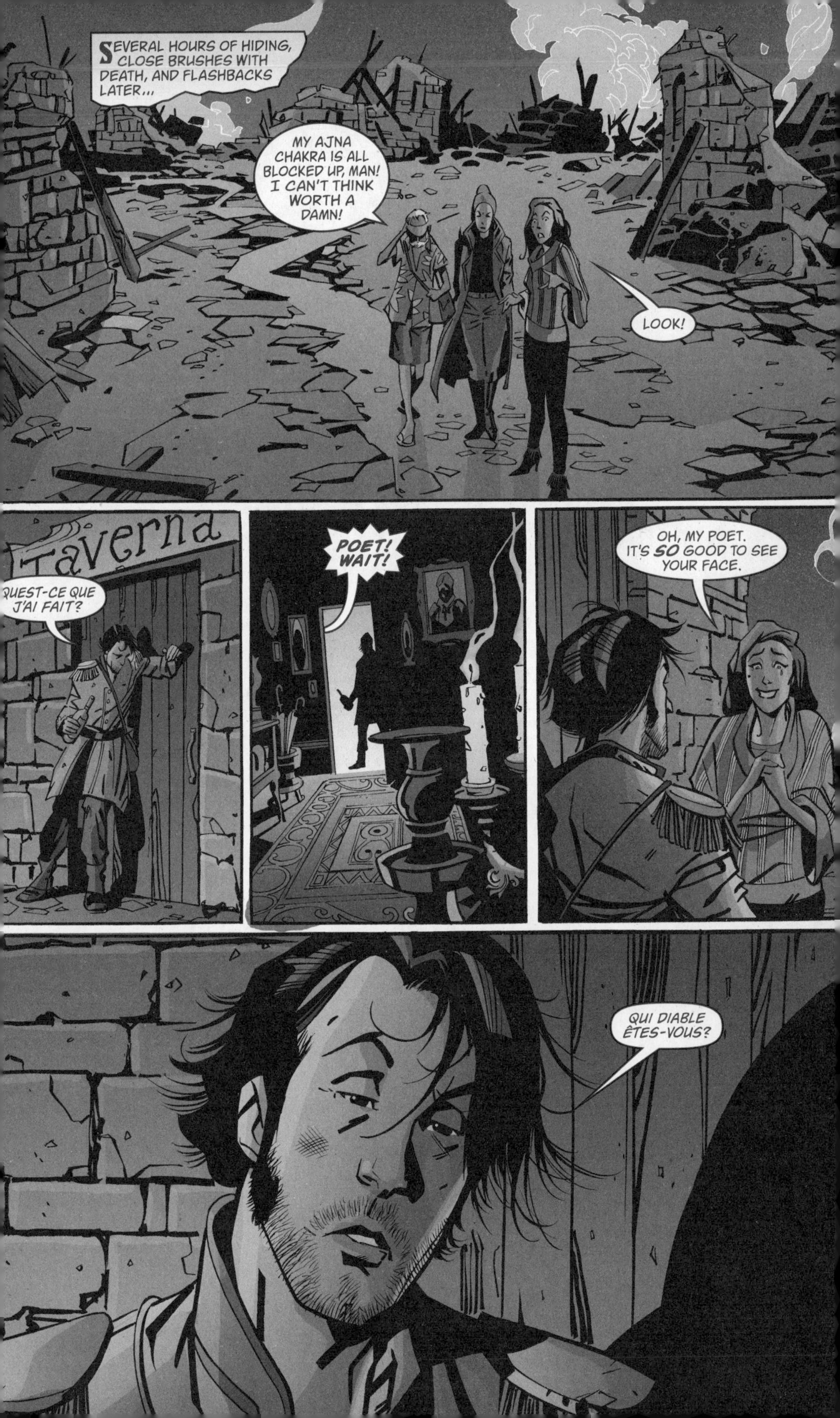
SEVERAL HOURS OF HIDING, CLOSE BRUSHES WITH DEATH, AND FLASHBACKS LATER...
MY AJNA CHAKRA IS ALL BLOCKED UP, MAN! I CAN'T THINK WORTH A DAMN!
LOOK!
Taverna
QUEST-CE QUE J'AI FAIT?
POET! WAIT!
OH, MY POET. IT'S SO GOOD TO SEE YOUR FACE.
QUI DIABLE ÊTES-VOUS?

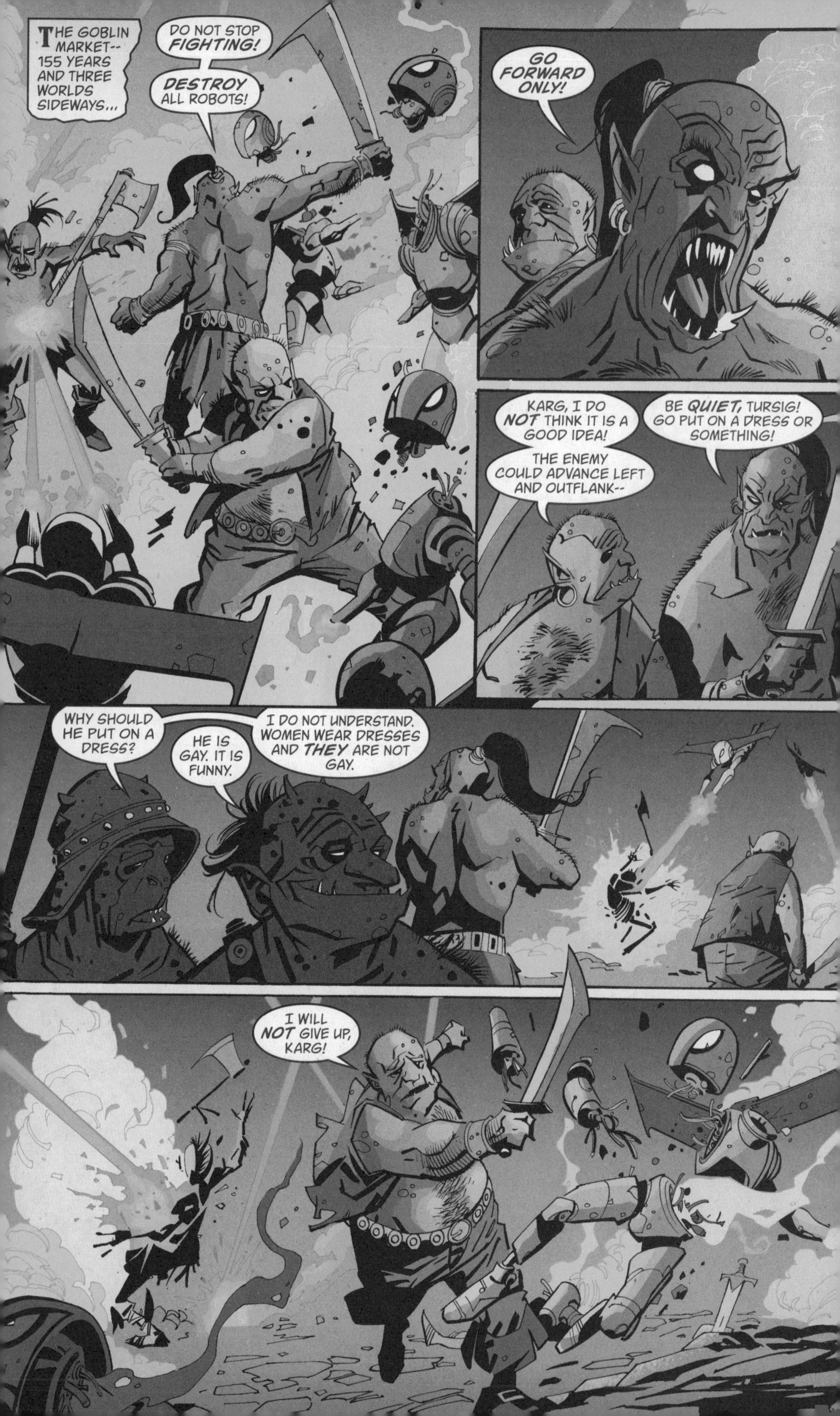
THE GOBLIN MARKET-- 155 YEARS AND THREE WORLDS SIDEWAYS...
DO NOT STOP FIGHTING!
DESTROY ALL ROBOTS!
GO FORWARD ONLY!
KARG, I DO NOT THINK IT IS A GOOD IDEA!
THE ENEMY COULD ADVANCE LEFT AND OUTFLANK--
BE QUIET, TURSIG! GO PUT ON A DRESS OR SOMETHING!
WHY SHOULD HE PUT ON A DRESS?
HE IS GAY. IT IS FUNNY.
I DO NOT UNDERSTAND. WOMEN WEAR DRESSES AND THEY ARE NOT GAY.
I WILL NOT GIVE UP, KARG!

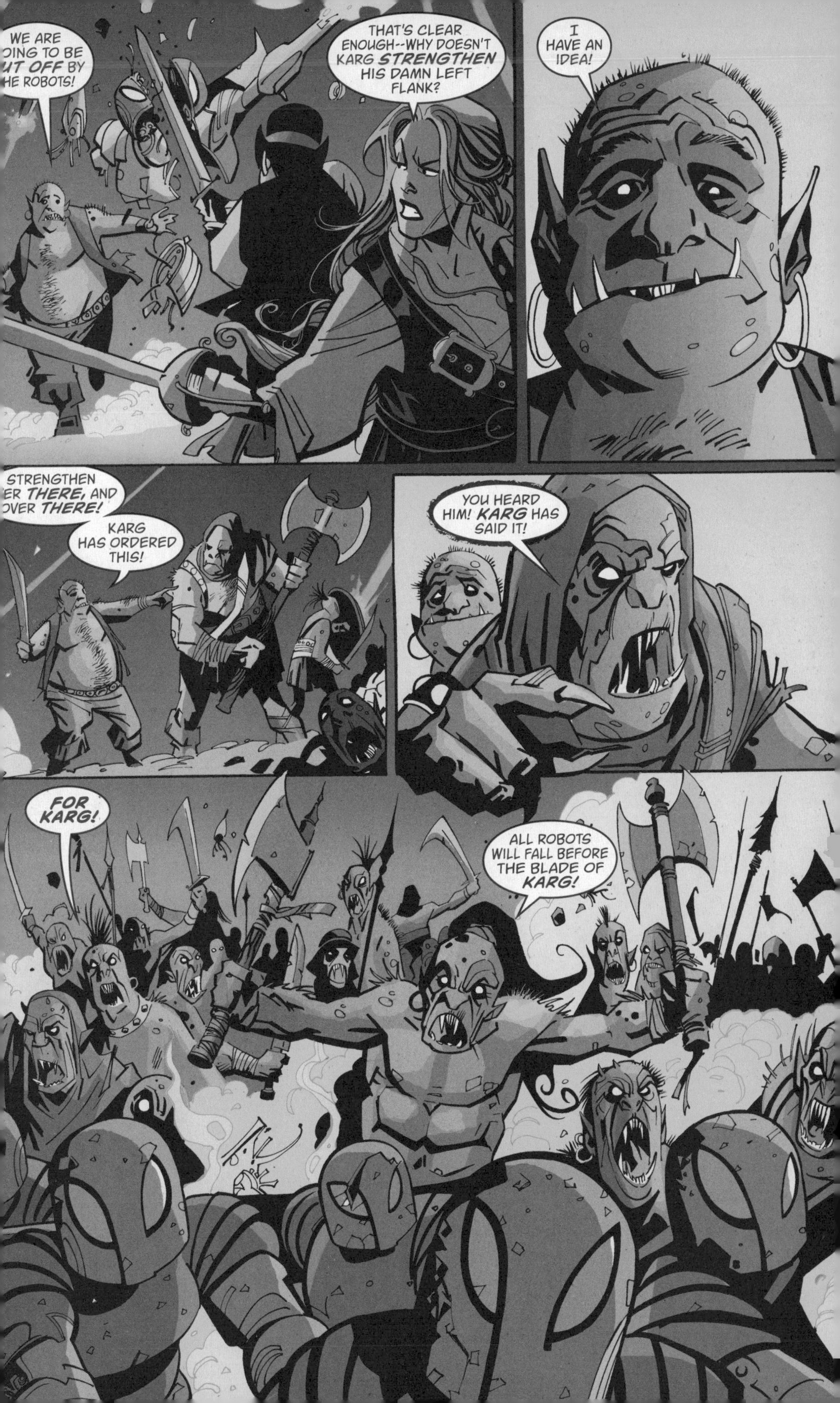
WE ARE GOING TO BE CUT OFF BY THE ROBOTS!
THAT'S CLEAR ENOUGH--WHY DOESN'T KARG STRENGTHEN HIS DAMN LEFT FLANK?
I HAVE AN IDEA!
STRENGTHEN OVER THERE, AND OVER THERE!
KARG HAS ORDERED THIS!
YOU HEARD HIM! KARG HAS SAID IT!
FOR KARG!
ALL ROBOTS WILL FALL BEFORE THE BLADE OF KARG!

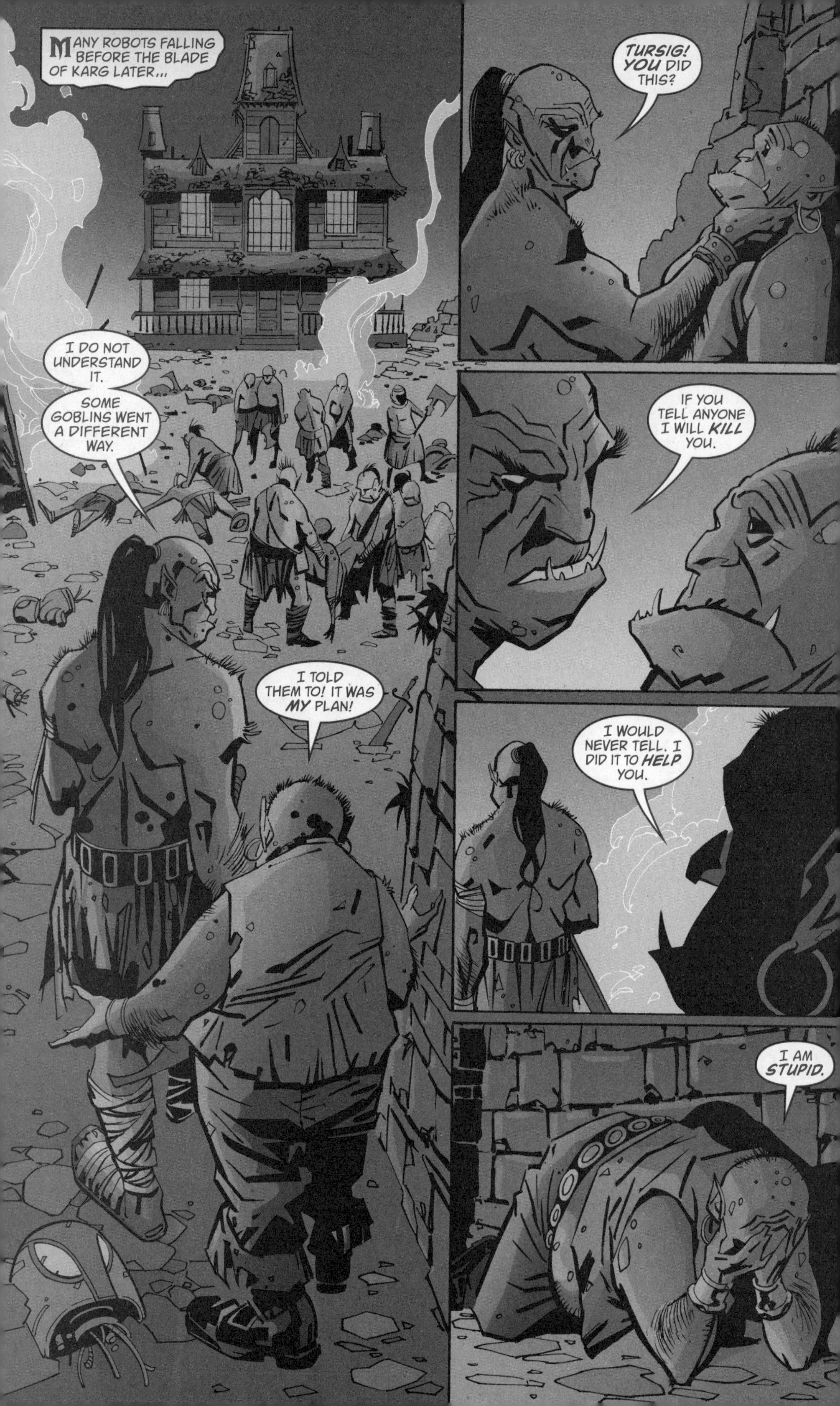
MANY ROBOTS FALLING BEFORE THE BLADE OF KARG LATER...
I DO NOT UNDERSTAND IT.
SOME GOBLINS WENT A DIFFERENT WAY.
I TOLD THEM TO! IT WAS MY PLAN!
TURSIG! YOU DID THIS?
IF YOU TELL ANYONE I WILL KILL YOU.
I WOULD NEVER TELL. I DID IT TO HELP YOU.
I AM STUPID.

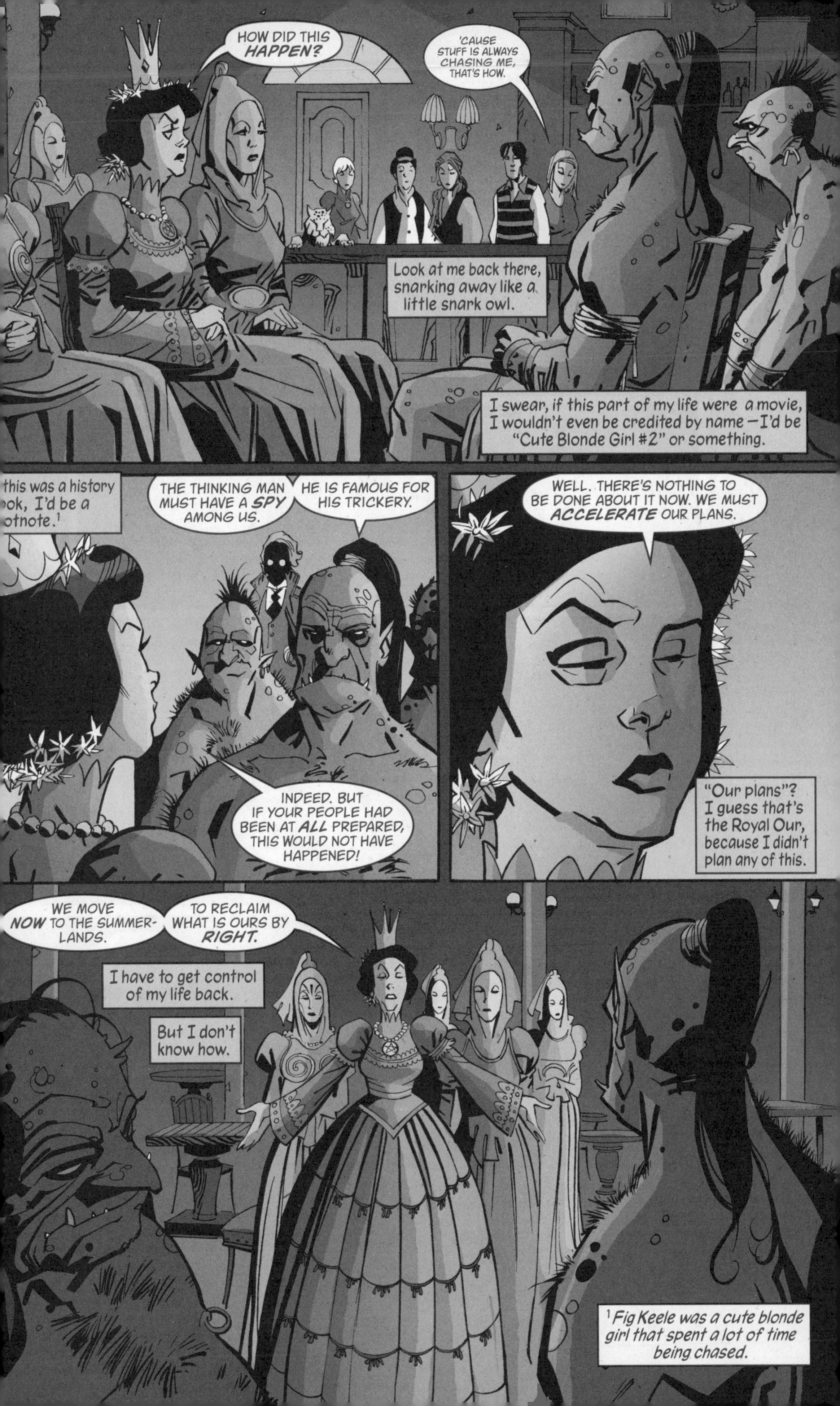
HOW DID THIS HAPPEN?
'CAUSE STUFF IS ALWAYS CHASING ME, THAT'S HOW.
Look at me back there, snarking away like a little snark owl.
I swear, if this part of my life were a movie, I wouldn't even be credited by name—I'd be "Cute Blonde Girl #2" or something.
this was a history ok, I'd be a otnote.[1]
THE THINKING MAN MUST HAVE A SPY AMONG US.
HE IS FAMOUS FOR HIS TRICKERY.
INDEED. BUT IF YOUR PEOPLE HAD BEEN AT ALL PREPARED, THIS WOULD NOT HAVE HAPPENED!
WELL. THERE'S NOTHING TO BE DONE ABOUT IT NOW. WE MUST ACCELERATE OUR PLANS.
"Our plans"? I guess that's the Royal Our, because I didn't plan any of this.
WE MOVE NOW TO THE SUMMER-LANDS.
TO RECLAIM WHAT IS OURS BY RIGHT.
I have to get control of my life back.
But I don't know how.
[1] Fig Keele was a cute blonde girl that spent a lot of time being chased.

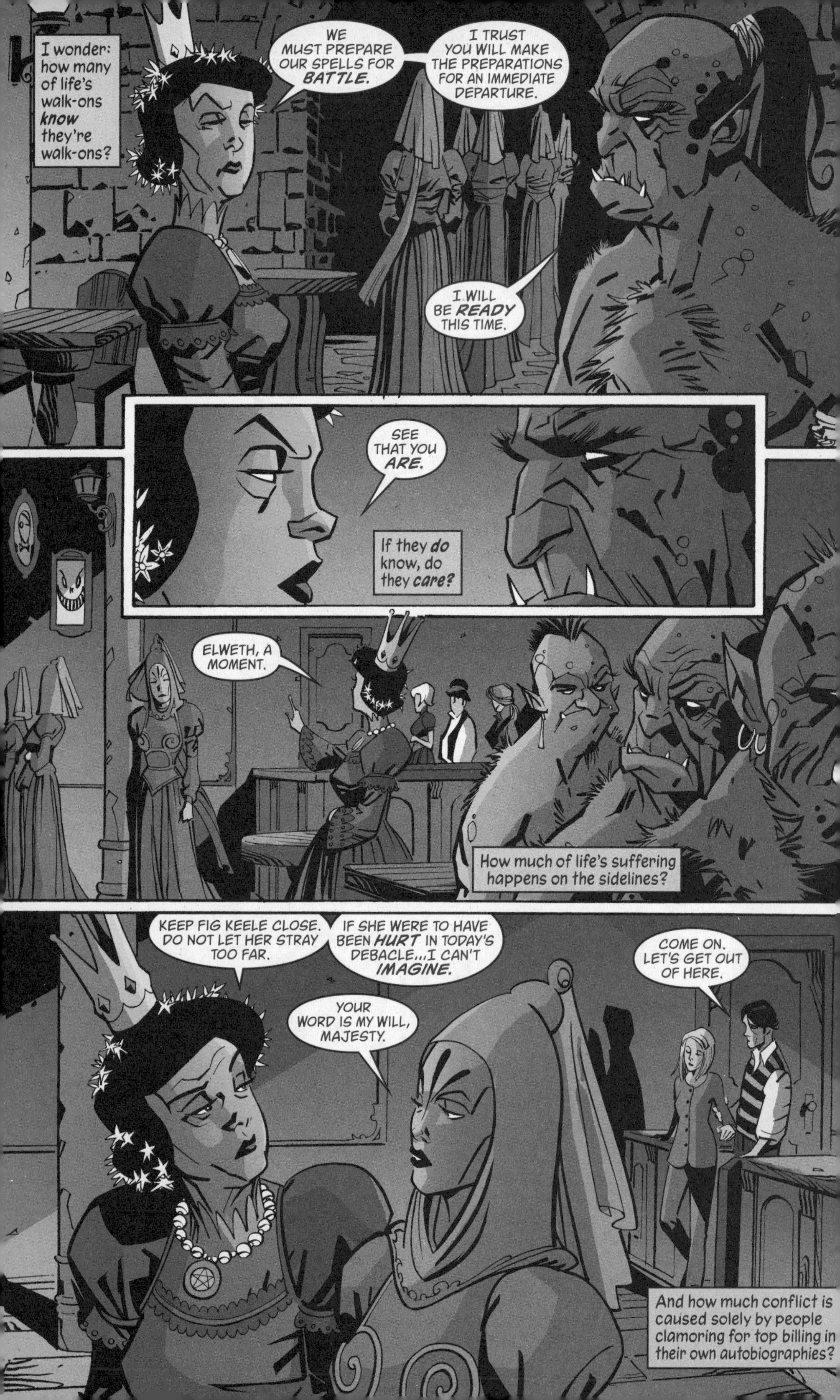

I wonder: how many of life's walk-ons *know* they're walk-ons?
WE MUST PREPARE OUR SPELLS FOR *BATTLE.*
I TRUST YOU WILL MAKE THE PREPARATIONS FOR AN IMMEDIATE DEPARTURE.
I WILL BE *READY* THIS TIME.
SEE THAT YOU *ARE.*
If they *do* know, do they *care?*
ELWETH, A MOMENT.
How much of life's suffering happens on the sidelines?
KEEP FIG KEELE CLOSE. DO NOT LET HER STRAY TOO FAR.
IF SHE WERE TO HAVE BEEN *HURT* IN TODAY'S DEBACLE... I CAN'T *IMAGINE.*
YOUR WORD IS MY WILL, MAJESTY.
COME ON. LET'S GET OUT OF HERE.
And how much conflict is caused solely by people clamoring for top billing in their own autobiographies?

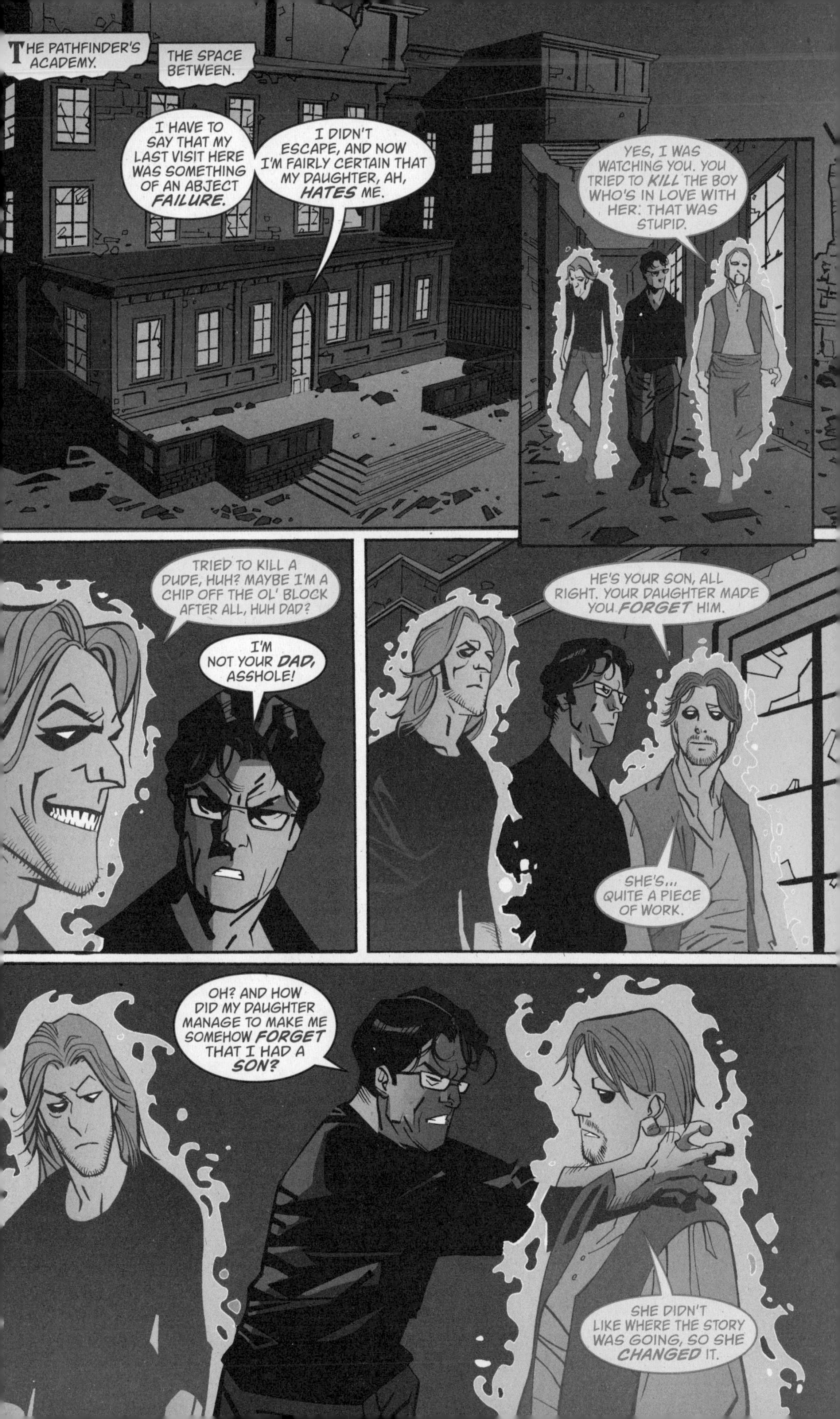
THE PATHFINDER'S ACADEMY.
THE SPACE BETWEEN.
I HAVE TO SAY THAT MY LAST VISIT HERE WAS SOMETHING OF AN ABJECT FAILURE.
I DIDN'T ESCAPE, AND NOW I'M FAIRLY CERTAIN THAT MY DAUGHTER, AH, HATES ME.
YES, I WAS WATCHING YOU. YOU TRIED TO KILL THE BOY WHO'S IN LOVE WITH HER. THAT WAS STUPID.
TRIED TO KILL A DUDE, HUH? MAYBE I'M A CHIP OFF THE OL' BLOCK AFTER ALL, HUH DAD?
I'M NOT YOUR DAD, ASSHOLE!
HE'S YOUR SON, ALL RIGHT. YOUR DAUGHTER MADE YOU FORGET HIM.
SHE'S... QUITE A PIECE OF WORK.
OH? AND HOW DID MY DAUGHTER MANAGE TO MAKE ME SOMEHOW FORGET THAT I HAD A SON?
SHE DIDN'T LIKE WHERE THE STORY WAS GOING, SO SHE CHANGED IT.

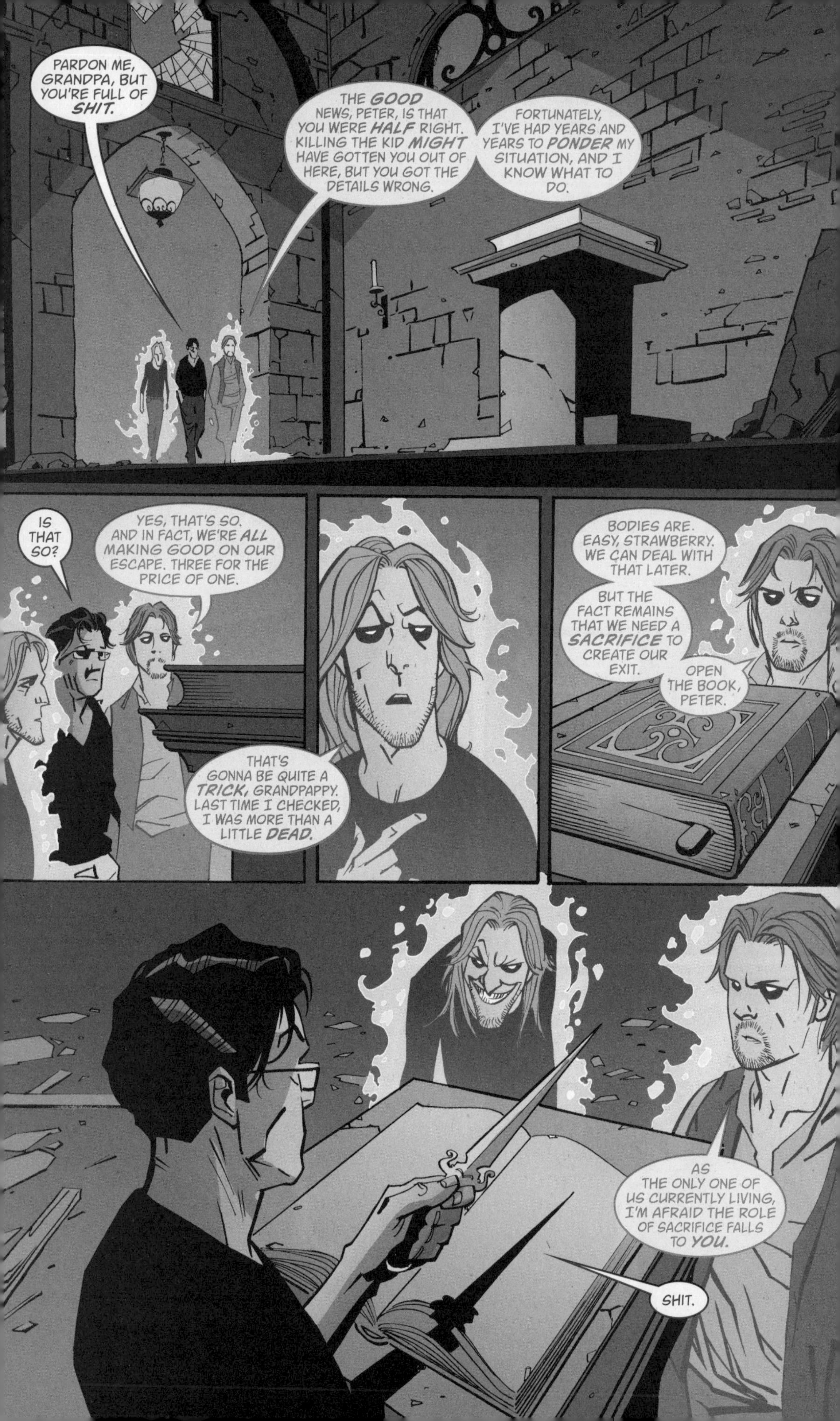
PARDON ME, GRANDPA, BUT YOU'RE FULL OF SHIT.
THE GOOD NEWS, PETER, IS THAT YOU WERE HALF RIGHT. KILLING THE KID MIGHT HAVE GOTTEN YOU OUT OF HERE, BUT YOU GOT THE DETAILS WRONG.
FORTUNATELY, I'VE HAD YEARS AND YEARS TO PONDER MY SITUATION, AND I KNOW WHAT TO DO.
IS THAT SO?
YES, THAT'S SO. AND IN FACT, WE'RE ALL MAKING GOOD ON OUR ESCAPE. THREE FOR THE PRICE OF ONE.
THAT'S GONNA BE QUITE A TRICK, GRANDPAPPY. LAST TIME I CHECKED, I WAS MORE THAN A LITTLE DEAD.
BODIES ARE. EASY, STRAWBERRY. WE CAN DEAL WITH THAT LATER.
BUT THE FACT REMAINS THAT WE NEED A SACRIFICE TO CREATE OUR EXIT.
OPEN THE BOOK, PETER.
AS THE ONLY ONE OF US CURRENTLY LIVING, I'M AFRAID THE ROLE OF SACRIFICE FALLS TO YOU.
SHIT.

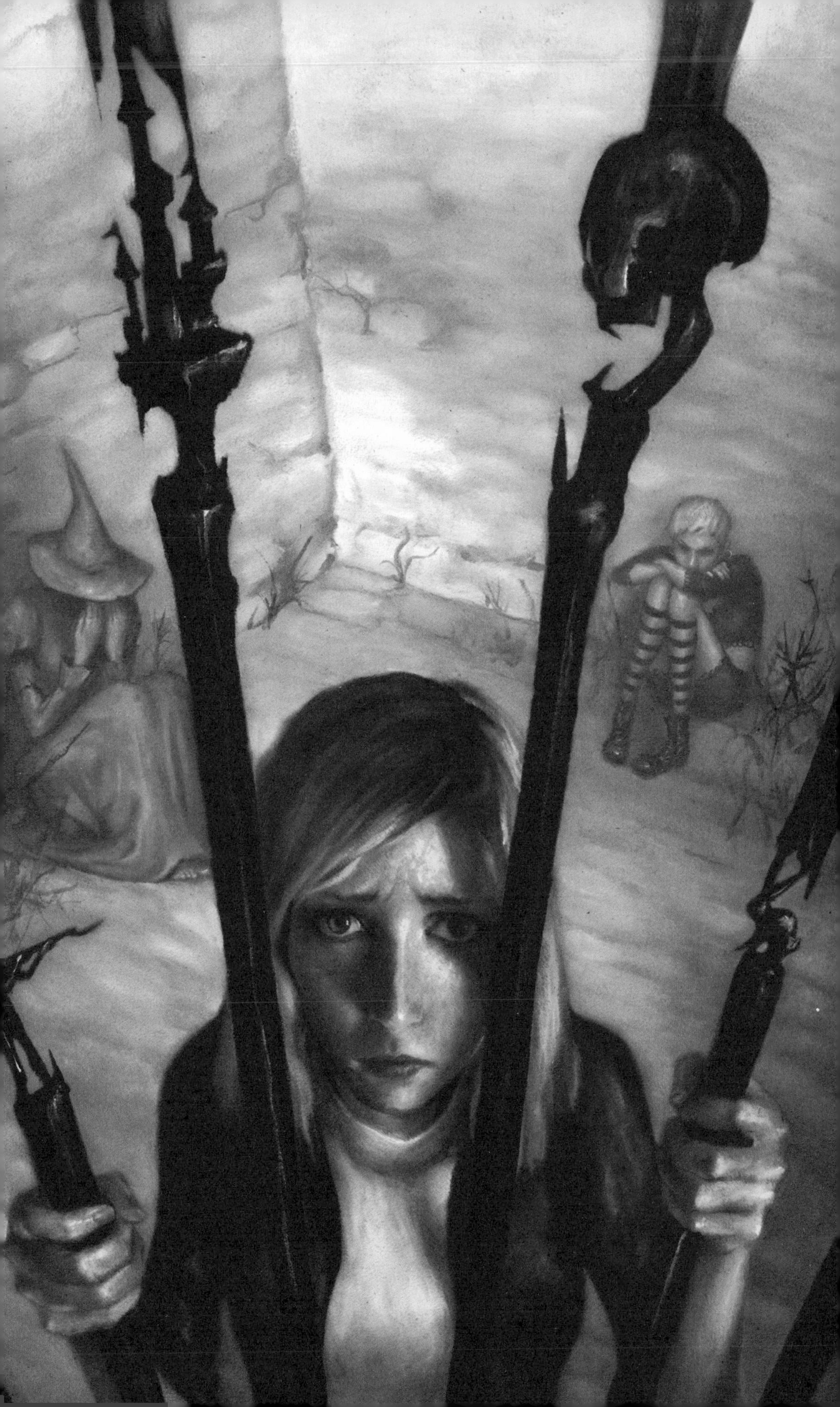

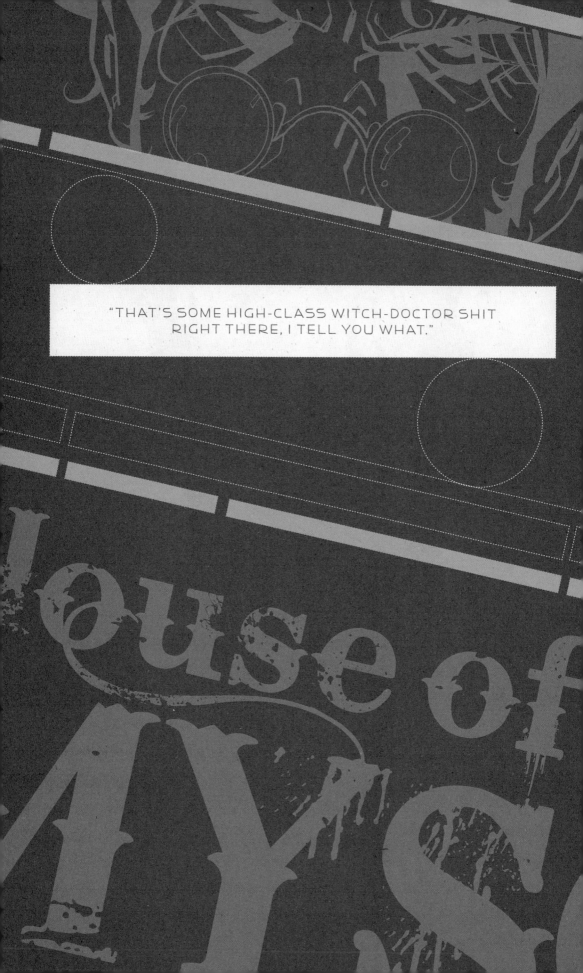

"THAT'S SOME HIGH-CLASS WITCH-DOCTOR SHIT RIGHT THERE, I TELL YOU WHAT."

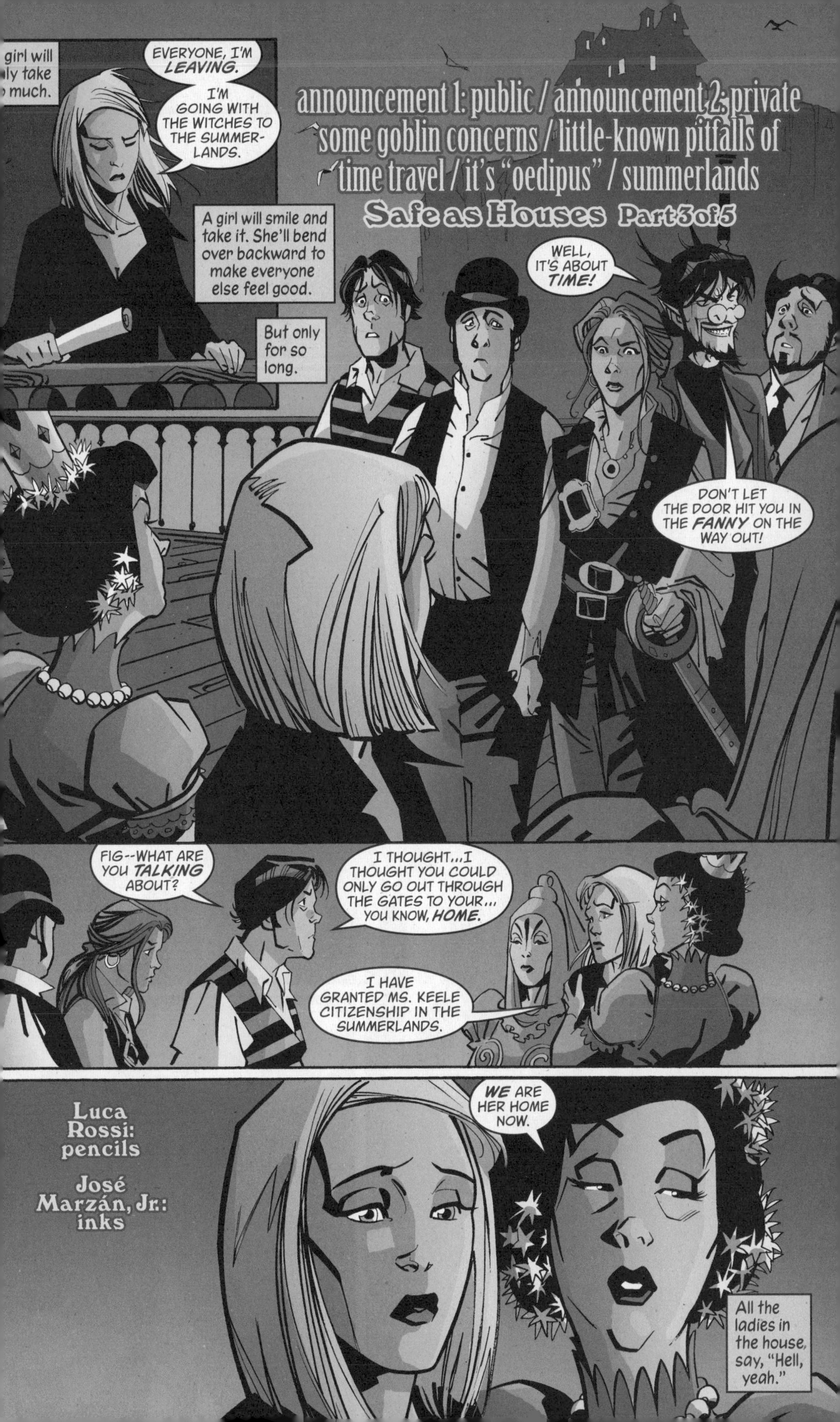
girl will
ly take
much.
EVERYONE, I'M LEAVING.
I'M GOING WITH THE WITCHES TO THE SUMMERLANDS.
announcement 1: public / announcement 2: private
some goblin concerns / little-known pitfalls of
time travel / it's "oedipus" / summerlands
Safe as Houses Part 3 of 5
A girl will smile and take it. She'll bend over backward to make everyone else feel good.
But only for so long.
WELL, IT'S ABOUT TIME!
DON'T LET THE DOOR HIT YOU IN THE FANNY ON THE WAY OUT!
FIG--WHAT ARE YOU TALKING ABOUT?
I THOUGHT...I THOUGHT YOU COULD ONLY GO OUT THROUGH THE GATES TO YOUR... YOU KNOW, HOME.
I HAVE GRANTED MS. KEELE CITIZENSHIP IN THE SUMMERLANDS.
Luca Rossi: pencils
José Marzán, Jr.: inks
WE ARE HER HOME NOW.
All the ladies in the house, say, "Hell, yeah."

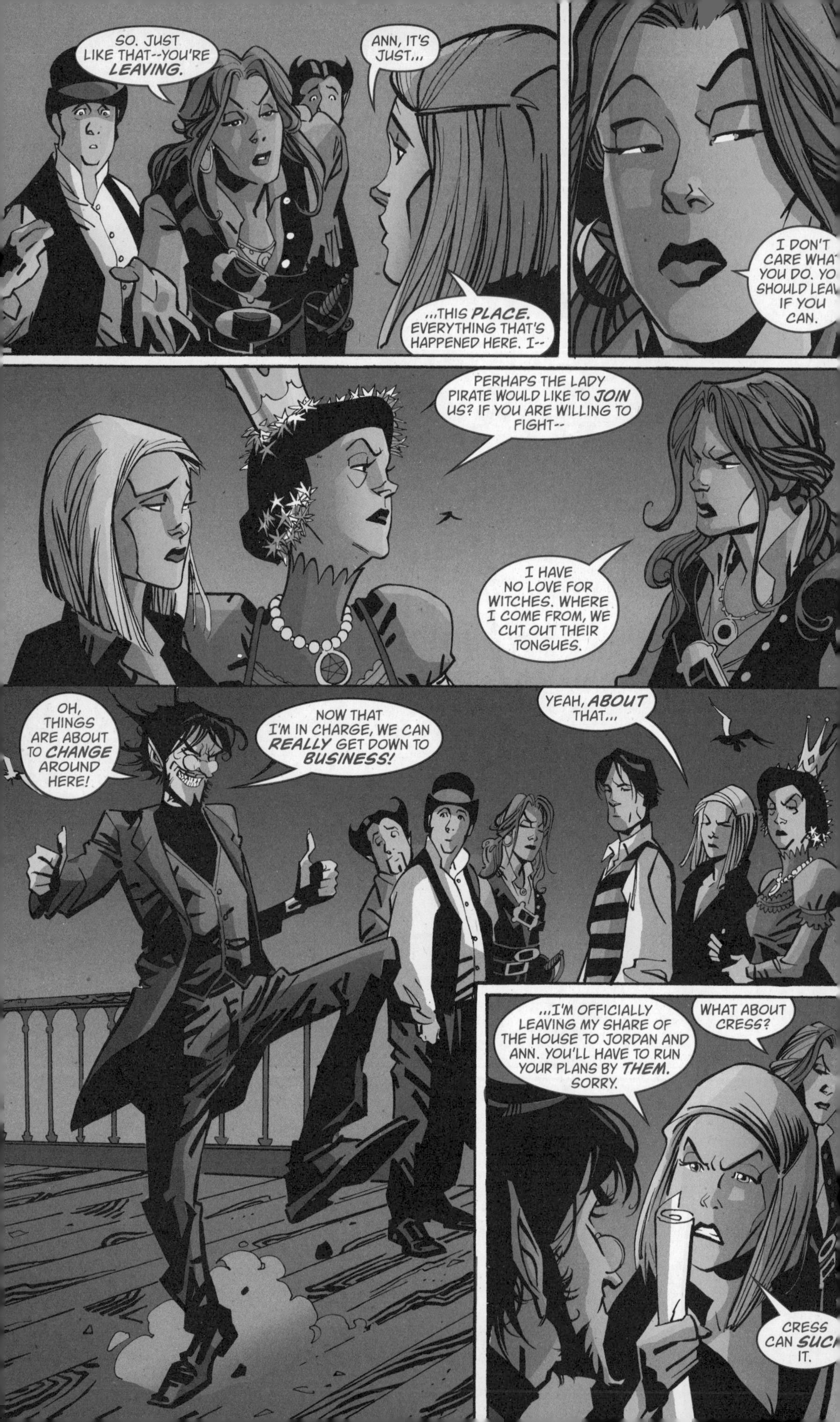
SO. JUST LIKE THAT--YOU'RE LEAVING.
ANN, IT'S JUST...
...THIS PLACE. EVERYTHING THAT'S HAPPENED HERE. I--
I DON'T CARE WHA YOU DO. YO SHOULD LEA IF YOU CAN.
PERHAPS THE LADY PIRATE WOULD LIKE TO JOIN US? IF YOU ARE WILLING TO FIGHT--
I HAVE NO LOVE FOR WITCHES. WHERE I COME FROM, WE CUT OUT THEIR TONGUES.
OH, THINGS ARE ABOUT TO CHANGE AROUND HERE!
NOW THAT I'M IN CHARGE, WE CAN REALLY GET DOWN TO BUSINESS!
YEAH, ABOUT THAT...
...I'M OFFICIALLY LEAVING MY SHARE OF THE HOUSE TO JORDAN AND ANN. YOU'LL HAVE TO RUN YOUR PLANS BY THEM. SORRY.
WHAT ABOUT CRESS?
CRESS CAN SUC IT.

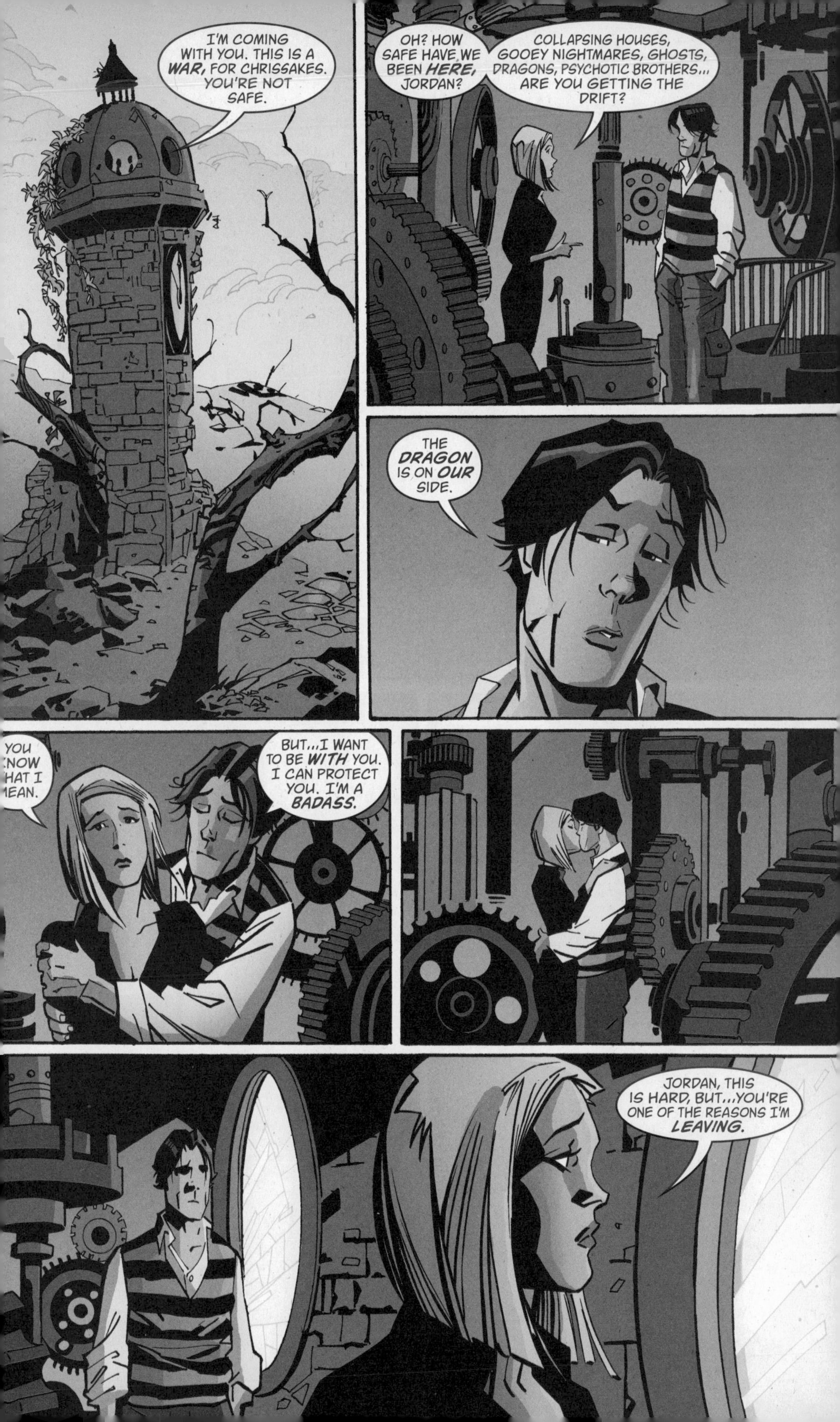

I'M COMING WITH YOU. THIS IS A **WAR,** FOR CHRISSAKES. YOU'RE NOT SAFE.
OH? HOW SAFE HAVE WE BEEN **HERE,** JORDAN?
COLLAPSING HOUSES, GOOEY NIGHTMARES, GHOSTS, DRAGONS, PSYCHOTIC BROTHERS... ARE YOU GETTING THE DRIFT?
THE **DRAGON** IS ON **OUR** SIDE.
YOU KNOW THAT I MEAN.
BUT...I WANT TO BE **WITH** YOU. I CAN PROTECT YOU. I'M A **BADASS.**
JORDAN, THIS IS HARD, BUT...YOU'RE ONE OF THE REASONS I'M **LEAVING.**

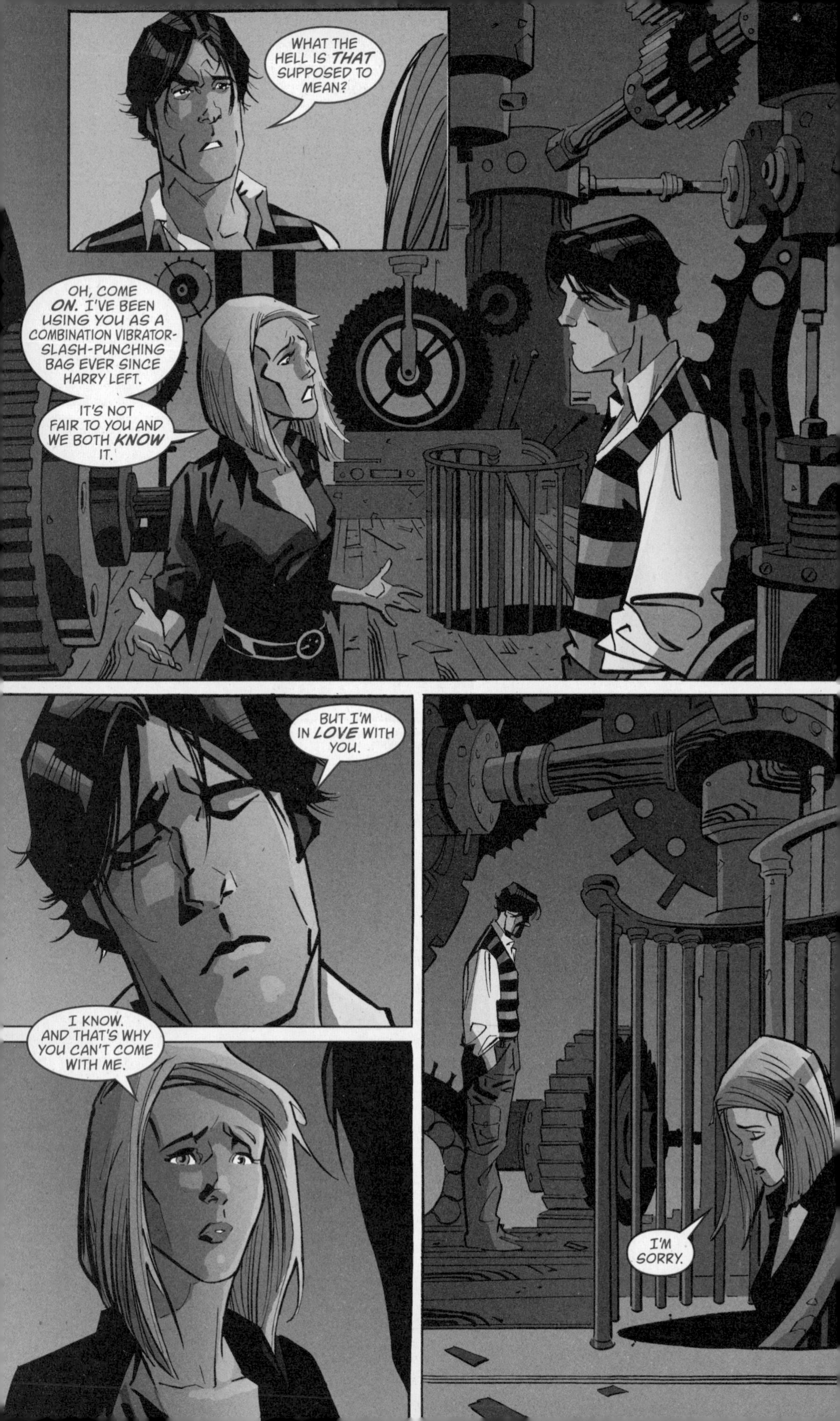

WHAT THE HELL IS **THAT** SUPPOSED TO MEAN?
OH, COME **ON.** I'VE BEEN USING YOU AS A COMBINATION VIBRATOR-SLASH-PUNCHING BAG EVER SINCE HARRY LEFT.
IT'S NOT FAIR TO YOU AND WE BOTH **KNOW** IT.
BUT I'M IN **LOVE** WITH YOU.
I KNOW. AND THAT'S WHY YOU CAN'T COME WITH ME.
I'M SORRY.

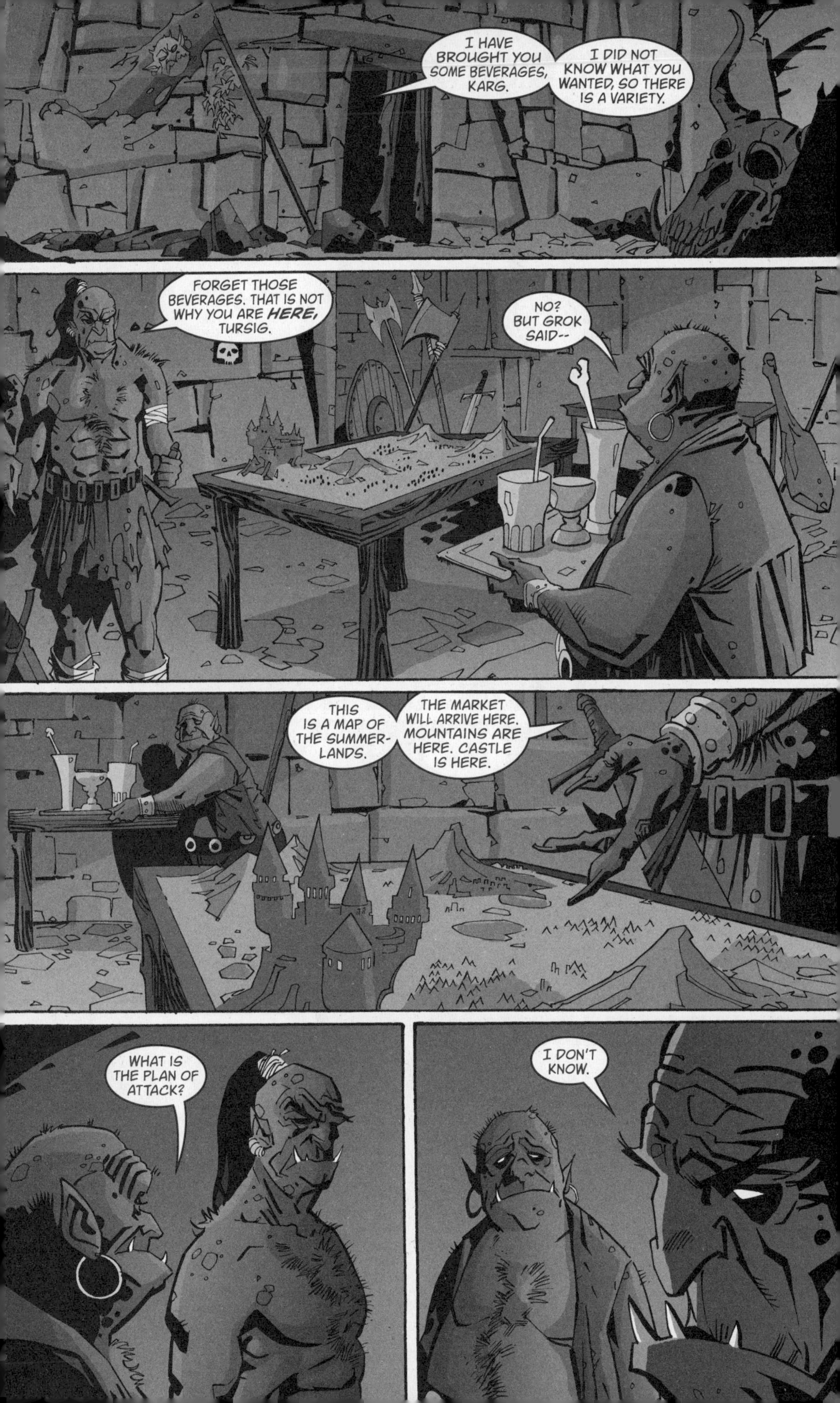

I HAVE BROUGHT YOU SOME BEVERAGES, KARG.
I DID NOT KNOW WHAT YOU WANTED, SO THERE IS A VARIETY.
FORGET THOSE BEVERAGES. THAT IS NOT WHY YOU ARE *HERE,* TURSIG.
NO? BUT GROK SAID--
THIS IS A MAP OF THE SUMMER-LANDS.
THE MARKET WILL ARRIVE HERE. MOUNTAINS ARE HERE. CASTLE IS HERE.
WHAT IS THE PLAN OF ATTACK?
I DON'T KNOW.

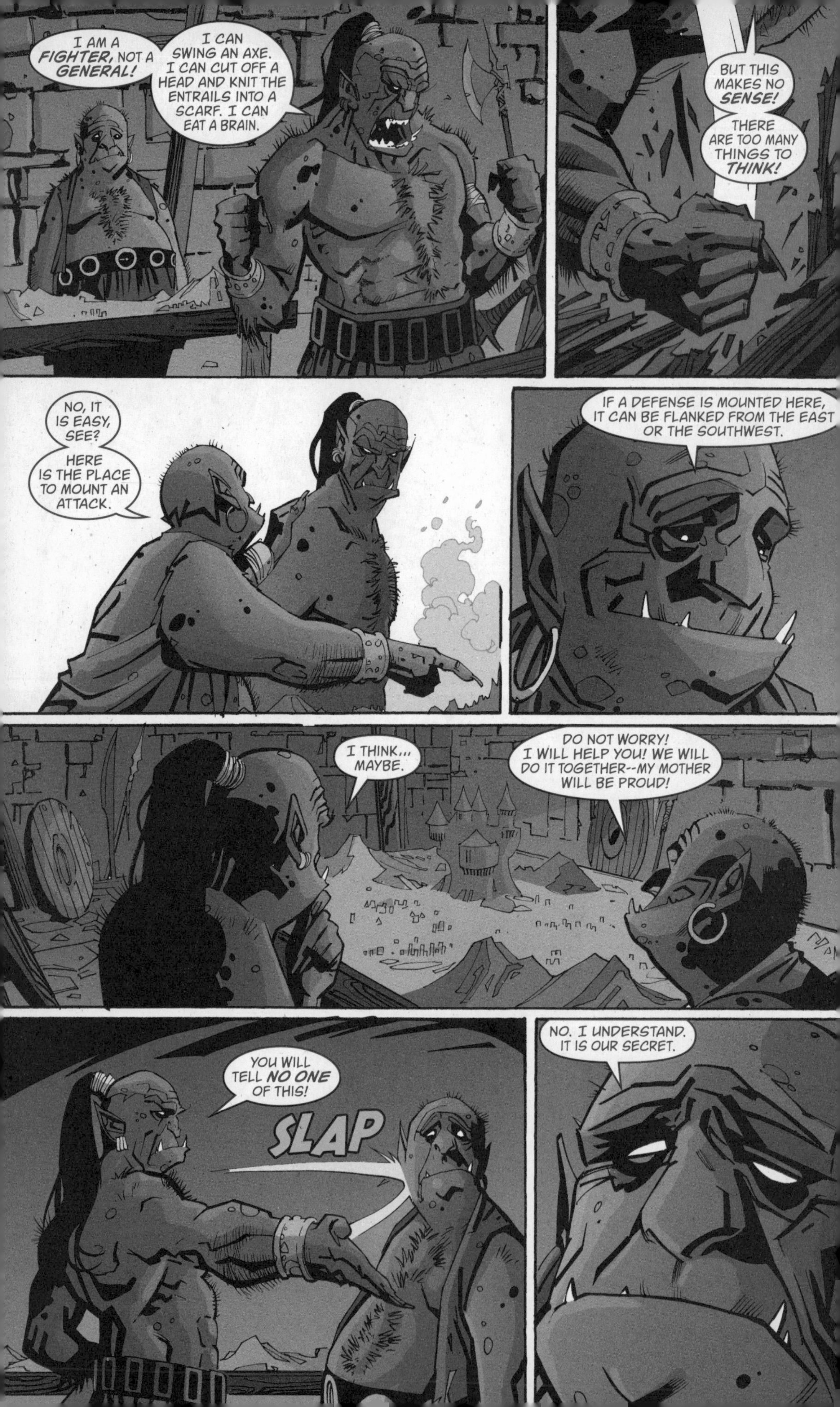
I AM A FIGHTER, NOT A GENERAL!
I CAN SWING AN AXE. I CAN CUT OFF A HEAD AND KNIT THE ENTRAILS INTO A SCARF. I CAN EAT A BRAIN.
BUT THIS MAKES NO SENSE!
THERE ARE TOO MANY THINGS TO THINK!
NO, IT IS EASY, SEE?
HERE IS THE PLACE TO MOUNT AN ATTACK.
IF A DEFENSE IS MOUNTED HERE, IT CAN BE FLANKED FROM THE EAST OR THE SOUTHWEST.
I THINK... MAYBE.
DO NOT WORRY! I WILL HELP YOU! WE WILL DO IT TOGETHER--MY MOTHER WILL BE PROUD!
YOU WILL TELL NO ONE OF THIS!
SLAP
NO. I UNDERSTAND. IT IS OUR SECRET.

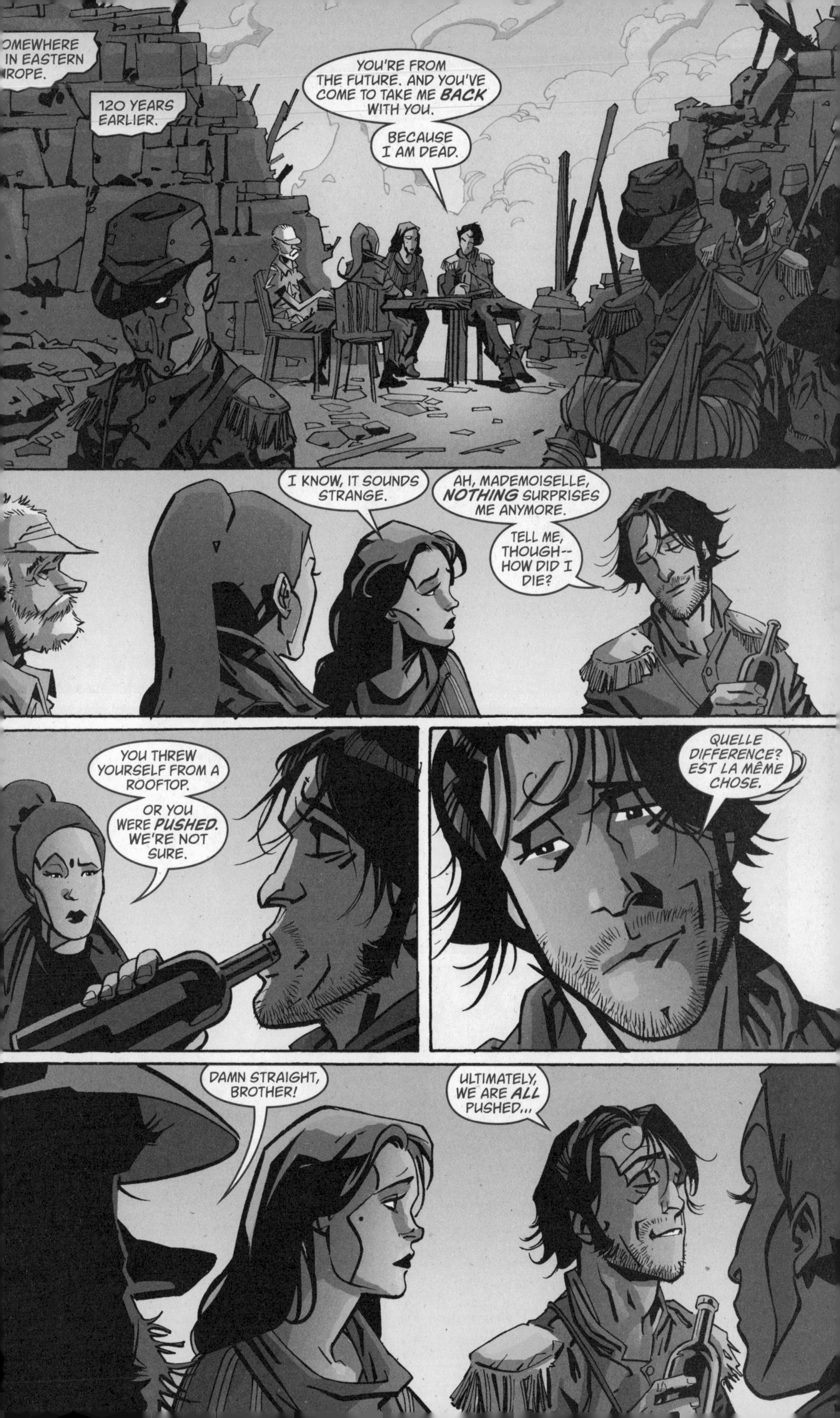
OMEWHERE IN EASTERN ROPE.
120 YEARS EARLIER.
YOU'RE FROM THE FUTURE. AND YOU'VE COME TO TAKE ME BACK WITH YOU.
BECAUSE I AM DEAD.
I KNOW, IT SOUNDS STRANGE.
AH, MADEMOISELLE, NOTHING SURPRISES ME ANYMORE.
TELL ME, THOUGH-- HOW DID I DIE?
YOU THREW YOURSELF FROM A ROOFTOP.
OR YOU WERE PUSHED. WE'RE NOT SURE.
QUELLE DIFFERENCE? EST LA MÊME CHOSE.
DAMN STRAIGHT, BROTHER!
ULTIMATELY, WE ARE ALL PUSHED...

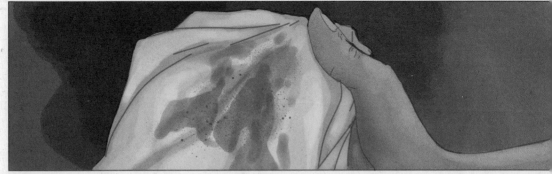

I'M AFRAID THE DIAGNOSIS IS INDISPUTABLE.

HOW LONG DO I HAVE?

SIX MONTHS? A *YEAR* AT THE LONGEST.

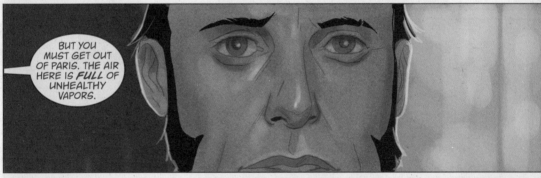

BUT YOU MUST GET OUT OF PARIS. THE AIR HERE IS *FULL* OF UNHEALTHY VAPORS.

PARDON ME FOR ASKING, BUT ARE YOU EDUARD ST. GERMAIN THE *PLAYWRIGHT?*

THE SAME.

WHY HAVE WE SEEN NO *PLAYS* OF YOURS IN THE PAST YEAR?

MY MUSE COMMITTED SUICIDE.

THANK YOU, DOCTOR.

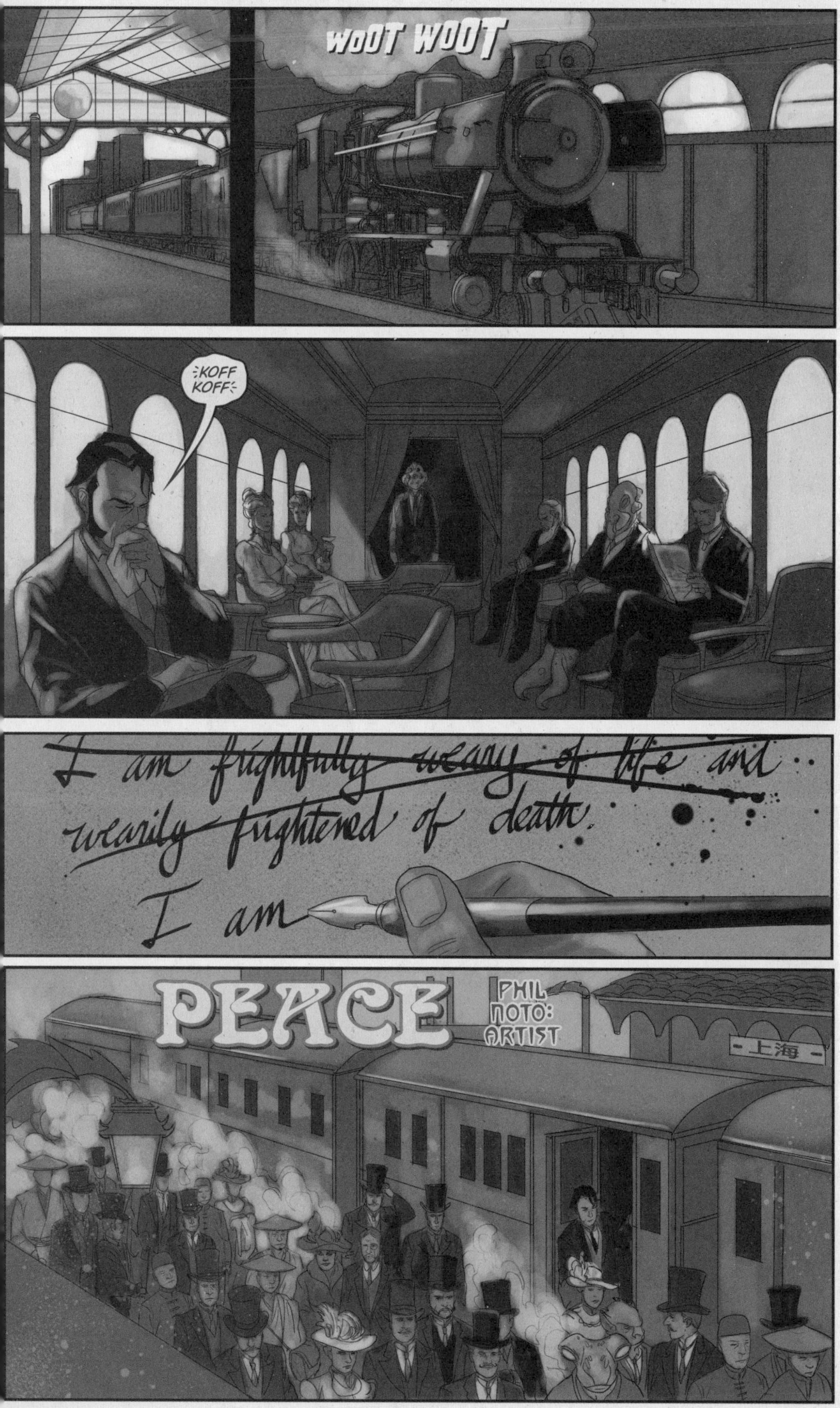
WOOT WOOT
KOFF KOFF
I am frightfully weary of life and wearily frightened of death
I am
PEACE
PHIL NOTO: ARTIST
上海

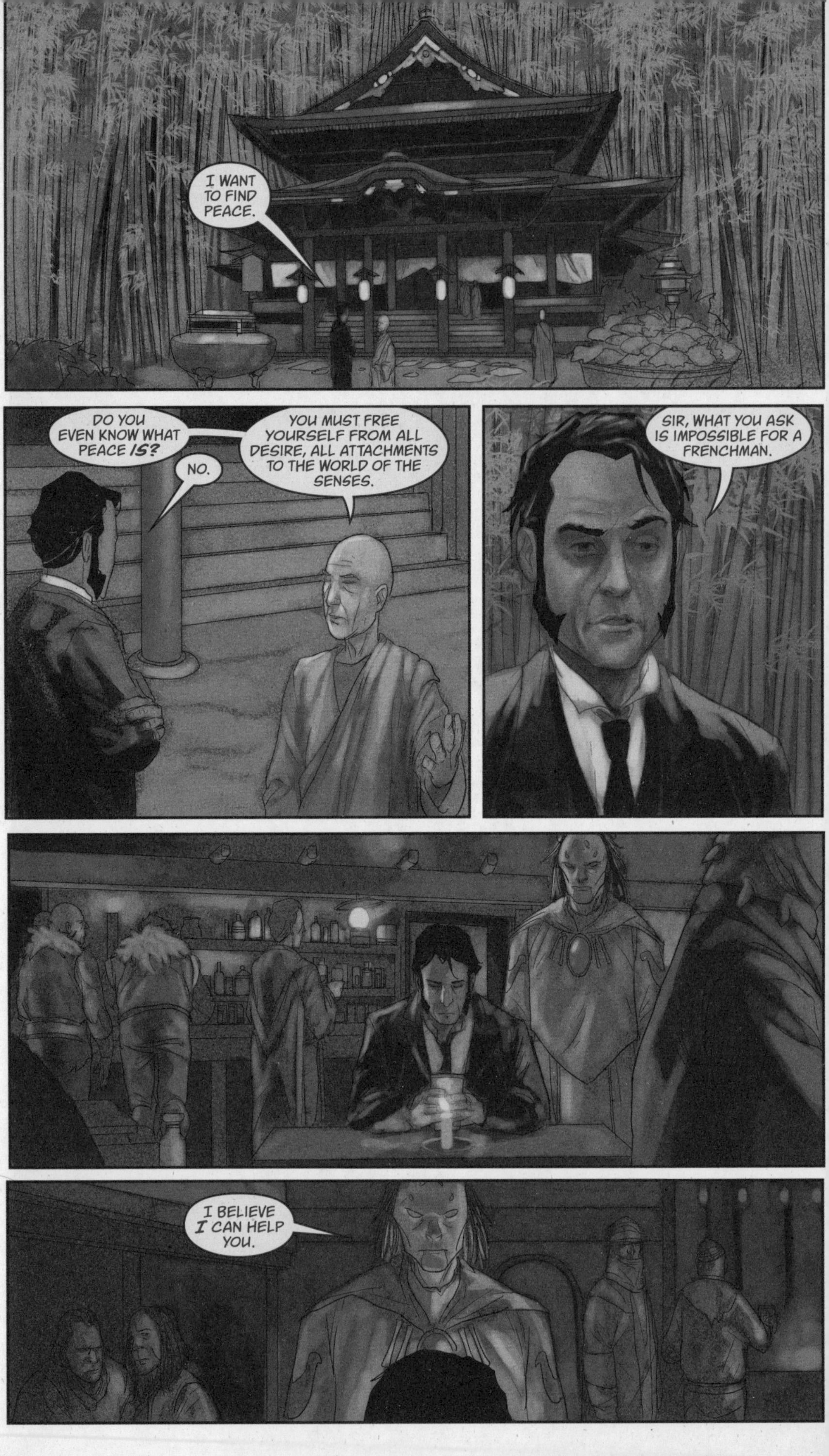

I WANT TO FIND PEACE.
DO YOU EVEN KNOW WHAT PEACE *IS?*
NO.
YOU MUST FREE YOURSELF FROM ALL DESIRE, ALL ATTACHMENTS TO THE WORLD OF THE SENSES.
SIR, WHAT YOU ASK IS IMPOSSIBLE FOR A FRENCHMAN.
I BELIEVE *I* CAN HELP YOU.

THERE IS A CURE FOR YOUR CONDITION.
BUT I DON'T KNOW IF YOU'RE PREPARED FOR THE COST.
TELL ME. I DON'T WANT TO DIE.
TAKE THE BONE.
WHEN THE TIME COMES, SMEAR IT WITH BLOOD. BREAK IT. THEN YOU WILL BE HEALED.
WHOSE BLOOD?
AH, THAT'S THE THING. THAT'S WHAT MAKES IT WORK.
THE BLOOD OF A MAN. A MAN YOU YOURSELF HAVE SLAIN. LIFE FOR LIFE. DEATH FOR DEATH. BALANCE.
YOU'RE MAD. I CAN'T KILL ANOTHER MAN TO SAVE MYSELF.
EITHER WAY, ONE LIVES AND ANOTHER DIES. WHAT DIFFERENCE DOES IT MAKE WHO?

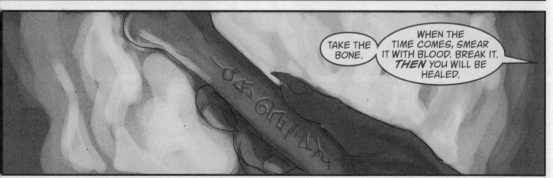

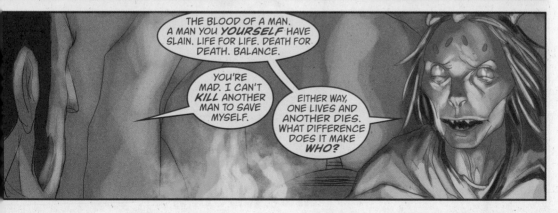

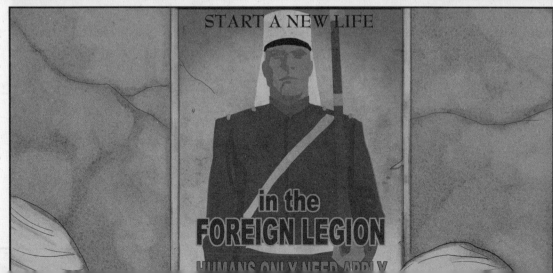

START A NEW LIFE

in the
FOREIGN LEGION

HUMANS ONLY NEED APPLY

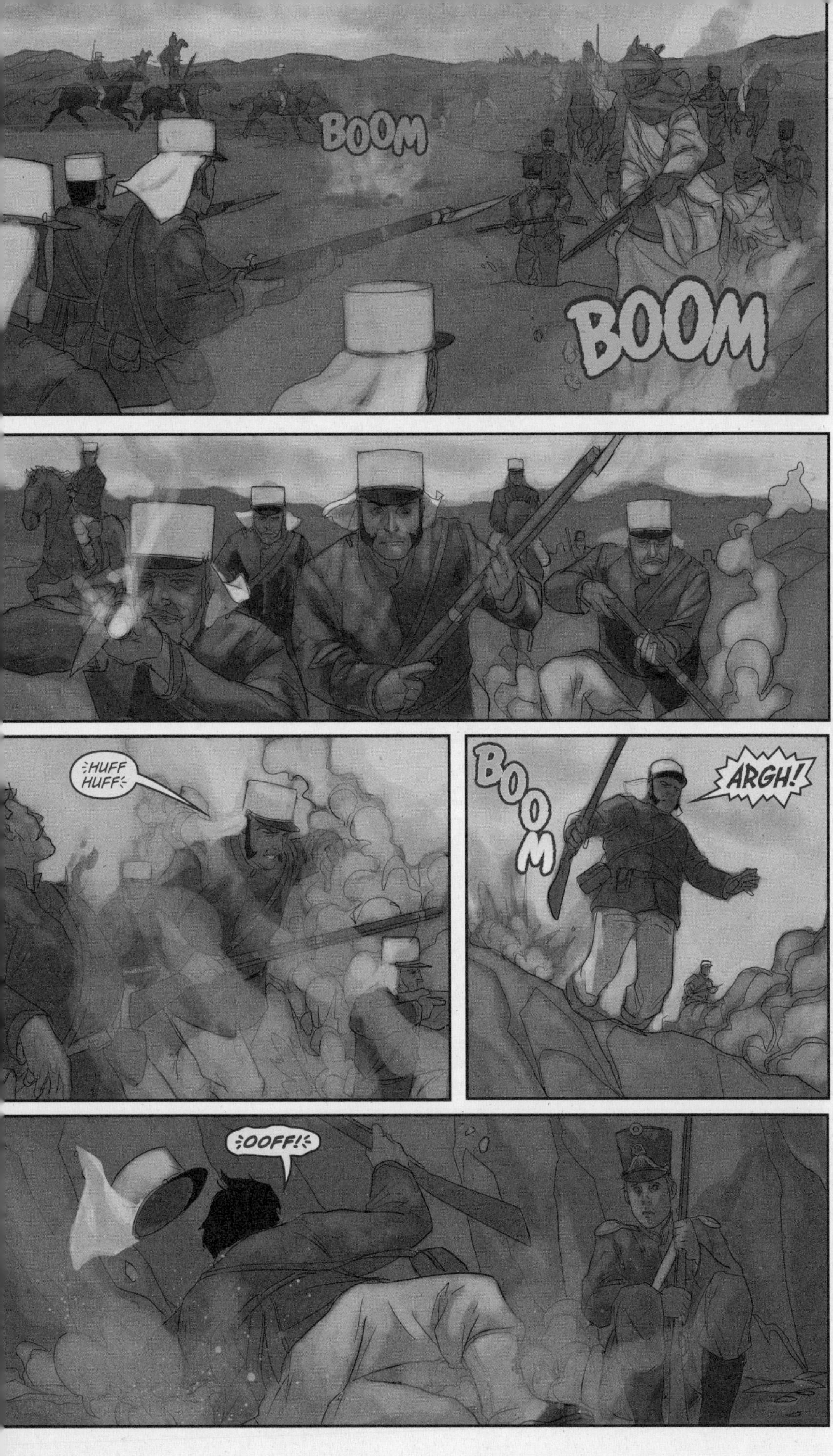
BOOM
BOOM
HUFF HUFF
BOOM
ARGH!
OOFF!

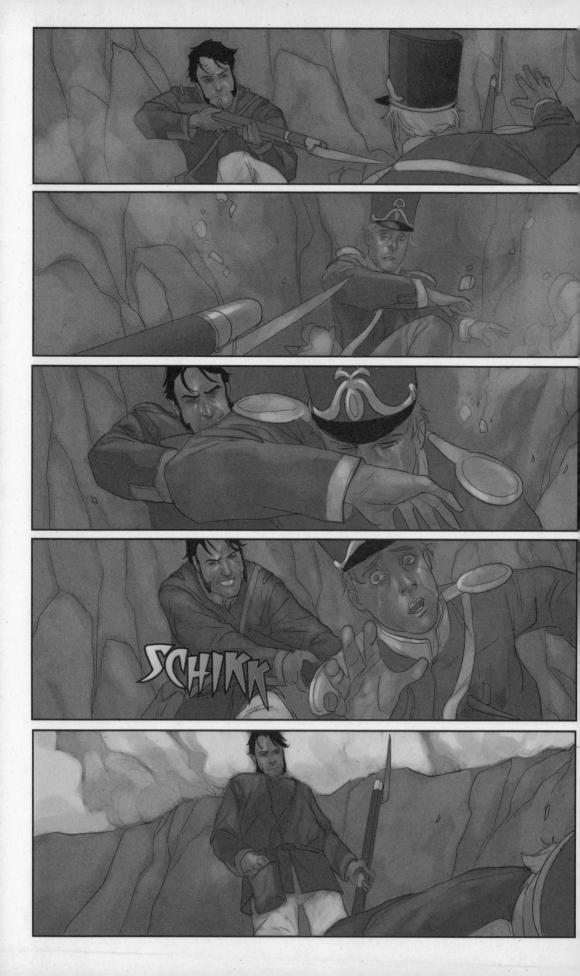

SCHIKK

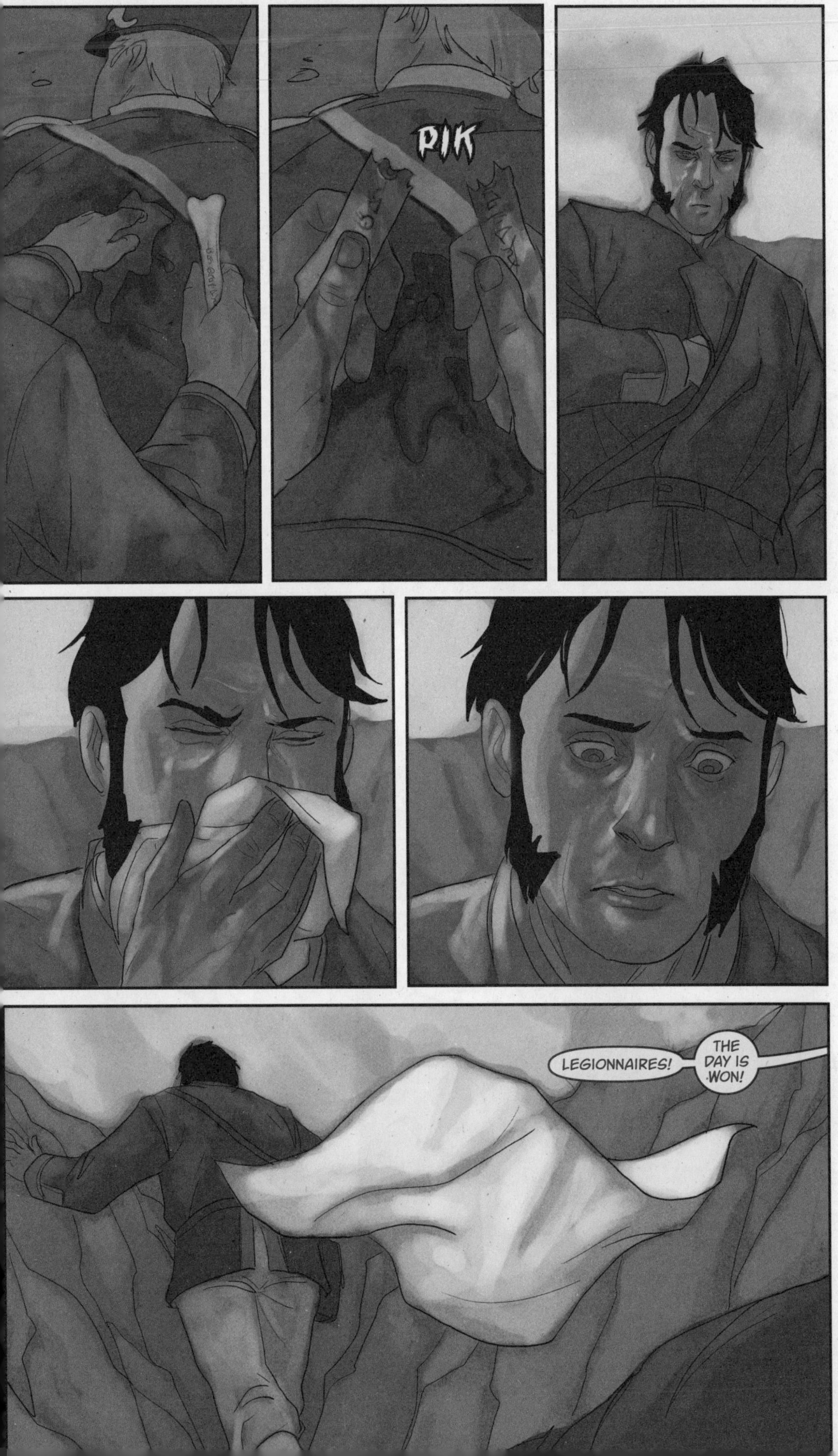
PIK
LEGIONNAIRES!
THE DAY IS WON!

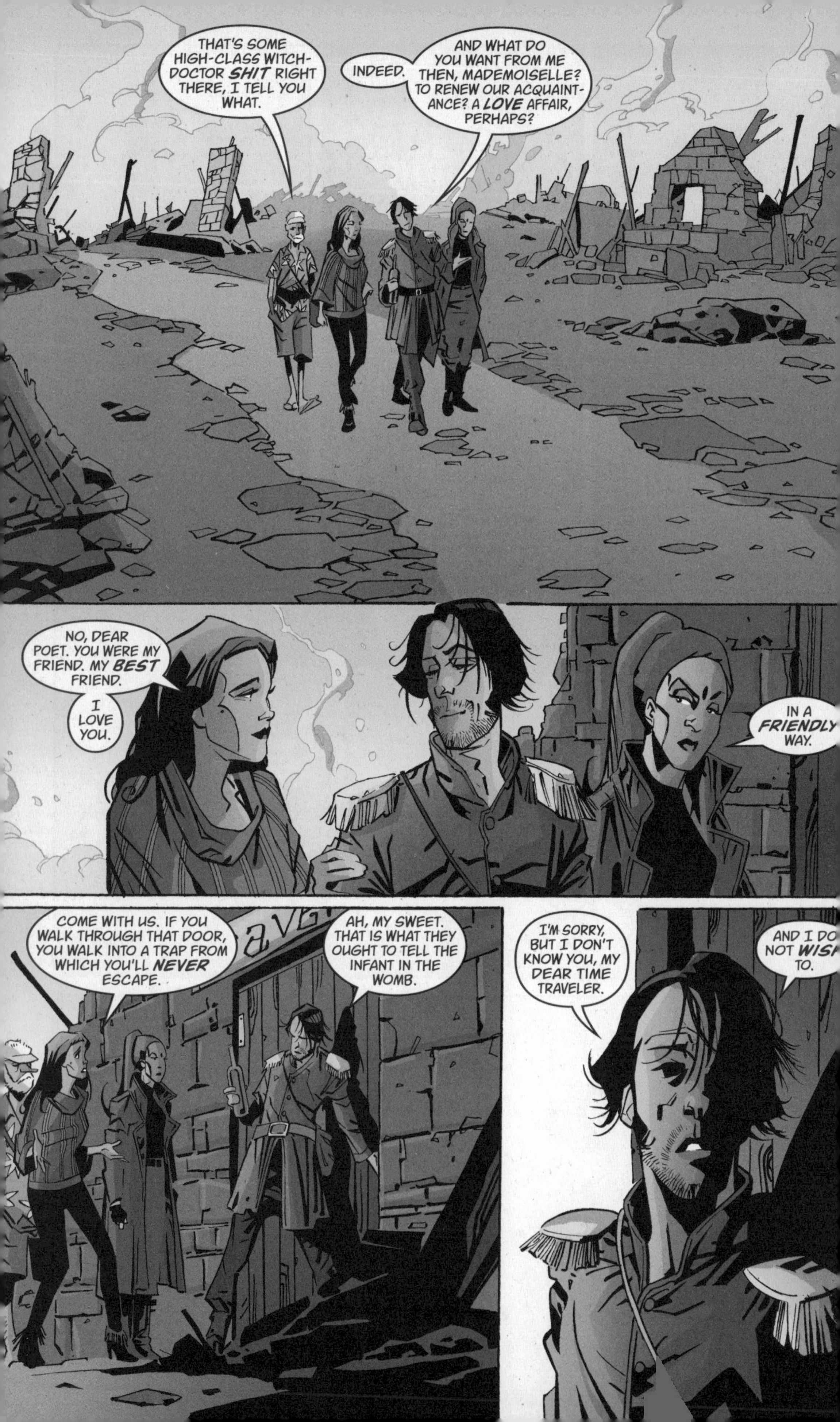
THAT'S SOME HIGH-CLASS WITCH-DOCTOR SHIT RIGHT THERE, I TELL YOU WHAT.
INDEED.
AND WHAT DO YOU WANT FROM ME THEN, MADEMOISELLE? TO RENEW OUR ACQUAINTANCE? A LOVE AFFAIR, PERHAPS?
NO, DEAR POET. YOU WERE MY FRIEND. MY BEST FRIEND.
I LOVE YOU.
IN A FRIENDLY WAY.
COME WITH US. IF YOU WALK THROUGH THAT DOOR, YOU WALK INTO A TRAP FROM WHICH YOU'LL NEVER ESCAPE.
AH, MY SWEET. THAT IS WHAT THEY OUGHT TO TELL THE INFANT IN THE WOMB.
I'M SORRY, BUT I DON'T KNOW YOU, MY DEAR TIME TRAVELER.
AND I DO NOT WISH TO.

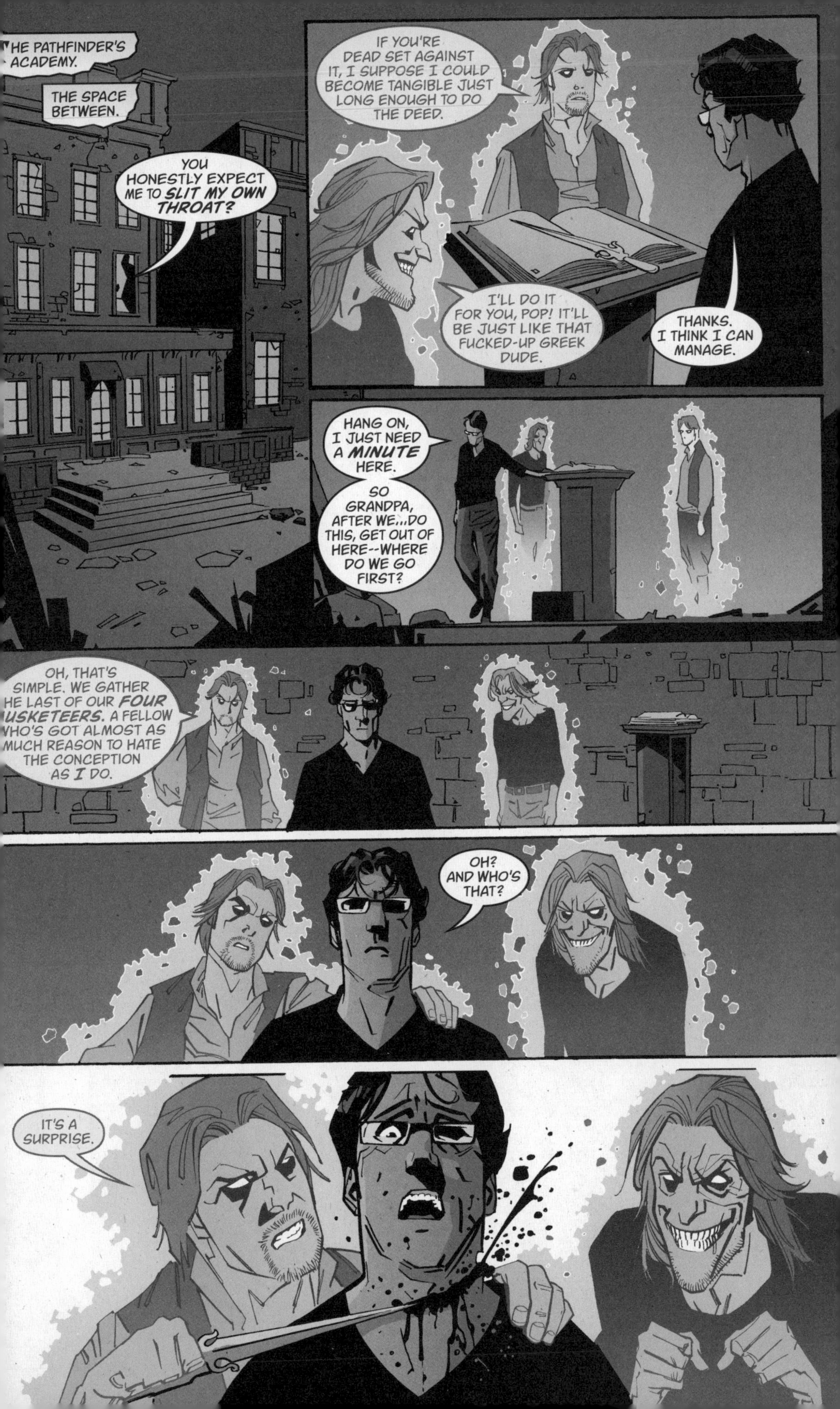
HE PATHFINDER'S ACADEMY.
THE SPACE BETWEEN.
YOU HONESTLY EXPECT ME TO SLIT MY OWN THROAT?
IF YOU'RE DEAD SET AGAINST IT, I SUPPOSE I COULD BECOME TANGIBLE JUST LONG ENOUGH TO DO THE DEED.
I'LL DO IT FOR YOU, POP! IT'LL BE JUST LIKE THAT FUCKED-UP GREEK DUDE.
THANKS. I THINK I CAN MANAGE.
HANG ON, I JUST NEED A MINUTE HERE.
SO GRANDPA, AFTER WE...DO THIS, GET OUT OF HERE--WHERE DO WE GO FIRST?
OH, THAT'S SIMPLE. WE GATHER HE LAST OF OUR FOUR USKETEERS. A FELLOW WHO'S GOT ALMOST AS MUCH REASON TO HATE THE CONCEPTION AS I DO.
OH? AND WHO'S THAT?
IT'S A SURPRISE.

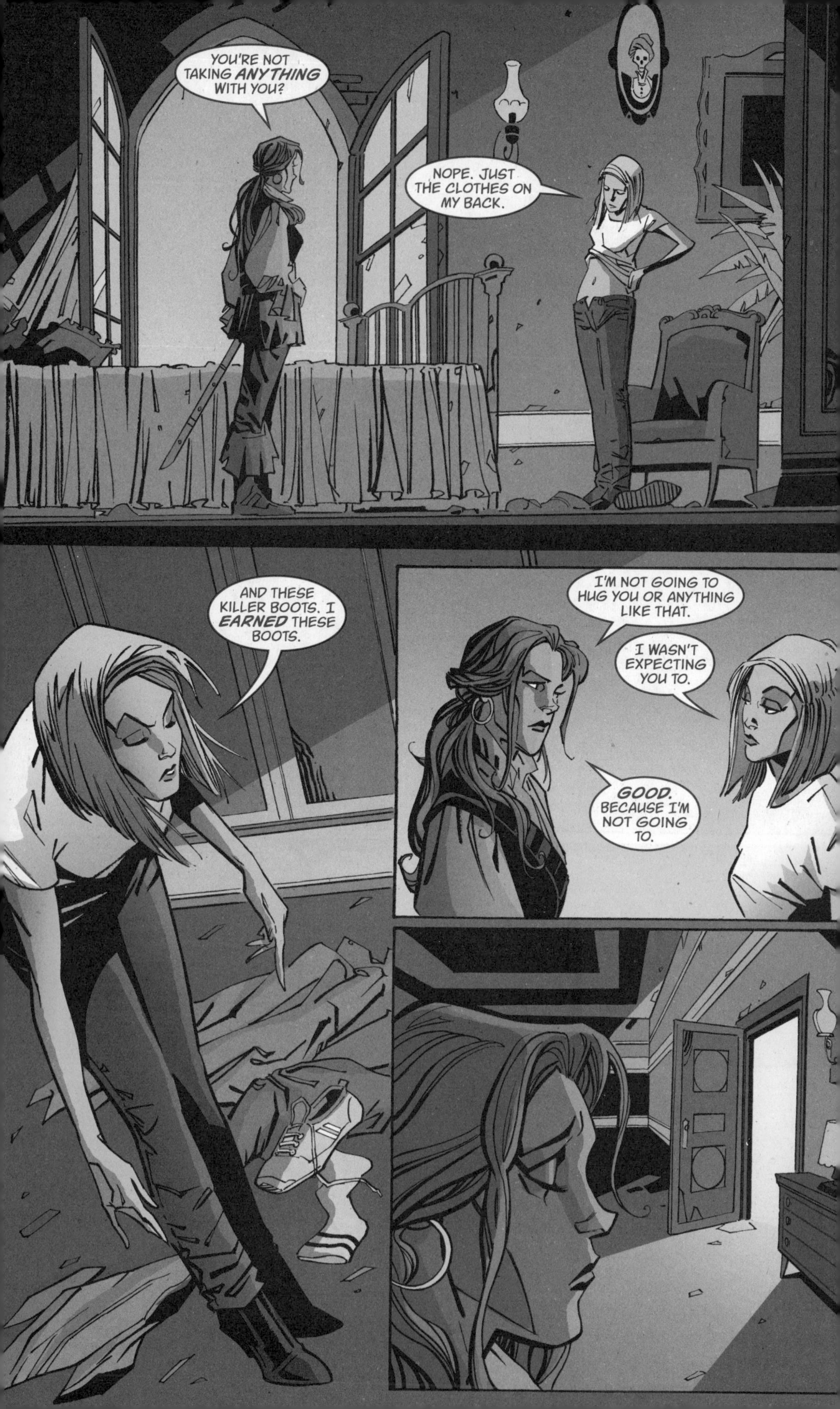
YOU'RE NOT TAKING ANYTHING WITH YOU?
NOPE. JUST THE CLOTHES ON MY BACK.
AND THESE KILLER BOOTS. I EARNED THESE BOOTS.
I'M NOT GOING TO HUG YOU OR ANYTHING LIKE THAT.
I WASN'T EXPECTING YOU TO.
GOOD. BECAUSE I'M NOT GOING TO.

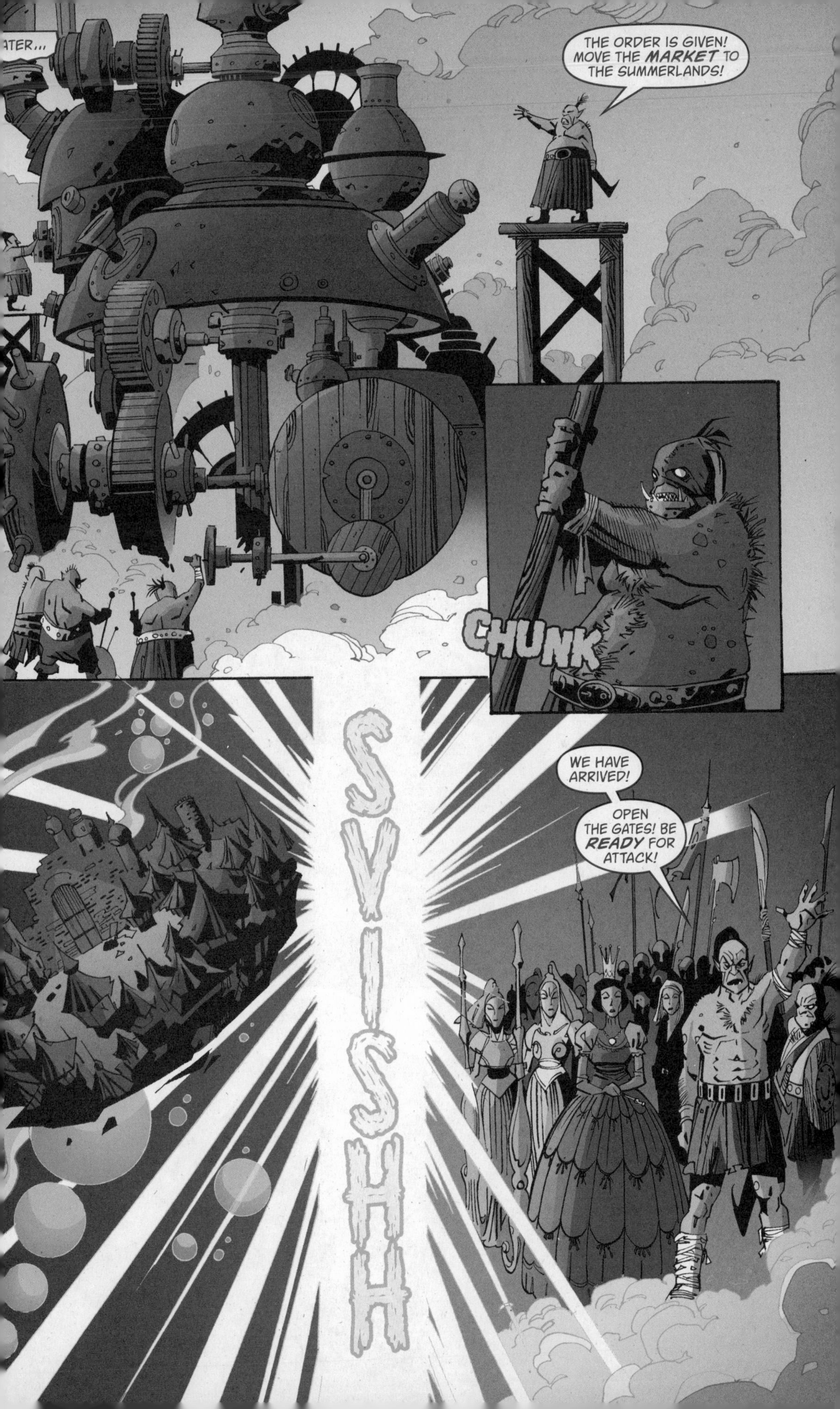

ATER...
THE ORDER IS GIVEN! MOVE THE MARKET TO THE SUMMERLANDS!
CHUNK
SVISSHH
WE HAVE ARRIVED!
OPEN THE GATES! BE READY FOR ATTACK!

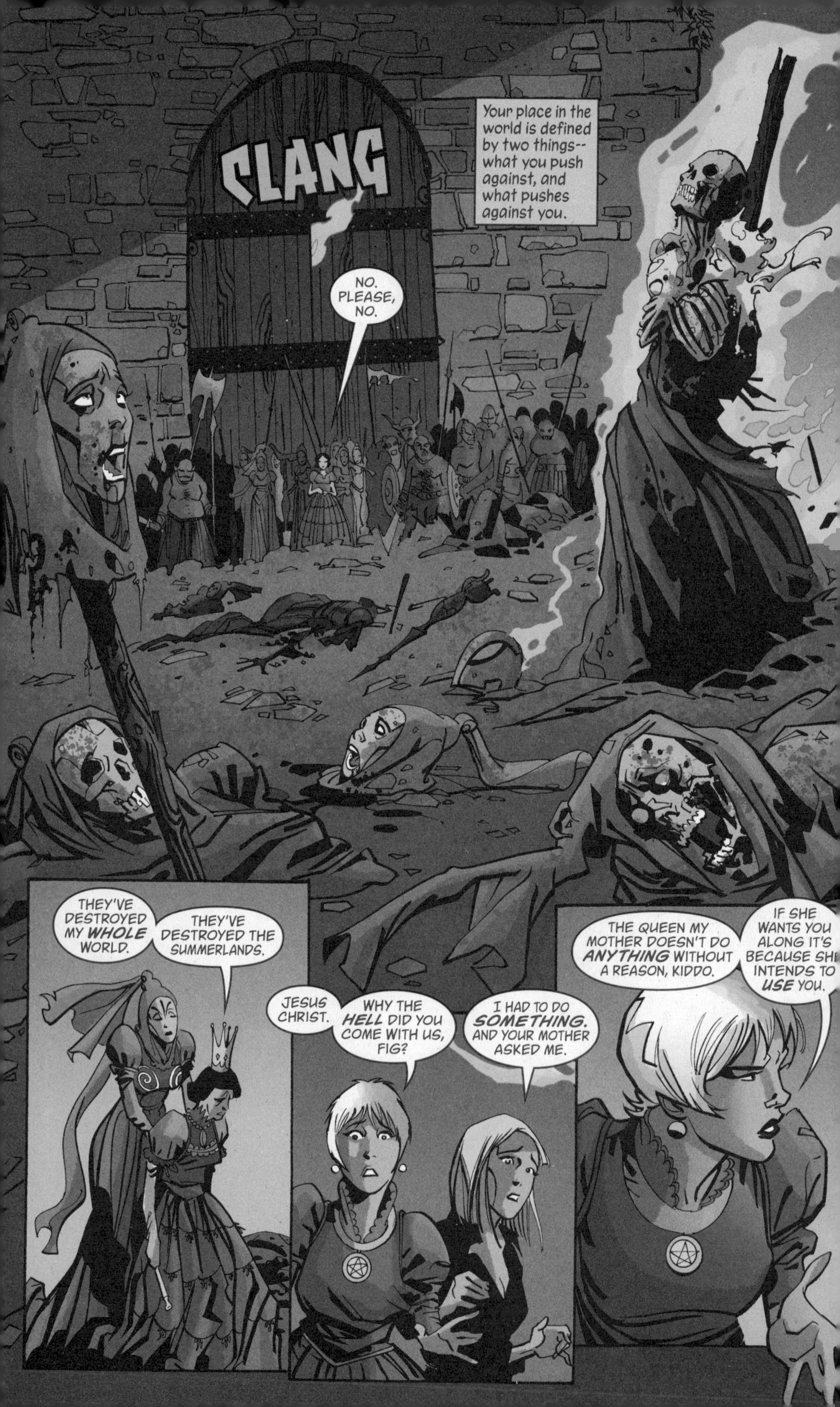
CLANG
Your place in the world is defined by two things-- what you push against, and what pushes against you.
NO. PLEASE, NO.
THEY'VE DESTROYED MY WHOLE WORLD.
THEY'VE DESTROYED THE SUMMERLANDS.
JESUS CHRIST.
WHY THE HELL DID YOU COME WITH US, FIG?
I HAD TO DO SOMETHING. AND YOUR MOTHER ASKED ME.
THE QUEEN MY MOTHER DOESN'T DO ANYTHING WITHOUT A REASON, KIDDO.
IF SHE WANTS YOU ALONG IT'S BECAUSE SHE INTENDS TO USE YOU.

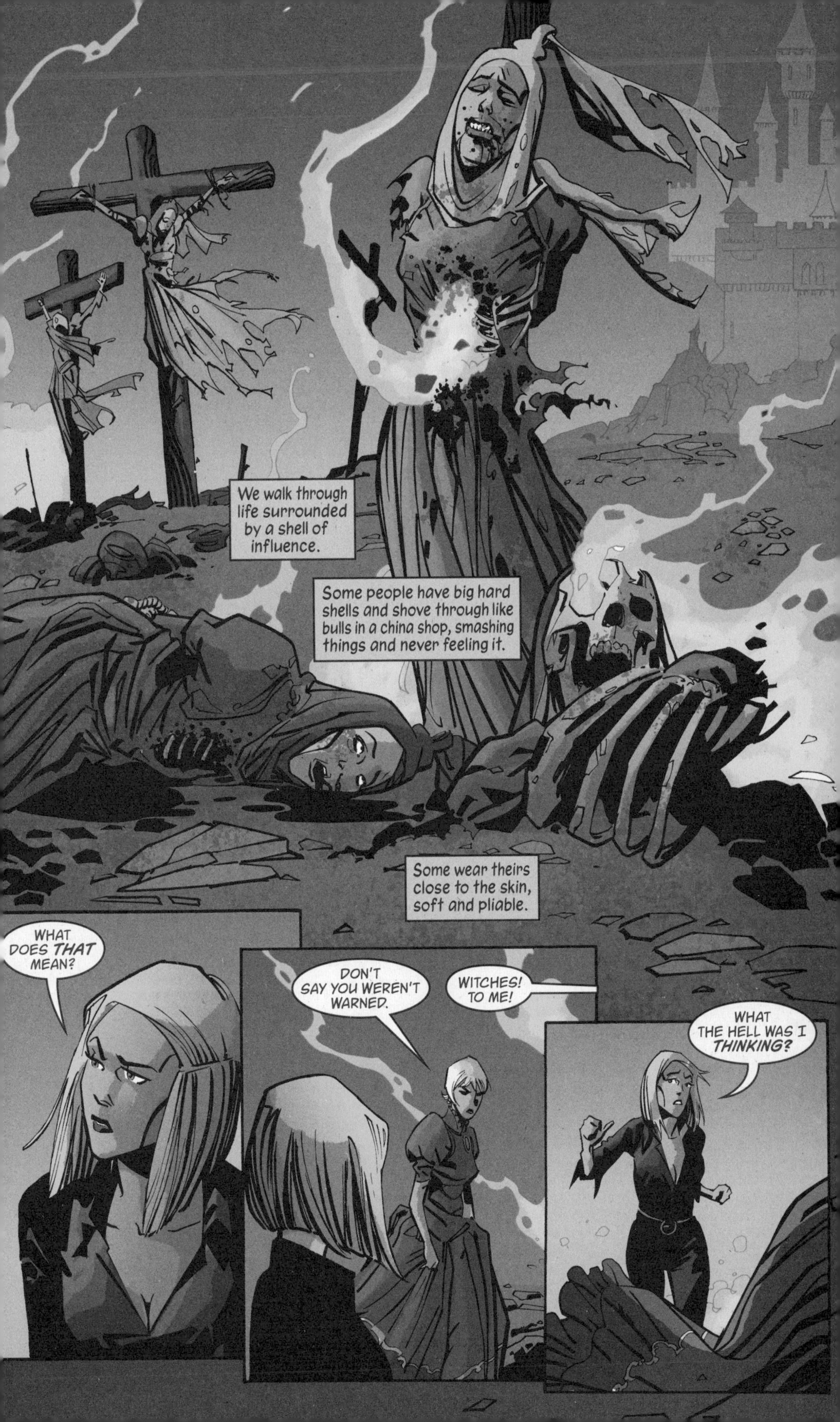
We walk through life surrounded by a shell of influence.
Some people have big hard shells and shove through like bulls in a china shop, smashing things and never feeling it.
Some wear theirs close to the skin, soft and pliable.
WHAT DOES THAT MEAN?
DON'T SAY YOU WEREN'T WARNED.
WITCHES! TO ME!
WHAT THE HELL WAS I THINKING?

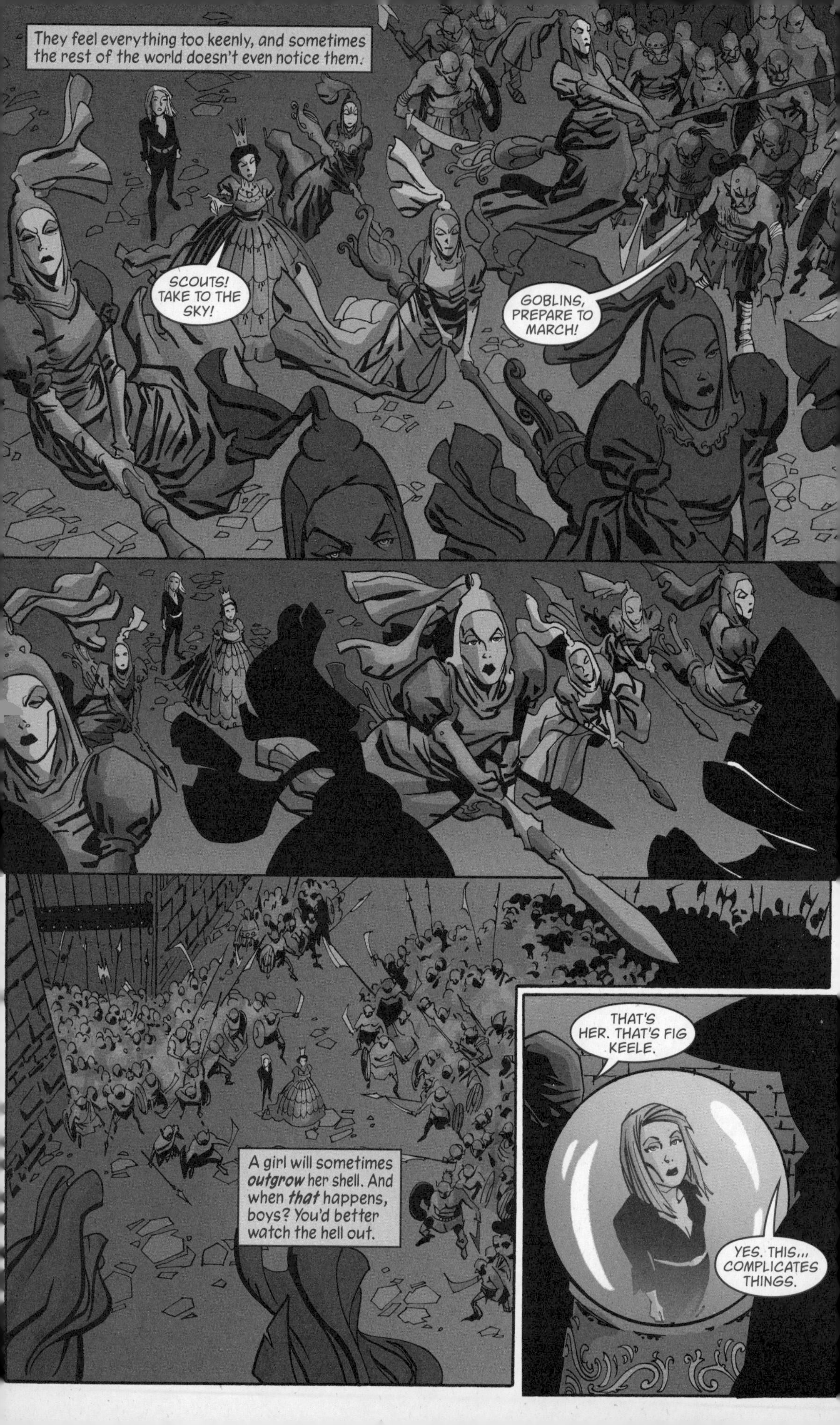
They feel everything too keenly, and sometimes the rest of the world doesn't even notice them.
SCOUTS! TAKE TO THE SKY!
GOBLINS, PREPARE TO MARCH!
A girl will sometimes *outgrow* her shell. And when *that* happens, boys? You'd better watch the hell out.
THAT'S HER. THAT'S FIG KEELE.
YES. THIS... COMPLICATES THINGS.

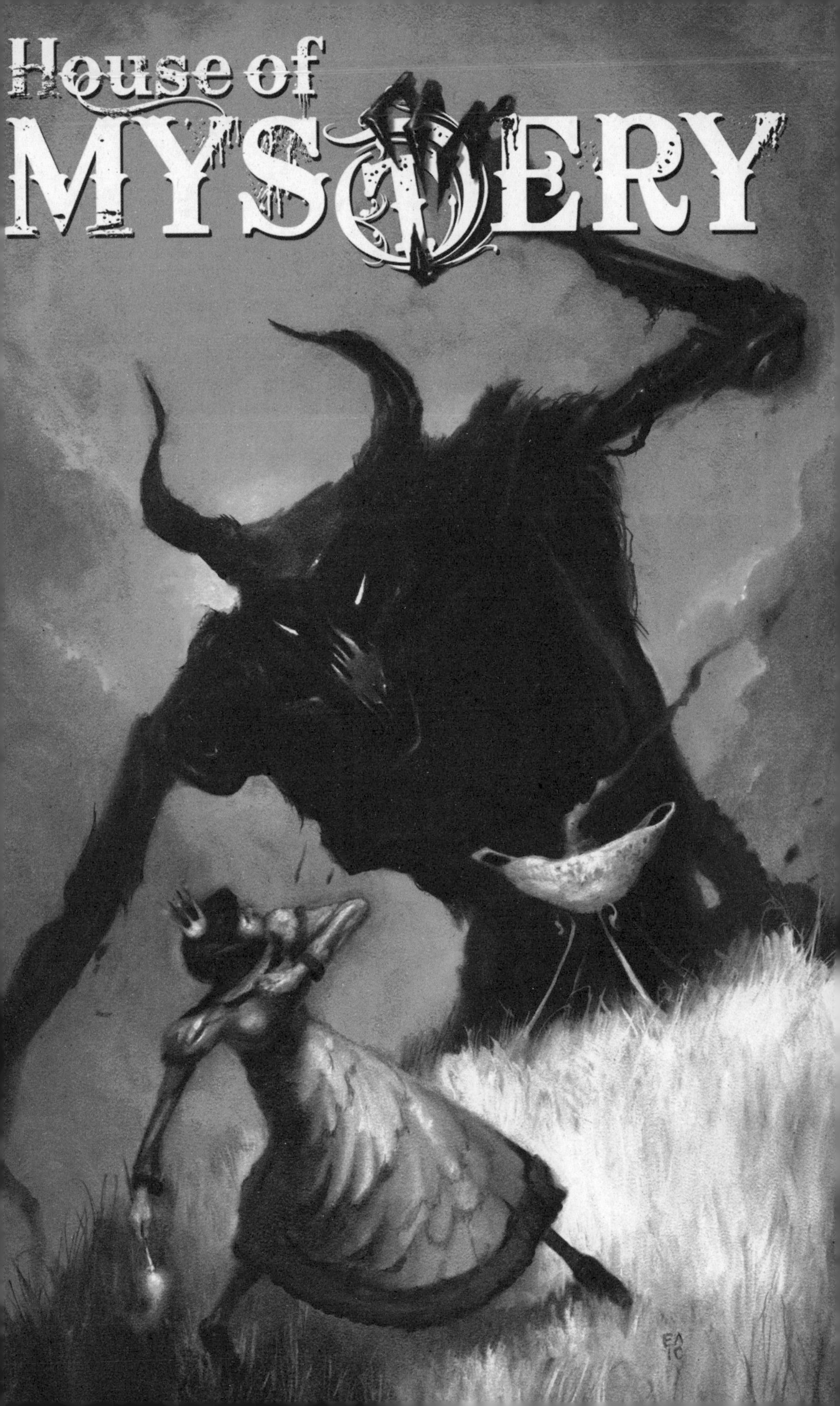
House of
MYSTERY

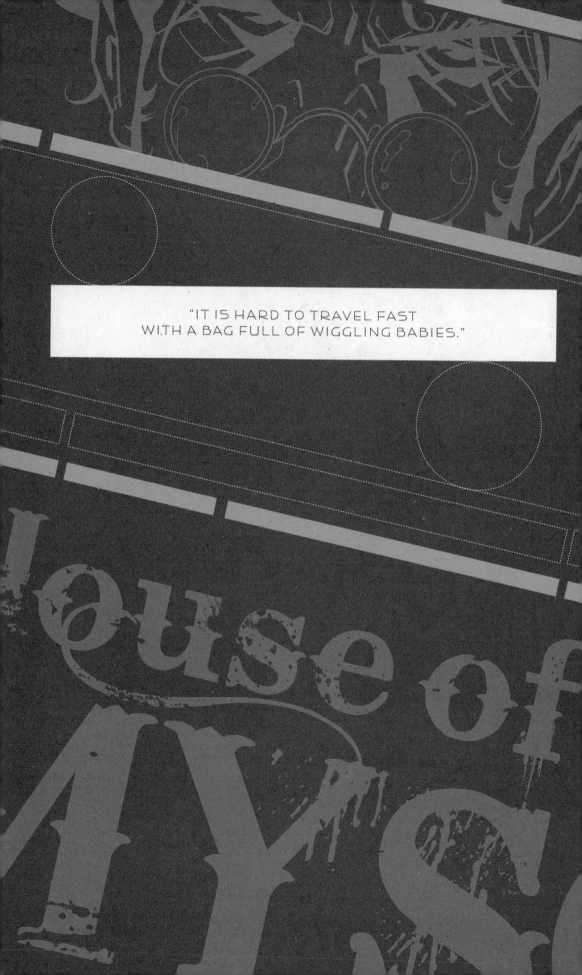

"IT IS HARD TO TRAVEL FAST
WITH A BAG FULL OF WIGGLING BABIES."

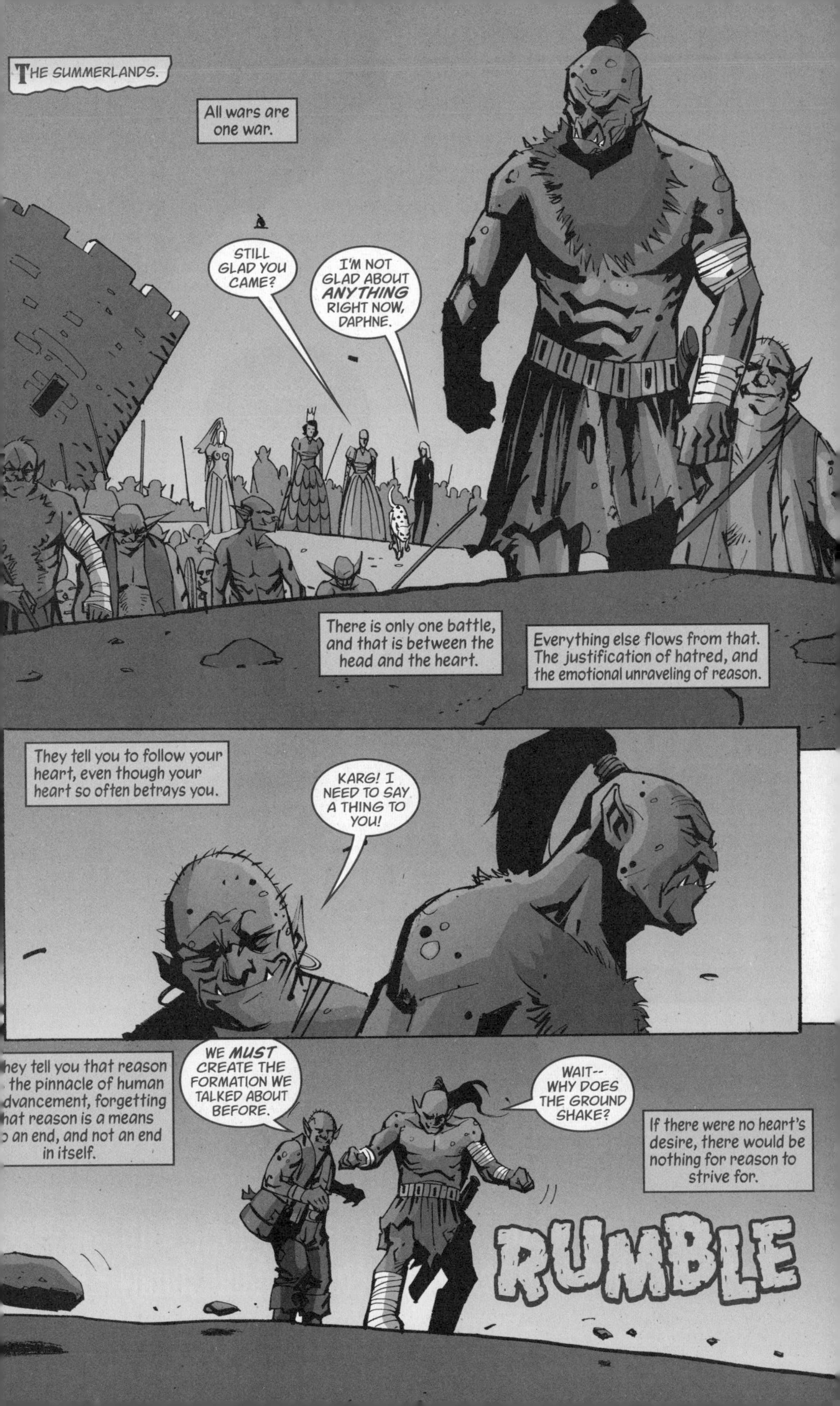

THE SUMMERLANDS.
All wars are one war.
STILL GLAD YOU CAME?
I'M NOT GLAD ABOUT ANYTHING RIGHT NOW, DAPHNE.
There is only one battle, and that is between the head and the heart.
Everything else flows from that. The justification of hatred, and the emotional unraveling of reason.
They tell you to follow your heart, even though your heart so often betrays you.
KARG! I NEED TO SAY A THING TO YOU!
hey tell you that reason the pinnacle of human dvancement, forgetting hat reason is a means o an end, and not an end in itself.
WE MUST CREATE THE FORMATION WE TALKED ABOUT BEFORE.
WAIT-- WHY DOES THE GROUND SHAKE?
If there were no heart's desire, there would be nothing for reason to strive for.
RUMBLE

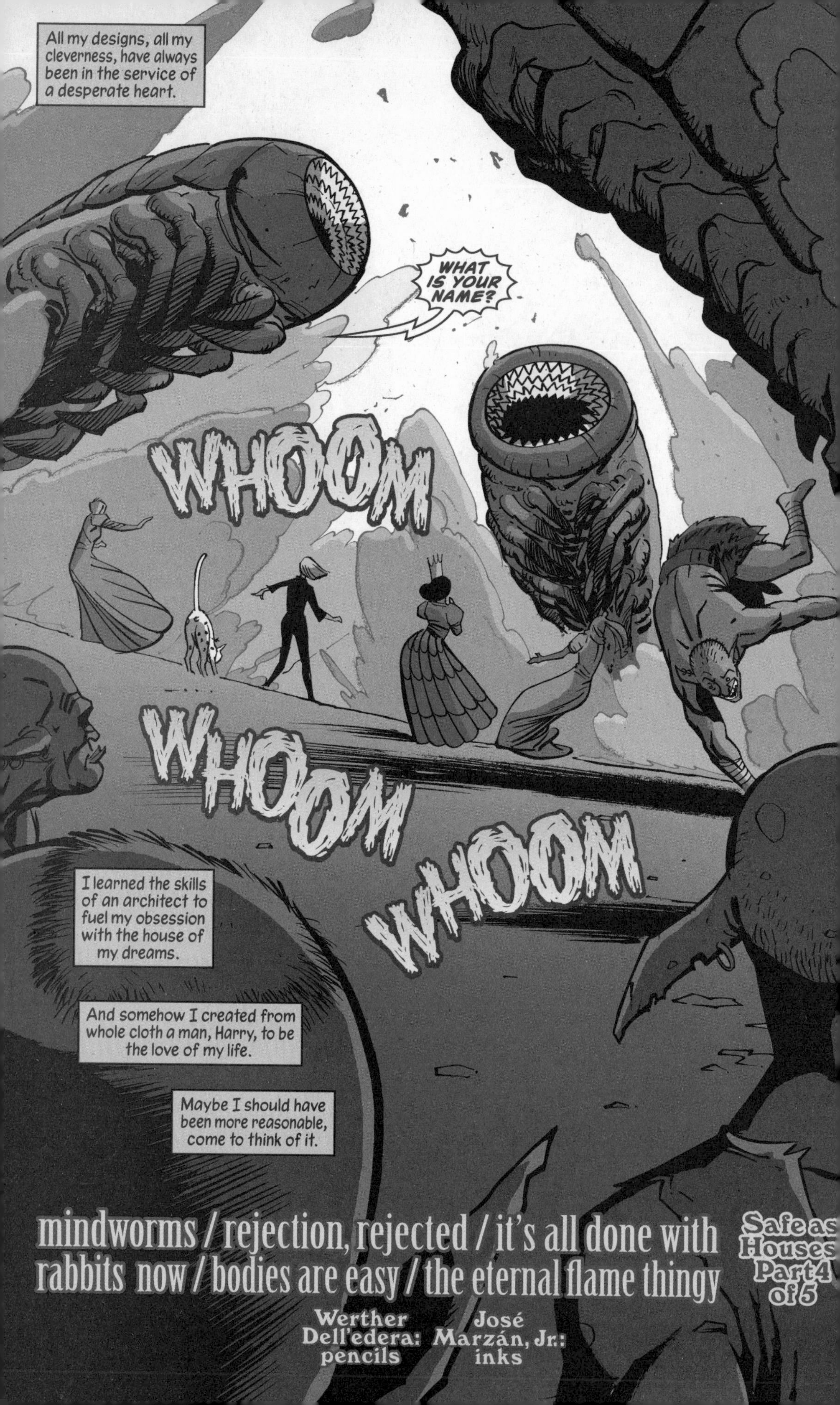

All my designs, all my cleverness, have always been in the service of a desperate heart.
WHAT IS YOUR NAME?
WHOOM
WHOOM
WHOOM
I learned the skills of an architect to fuel my obsession with the house of my dreams.
And somehow I created from whole cloth a man, Harry, to be the love of my life.
Maybe I should have been more reasonable, come to think of it.
mindworms / rejection, rejected / it's all done with rabbits now / bodies are easy / the eternal flame thingy
Safe as Houses Part 4 of 5
Werther Dell'edera: pencils
José Marzán, Jr.: inks

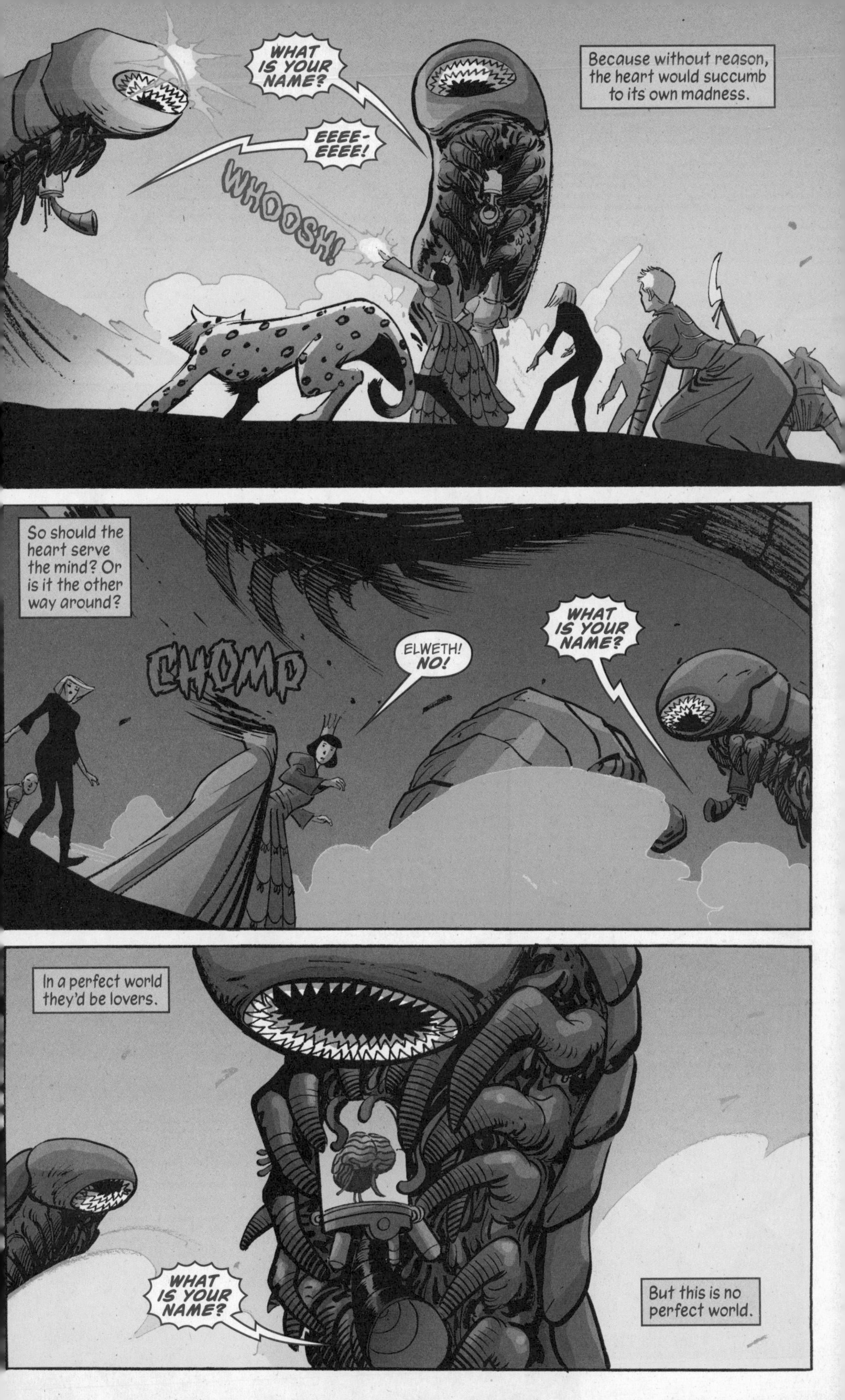
WHAT IS YOUR NAME?
Because without reason, the heart would succumb to its own madness.
EEEE-EEEE!
WHOOSH!
So should the heart serve the mind? Or is it the other way around?
CHOMP
ELWETH! NO!
WHAT IS YOUR NAME?
In a perfect world they'd be lovers.
WHAT IS YOUR NAME?
But this is no perfect world.

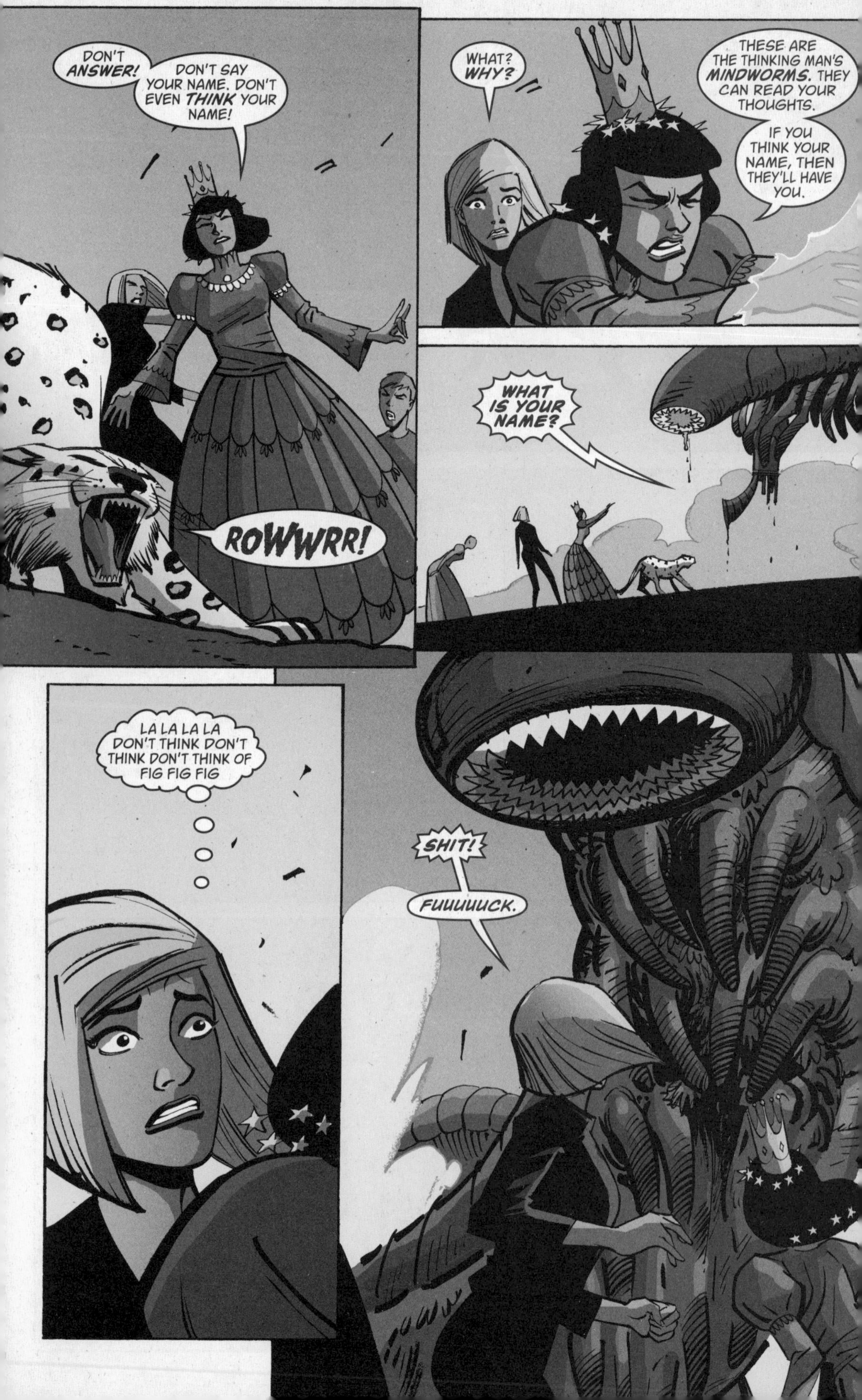
DON'T ANSWER!
DON'T SAY YOUR NAME. DON'T EVEN THINK YOUR NAME!
ROWWRR!
WHAT? WHY?
THESE ARE THE THINKING MAN'S MINDWORMS. THEY CAN READ YOUR THOUGHTS.
IF YOU THINK YOUR NAME, THEN THEY'LL HAVE YOU.
WHAT IS YOUR NAME?
LA LA LA LA DON'T THINK DON'T THINK DON'T THINK OF FIG FIG FIG
SHIT!
FUUUUUCK.

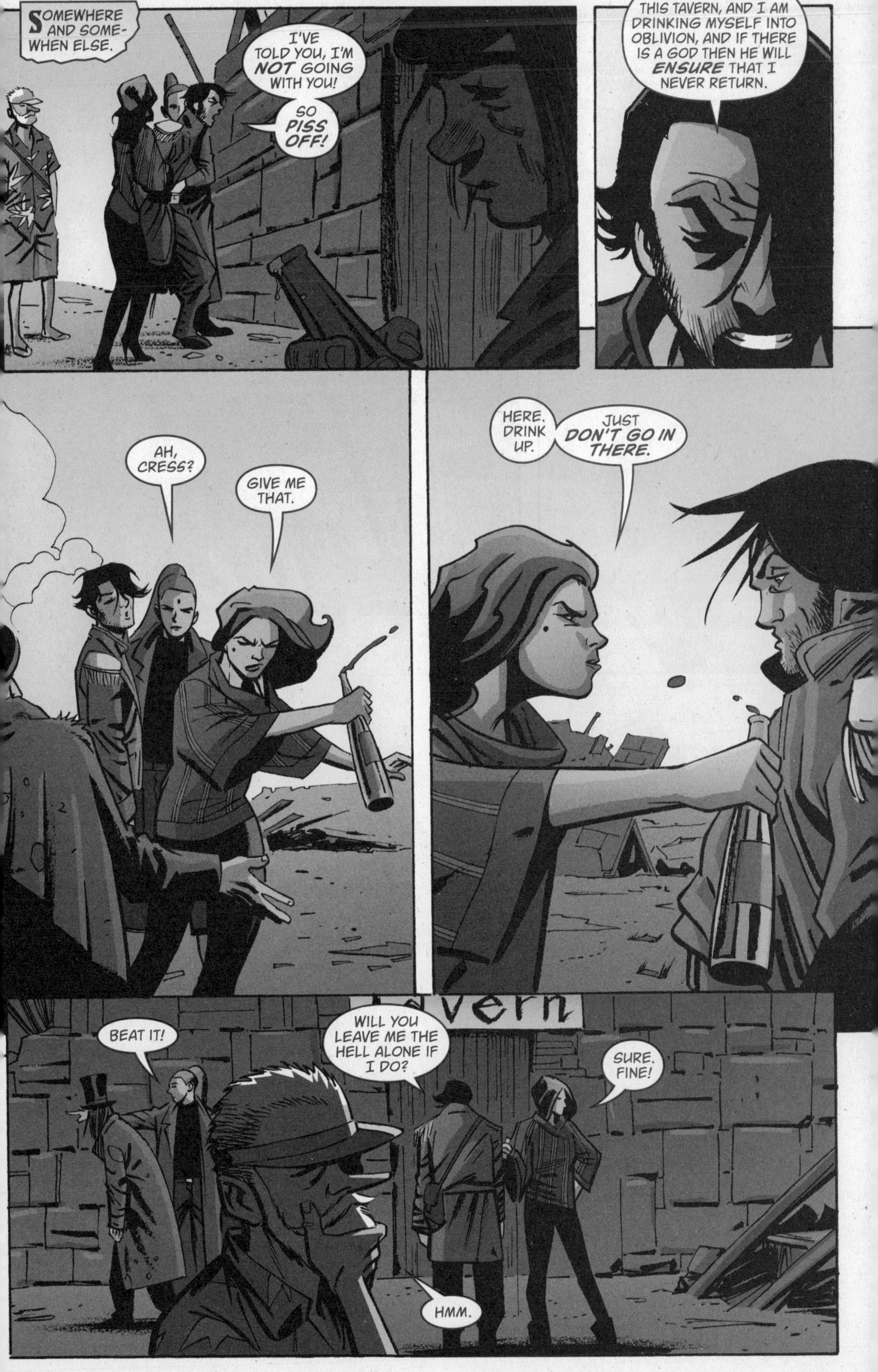
SOMEWHERE AND SOMEWHEN ELSE.
I'VE TOLD YOU, I'M NOT GOING WITH YOU!
SO PISS OFF!
I AM GOING INTO THIS TAVERN, AND I AM DRINKING MYSELF INTO OBLIVION, AND IF THERE IS A GOD THEN HE WILL ENSURE THAT I NEVER RETURN.
AH, CRESS?
GIVE ME THAT.
HERE. DRINK UP.
JUST DON'T GO IN THERE.
vern
BEAT IT!
WILL YOU LEAVE ME THE HELL ALONE IF I DO?
SURE. FINE!
HMM.

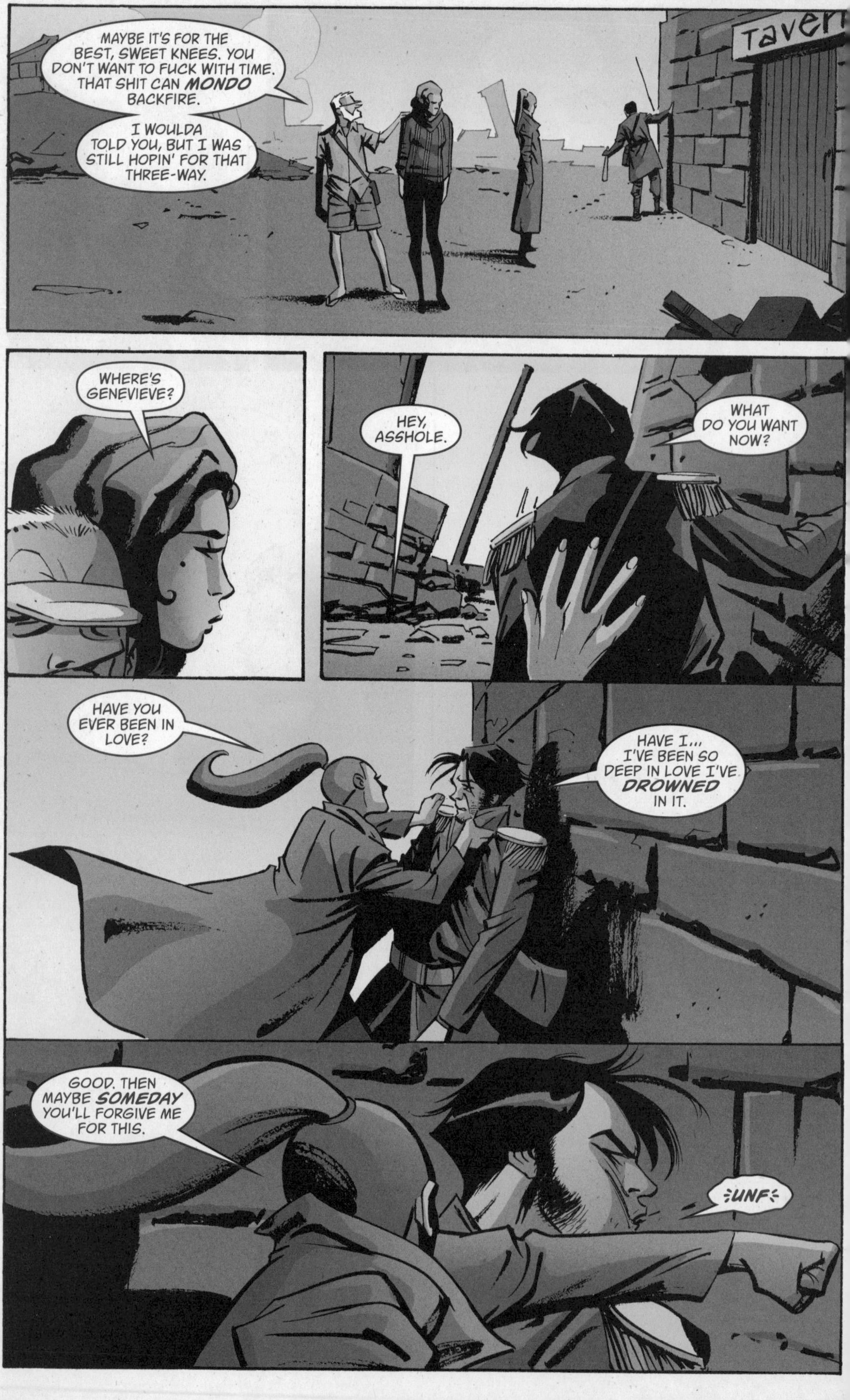

TAVER
MAYBE IT'S FOR THE BEST, SWEET KNEES. YOU DON'T WANT TO FUCK WITH TIME. THAT SHIT CAN *MONDO* BACKFIRE.
I WOULDA TOLD YOU, BUT I WAS STILL HOPIN' FOR THAT THREE-WAY.
WHERE'S GENEVIEVE?
HEY, ASSHOLE.
WHAT DO YOU WANT NOW?
HAVE YOU EVER BEEN IN LOVE?
HAVE I... I'VE BEEN SO DEEP IN LOVE I'VE *DROWNED* IN IT.
GOOD. THEN MAYBE *SOMEDAY* YOU'LL FORGIVE ME FOR THIS.
UNF

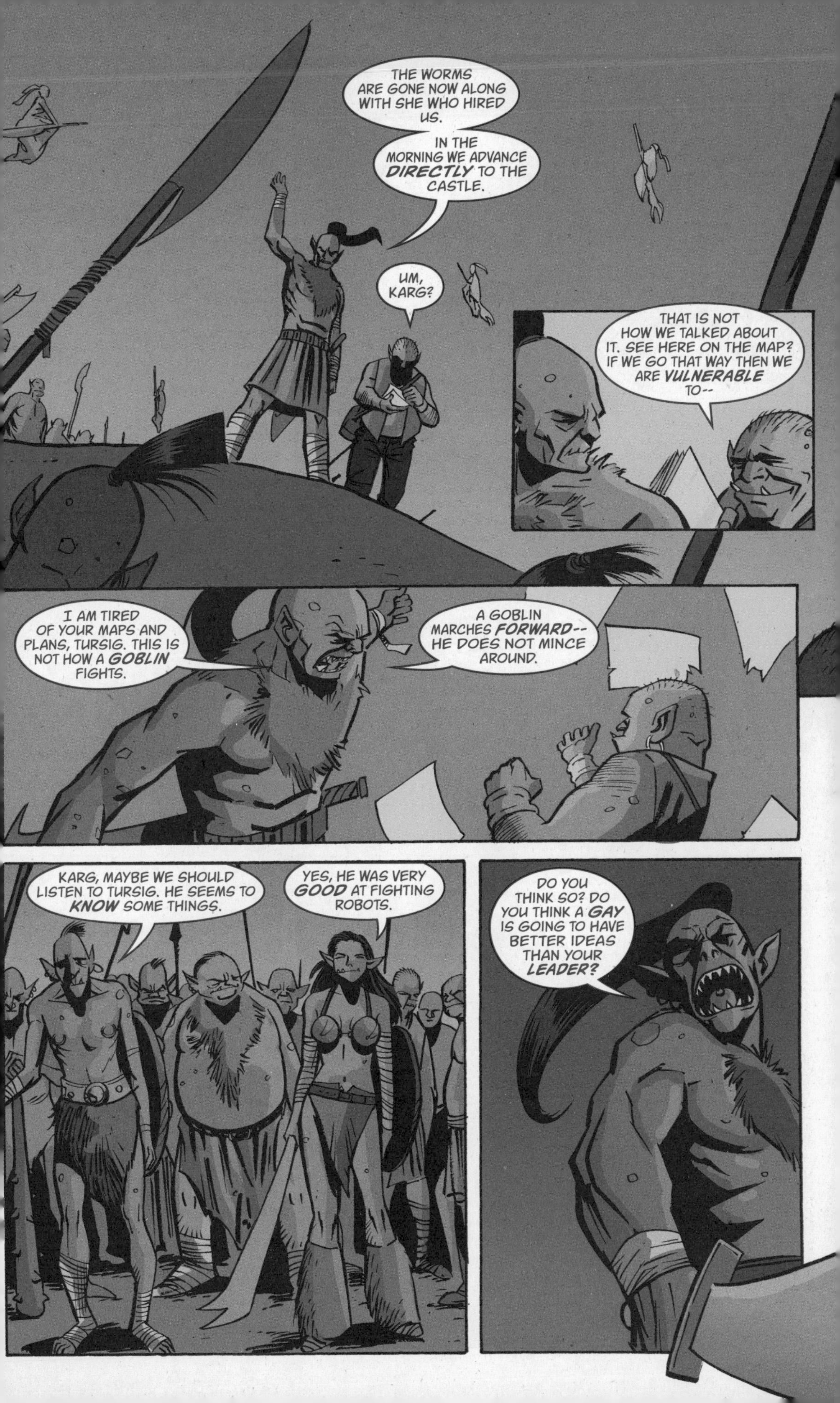
THE WORMS ARE GONE NOW ALONG WITH SHE WHO HIRED US.
IN THE MORNING WE ADVANCE DIRECTLY TO THE CASTLE.
UM, KARG?
THAT IS NOT HOW WE TALKED ABOUT IT. SEE HERE ON THE MAP? IF WE GO THAT WAY THEN WE ARE VULNERABLE TO--
I AM TIRED OF YOUR MAPS AND PLANS, TURSIG. THIS IS NOT HOW A GOBLIN FIGHTS.
A GOBLIN MARCHES FORWARD-- HE DOES NOT MINCE AROUND.
KARG, MAYBE WE SHOULD LISTEN TO TURSIG. HE SEEMS TO KNOW SOME THINGS.
YES, HE WAS VERY GOOD AT FIGHTING ROBOTS.
DO YOU THINK SO? DO YOU THINK A GAY IS GOING TO HAVE BETTER IDEAS THAN YOUR LEADER?

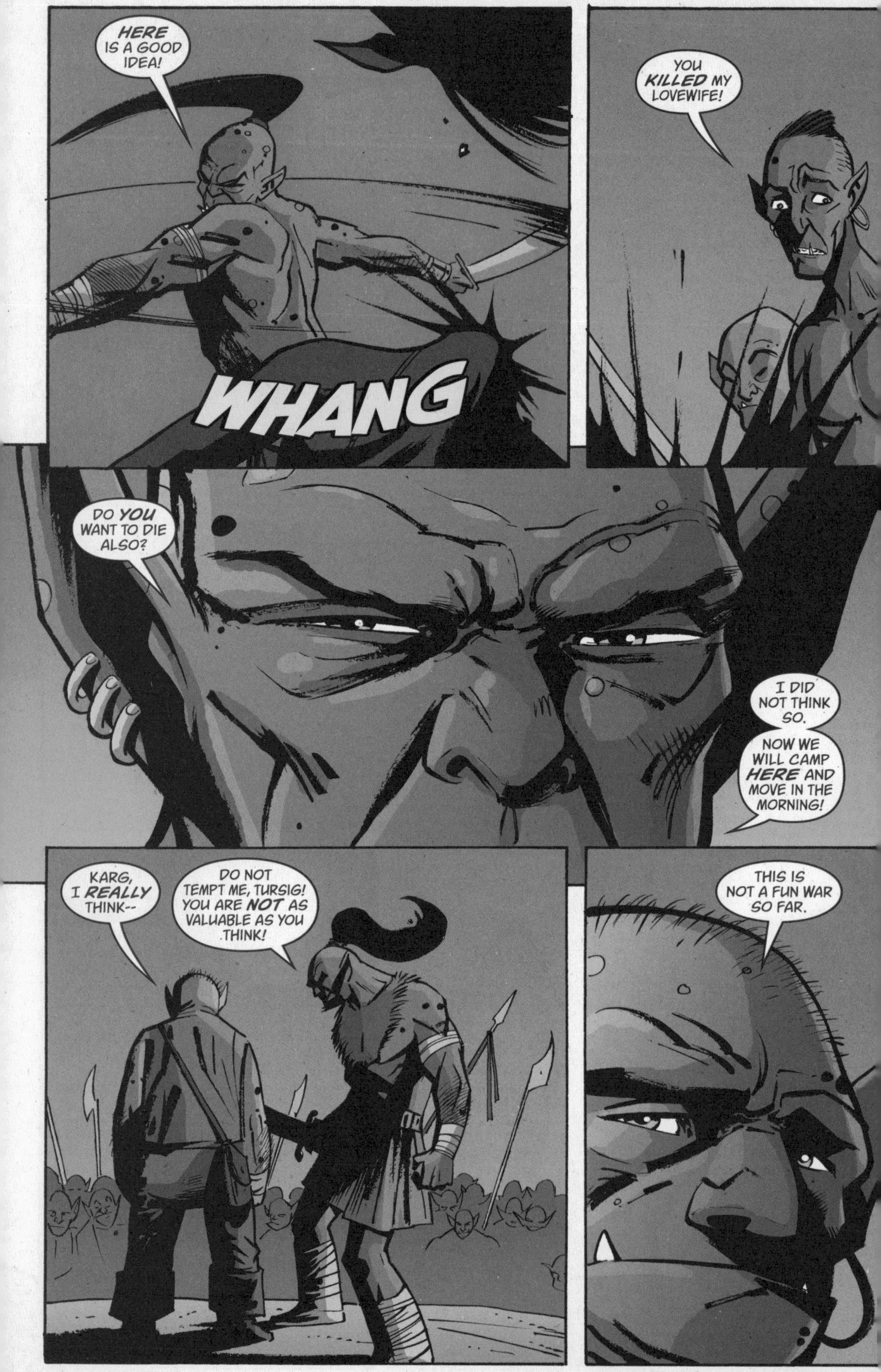
HERE IS A GOOD IDEA!
WHANG
YOU KILLED MY LOVEWIFE!
DO YOU WANT TO DIE ALSO?
I DID NOT THINK SO.
NOW WE WILL CAMP HERE AND MOVE IN THE MORNING!
KARG, I REALLY THINK--
DO NOT TEMPT ME, TURSIG! YOU ARE NOT AS VALUABLE AS YOU THINK!
THIS IS NOT A FUN WAR SO FAR.

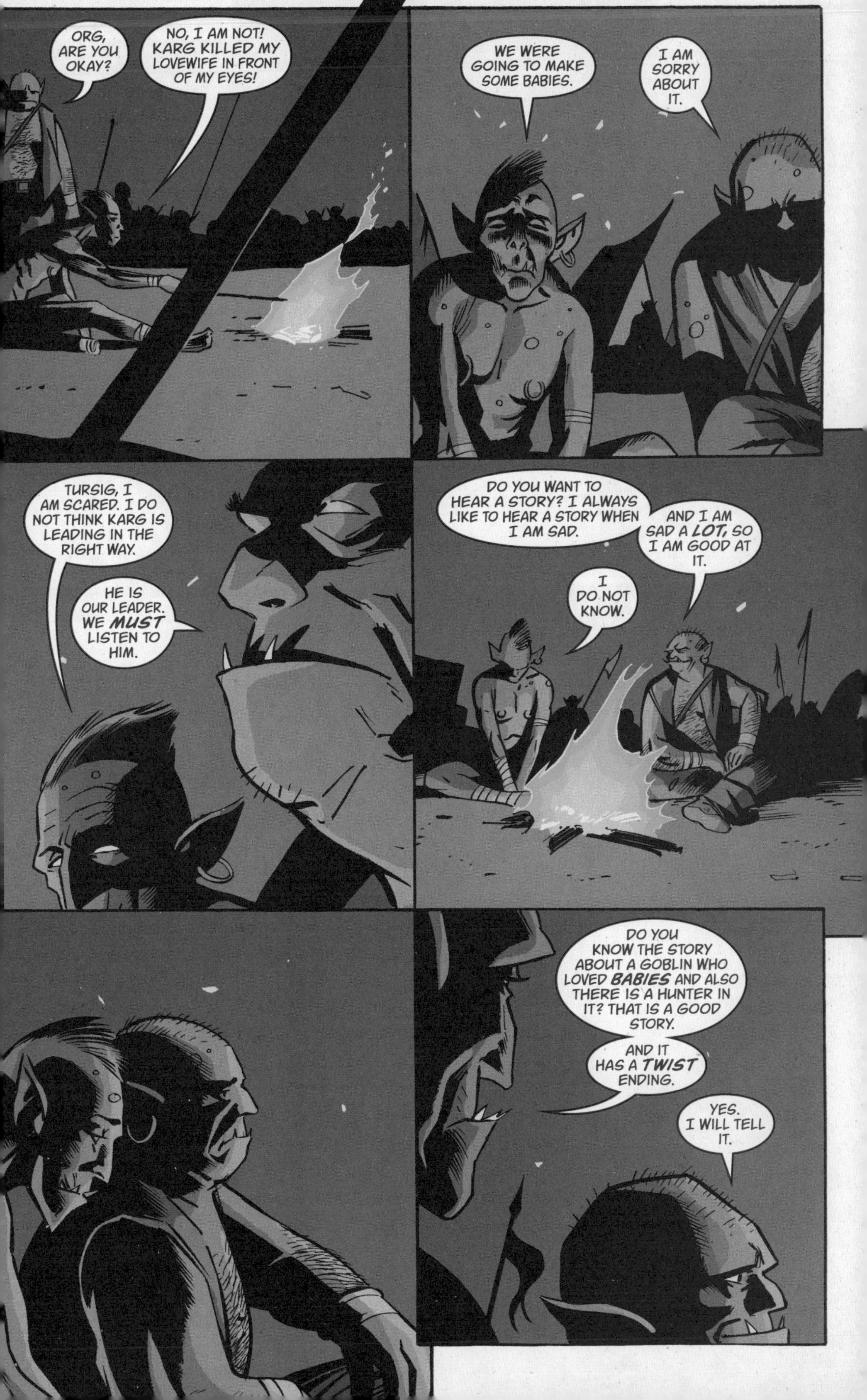
ORG, ARE YOU OKAY?
NO, I AM NOT! KARG KILLED MY LOVEWIFE IN FRONT OF MY EYES!
WE WERE GOING TO MAKE SOME BABIES.
I AM SORRY ABOUT IT.
TURSIG, I AM SCARED. I DO NOT THINK KARG IS LEADING IN THE RIGHT WAY.
HE IS OUR LEADER. WE MUST LISTEN TO HIM.
DO YOU WANT TO HEAR A STORY? I ALWAYS LIKE TO HEAR A STORY WHEN I AM SAD.
AND I AM SAD A LOT, SO I AM GOOD AT IT.
I DO NOT KNOW.
DO YOU KNOW THE STORY ABOUT A GOBLIN WHO LOVED BABIES AND ALSO THERE IS A HUNTER IN IT? THAT IS A GOOD STORY.
AND IT HAS A TWIST ENDING.
YES. I WILL TELL IT.

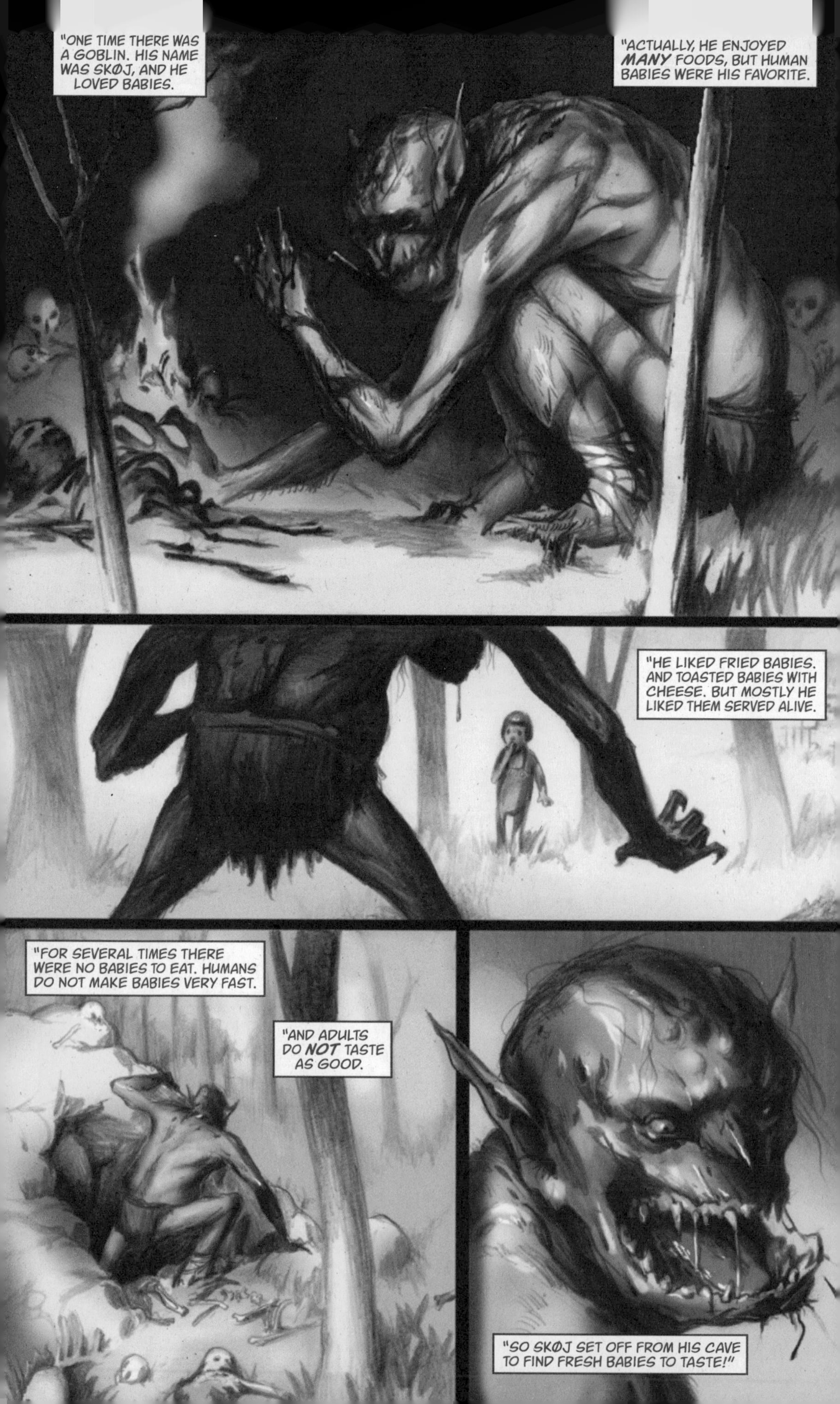
"ONE TIME THERE WAS A GOBLIN. HIS NAME WAS SKØJ, AND HE LOVED BABIES.
"ACTUALLY, HE ENJOYED MANY FOODS, BUT HUMAN BABIES WERE HIS FAVORITE.
"HE LIKED FRIED BABIES. AND TOASTED BABIES WITH CHEESE. BUT MOSTLY HE LIKED THEM SERVED ALIVE.
"FOR SEVERAL TIMES THERE WERE NO BABIES TO EAT. HUMANS DO NOT MAKE BABIES VERY FAST.
"AND ADULTS DO NOT TASTE AS GOOD.
"SO SKØJ SET OFF FROM HIS CAVE TO FIND FRESH BABIES TO TASTE!"

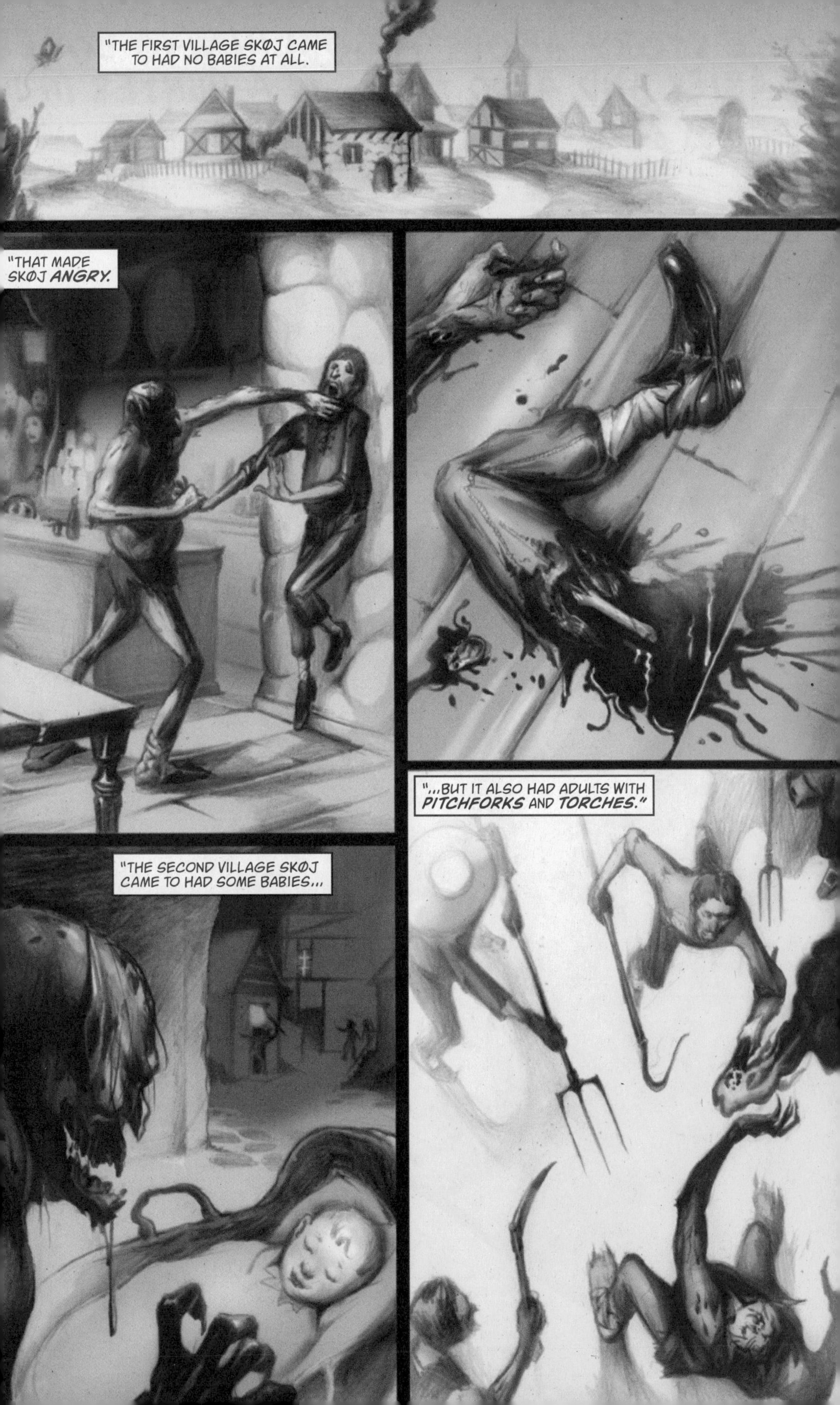
"THE FIRST VILLAGE SKØJ CAME TO HAD NO BABIES AT ALL.
"THAT MADE SKØJ ANGRY.
"THE SECOND VILLAGE SKØJ CAME TO HAD SOME BABIES...
"...BUT IT ALSO HAD ADULTS WITH PITCHFORKS AND TORCHES."

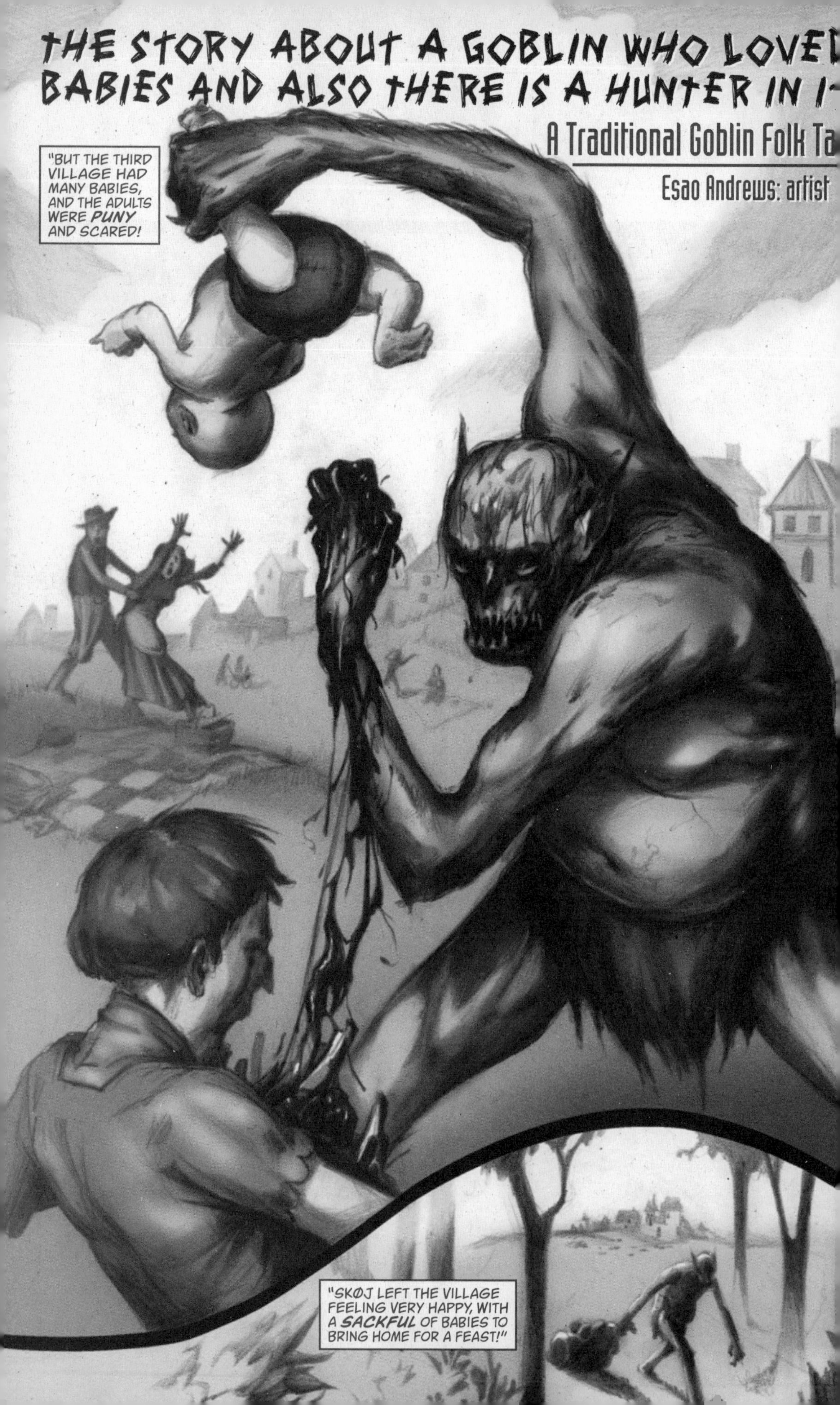
THE STORY ABOUT A GOBLIN WHO LOVE
BABIES AND ALSO THERE IS A HUNTER IN I
A Traditional Goblin Folk Ta
Esao Andrews: artist
"BUT THE THIRD VILLAGE HAD MANY BABIES, AND THE ADULTS WERE PUNY AND SCARED!
"SKØJ LEFT THE VILLAGE FEELING VERY HAPPY, WITH A SACKFUL OF BABIES TO BRING HOME FOR A FEAST!"

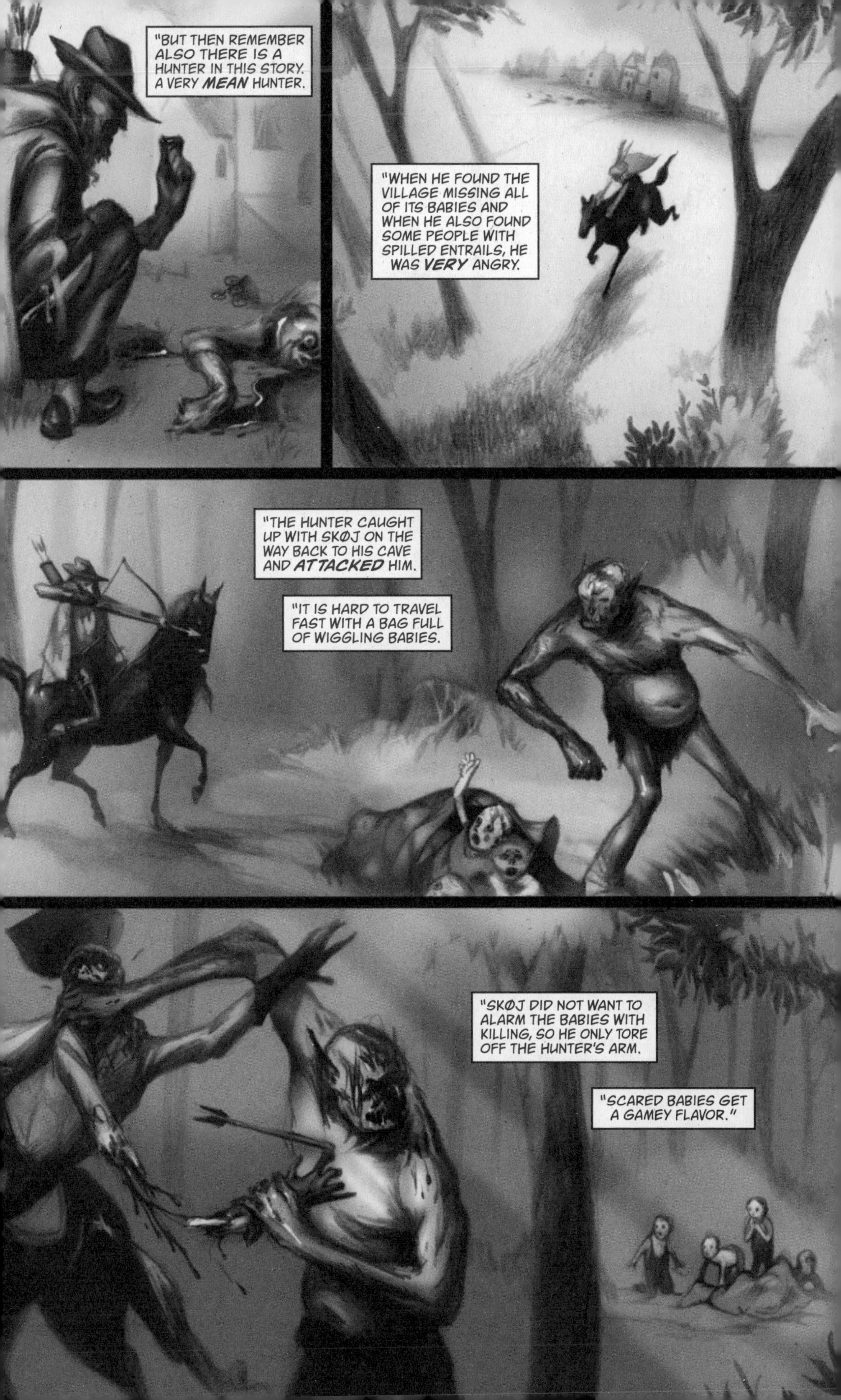
"BUT THEN REMEMBER ALSO THERE IS A HUNTER IN THIS STORY. A VERY MEAN HUNTER.
"WHEN HE FOUND THE VILLAGE MISSING ALL OF ITS BABIES AND WHEN HE ALSO FOUND SOME PEOPLE WITH SPILLED ENTRAILS, HE WAS VERY ANGRY.
"THE HUNTER CAUGHT UP WITH SKØJ ON THE WAY BACK TO HIS CAVE AND ATTACKED HIM.
"IT IS HARD TO TRAVEL FAST WITH A BAG FULL OF WIGGLING BABIES.
"SKØJ DID NOT WANT TO ALARM THE BABIES WITH KILLING, SO HE ONLY TORE OFF THE HUNTER'S ARM.
"SCARED BABIES GET A GAMEY FLAVOR."

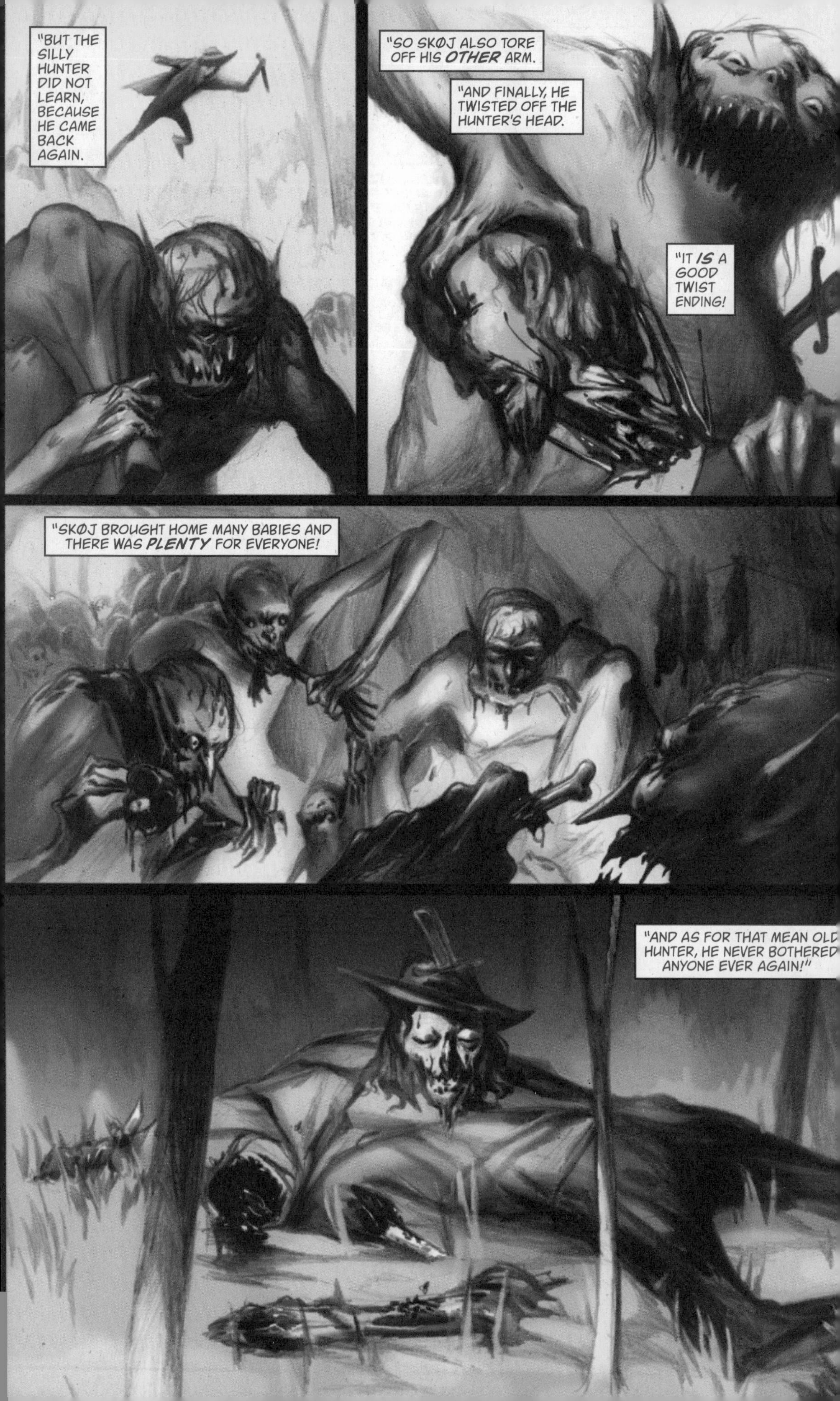
"BUT THE SILLY HUNTER DID NOT LEARN, BECAUSE HE CAME BACK AGAIN.
"SO SKØJ ALSO TORE OFF HIS OTHER ARM.
"AND FINALLY, HE TWISTED OFF THE HUNTER'S HEAD.
"IT IS A GOOD TWIST ENDING!
"SKØJ BROUGHT HOME MANY BABIES AND THERE WAS PLENTY FOR EVERYONE!
"AND AS FOR THAT MEAN OLD HUNTER, HE NEVER BOTHERED ANYONE EVER AGAIN!"

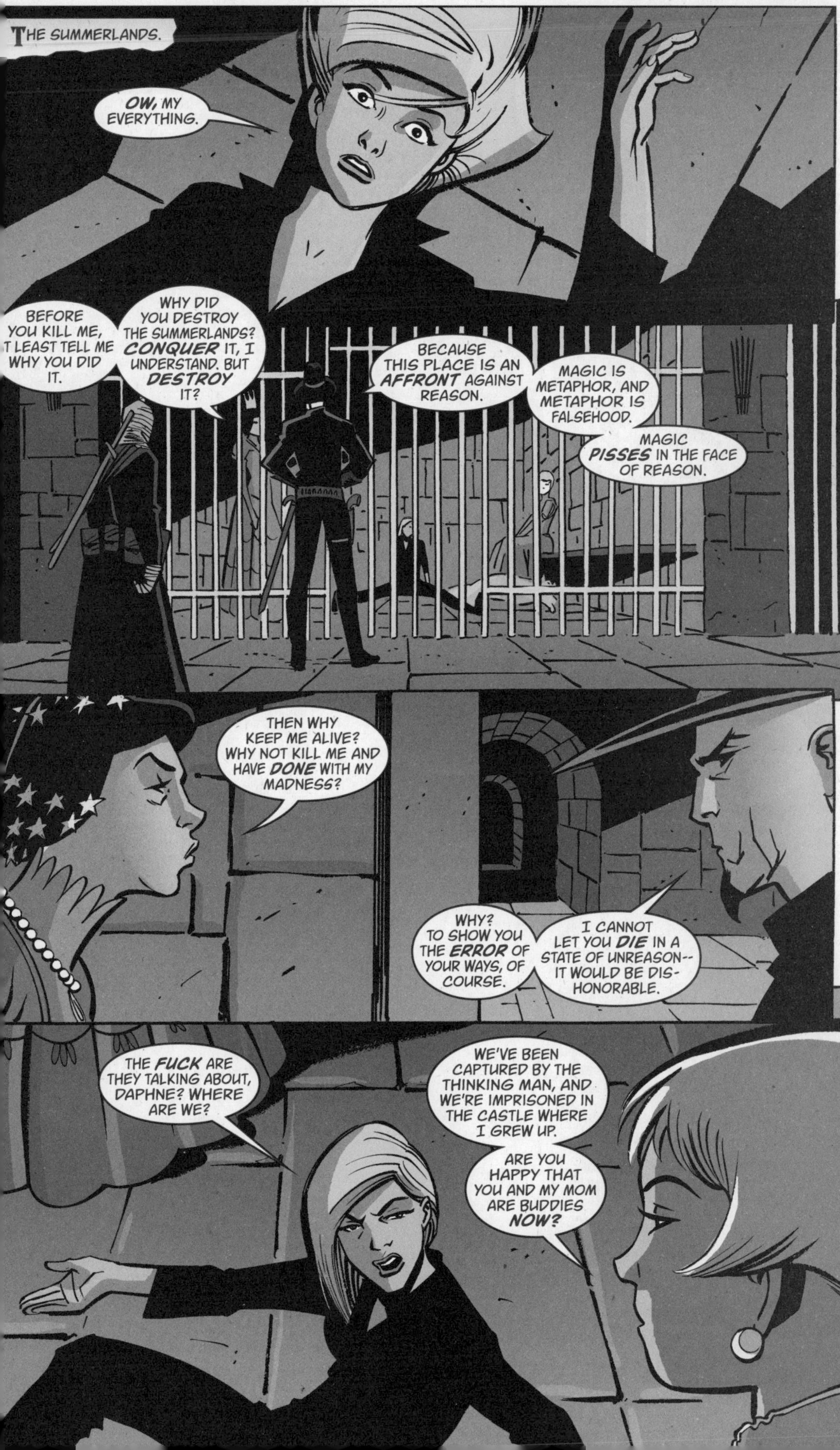
THE SUMMERLANDS.
OW, MY EVERYTHING.
BEFORE YOU KILL ME, AT LEAST TELL ME WHY YOU DID IT.
WHY DID YOU DESTROY THE SUMMERLANDS? CONQUER IT, I UNDERSTAND. BUT DESTROY IT?
BECAUSE THIS PLACE IS AN AFFRONT AGAINST REASON.
MAGIC IS METAPHOR, AND METAPHOR IS FALSEHOOD.
MAGIC PISSES IN THE FACE OF REASON.
THEN WHY KEEP ME ALIVE? WHY NOT KILL ME AND HAVE DONE WITH MY MADNESS?
WHY? TO SHOW YOU THE ERROR OF YOUR WAYS, OF COURSE.
I CANNOT LET YOU DIE IN A STATE OF UNREASON-- IT WOULD BE DISHONORABLE.
THE FUCK ARE THEY TALKING ABOUT, DAPHNE? WHERE ARE WE?
WE'VE BEEN CAPTURED BY THE THINKING MAN, AND WE'RE IMPRISONED IN THE CASTLE WHERE I GREW UP.
ARE YOU HAPPY THAT YOU AND MY MOM ARE BUDDIES NOW?

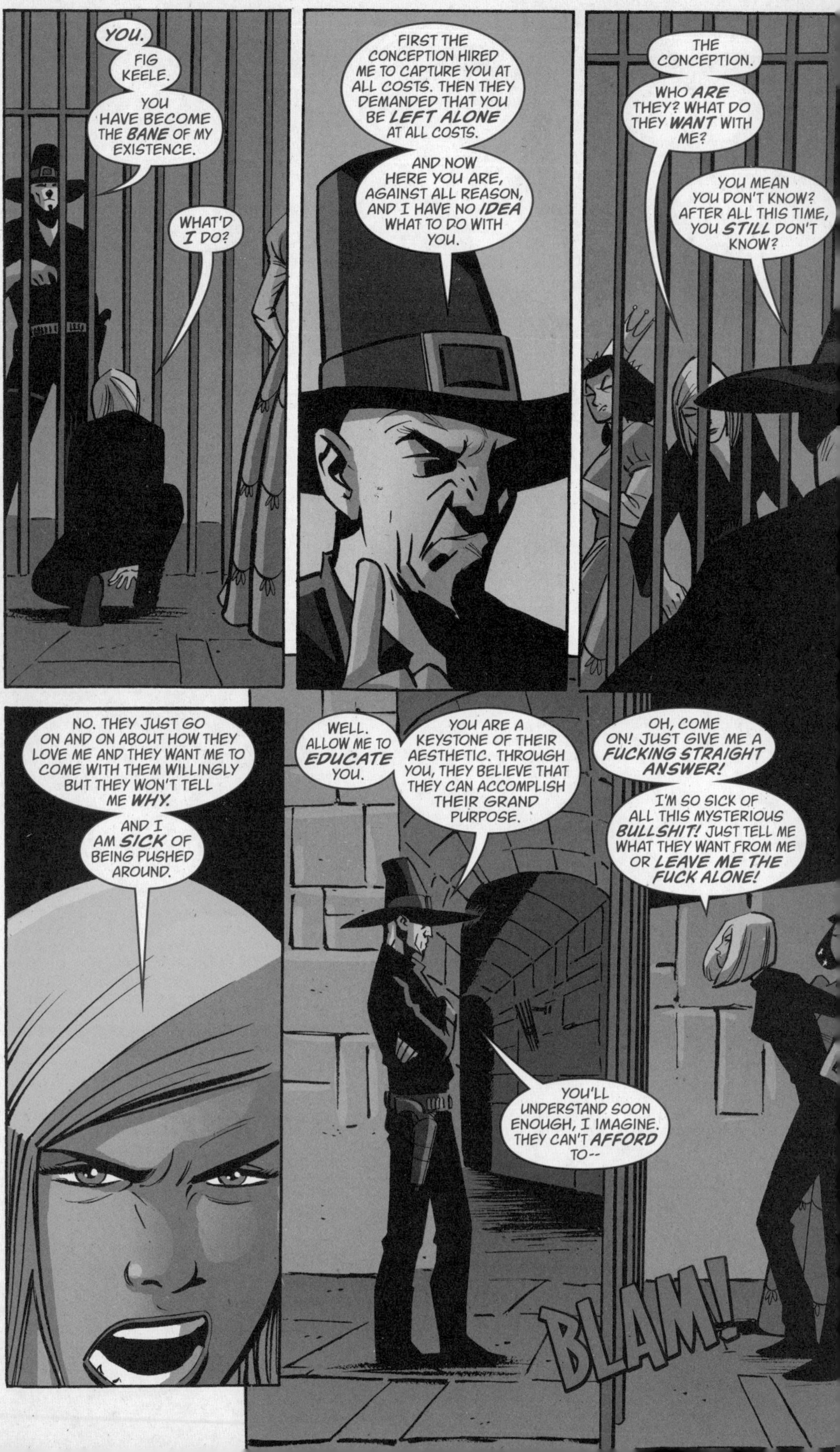
YOU.
FIG KEELE.
YOU HAVE BECOME THE BANE OF MY EXISTENCE.
WHAT'D I DO?
FIRST THE CONCEPTION HIRED ME TO CAPTURE YOU AT ALL COSTS. THEN THEY DEMANDED THAT YOU BE LEFT ALONE AT ALL COSTS.
AND NOW HERE YOU ARE, AGAINST ALL REASON, AND I HAVE NO IDEA WHAT TO DO WITH YOU.
THE CONCEPTION.
WHO ARE THEY? WHAT DO THEY WANT WITH ME?
YOU MEAN YOU DON'T KNOW? AFTER ALL THIS TIME, YOU STILL DON'T KNOW?
NO. THEY JUST GO ON AND ON ABOUT HOW THEY LOVE ME AND THEY WANT ME TO COME WITH THEM WILLINGLY BUT THEY WON'T TELL ME WHY.
AND I AM SICK OF BEING PUSHED AROUND.
WELL. ALLOW ME TO EDUCATE YOU.
YOU ARE A KEYSTONE OF THEIR AESTHETIC. THROUGH YOU, THEY BELIEVE THAT THEY CAN ACCOMPLISH THEIR GRAND PURPOSE.
OH, COME ON! JUST GIVE ME A FUCKING STRAIGHT ANSWER!
I'M SO SICK OF ALL THIS MYSTERIOUS BULLSHIT! JUST TELL ME WHAT THEY WANT FROM ME OR LEAVE ME THE FUCK ALONE!
YOU'LL UNDERSTAND SOON ENOUGH, I IMAGINE. THEY CAN'T AFFORD TO--
BLAM!

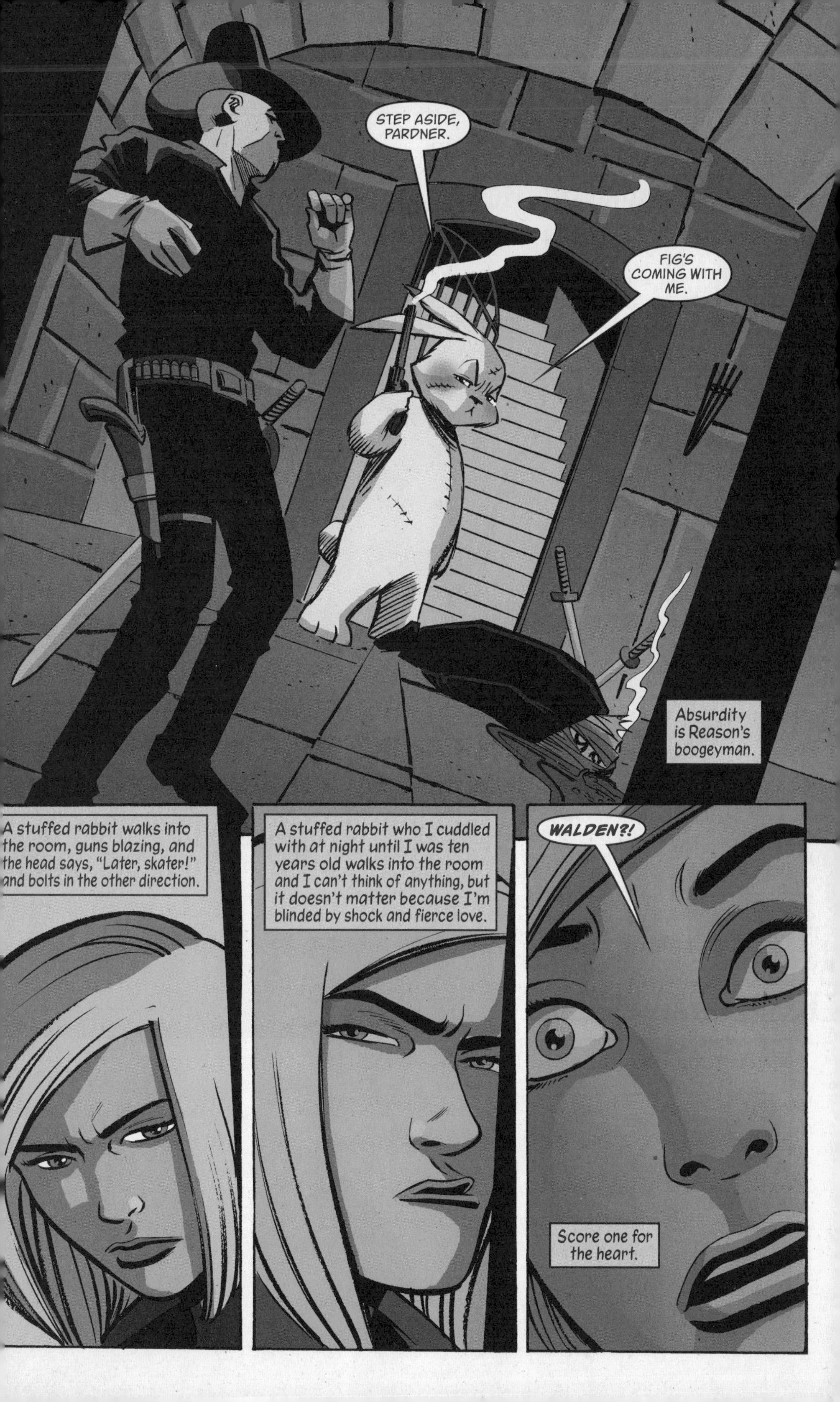
STEP ASIDE, PARDNER.
FIG'S COMING WITH ME.
Absurdity is Reason's boogeyman.
A stuffed rabbit walks into the room, guns blazing, and the head says, "Later, skater!" and bolts in the other direction.
A stuffed rabbit who I cuddled with at night until I was ten years old walks into the room and I can't think of anything, but it doesn't matter because I'm blinded by shock and fierce love.
WALDEN?!
Score one for the heart.

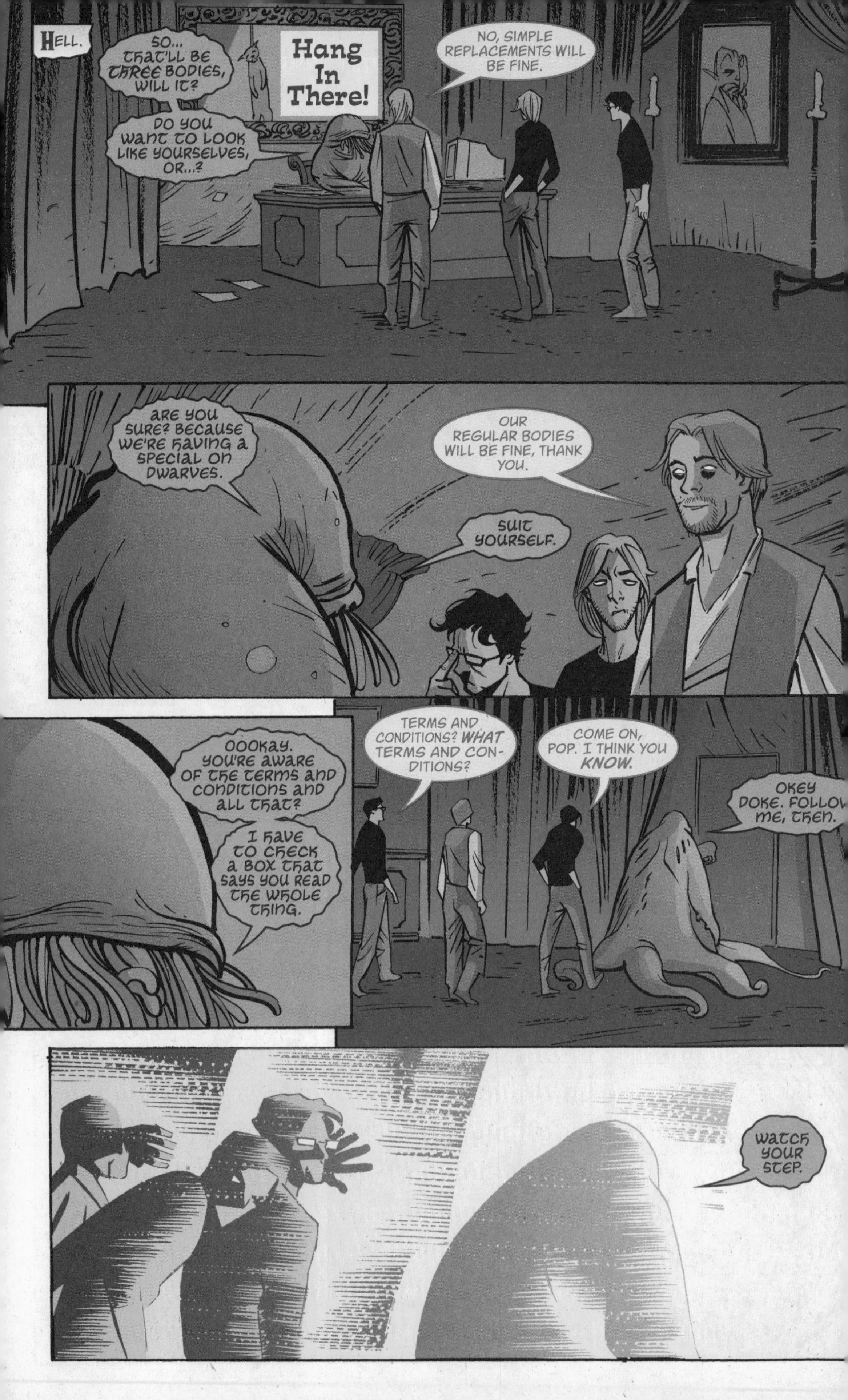
HELL.
SO... THAT'LL BE THREE BODIES, WILL IT?
DO YOU WANT TO LOOK LIKE YOURSELVES, OR...?
Hang In There!
NO, SIMPLE REPLACEMENTS WILL BE FINE.
ARE YOU SURE? BECAUSE WE'RE HAVING A SPECIAL ON DWARVES.
OUR REGULAR BODIES WILL BE FINE, THANK YOU.
SUIT YOURSELF.
OOOKAY. YOU'RE AWARE OF THE TERMS AND CONDITIONS AND ALL THAT?
I HAVE TO CHECK A BOX THAT SAYS YOU READ THE WHOLE THING.
TERMS AND CONDITIONS? WHAT TERMS AND CONDITIONS?
COME ON, POP. I THINK YOU KNOW.
OKEY DOKE. FOLLOW ME, THEN.
WATCH YOUR STEP.

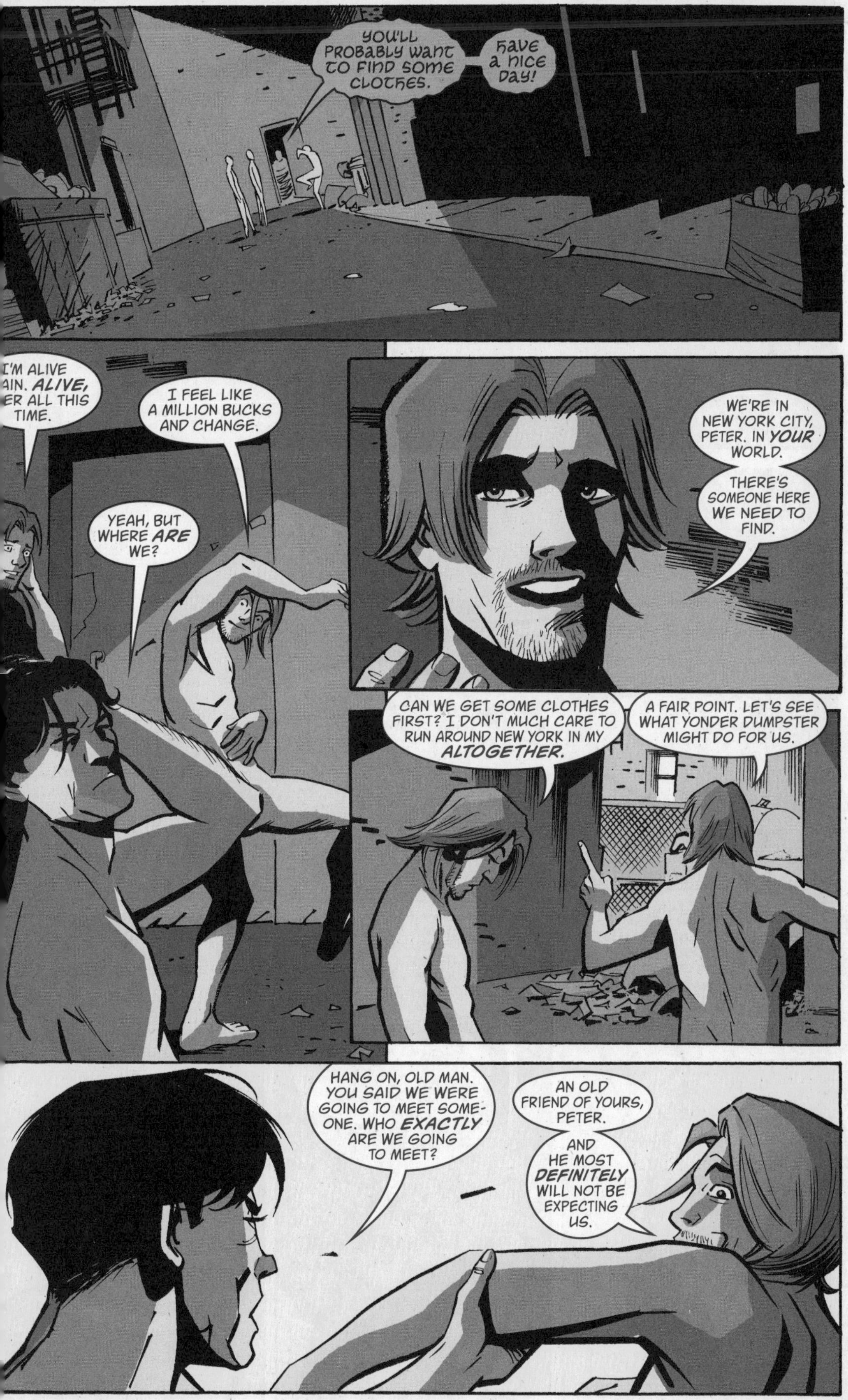
YOU'LL PROBABLY WANT TO FIND SOME CLOTHES.
HAVE A NICE DAY!
I'M ALIVE AIN. *ALIVE,* ER ALL THIS TIME.
I FEEL LIKE A MILLION BUCKS AND CHANGE.
YEAH, BUT WHERE *ARE* WE?
WE'RE IN NEW YORK CITY, PETER. IN *YOUR* WORLD.
THERE'S SOMEONE HERE WE NEED TO FIND.
CAN WE GET SOME CLOTHES FIRST? I DON'T MUCH CARE TO RUN AROUND NEW YORK IN MY *ALTOGETHER.*
A FAIR POINT. LET'S SEE WHAT YONDER DUMPSTER MIGHT DO FOR US.
HANG ON, OLD MAN. YOU SAID WE WERE GOING TO MEET SOME-ONE. WHO *EXACTLY* ARE WE GOING TO MEET?
AN OLD FRIEND OF YOURS, PETER.
AND HE MOST *DEFINITELY* WILL NOT BE EXPECTING US.

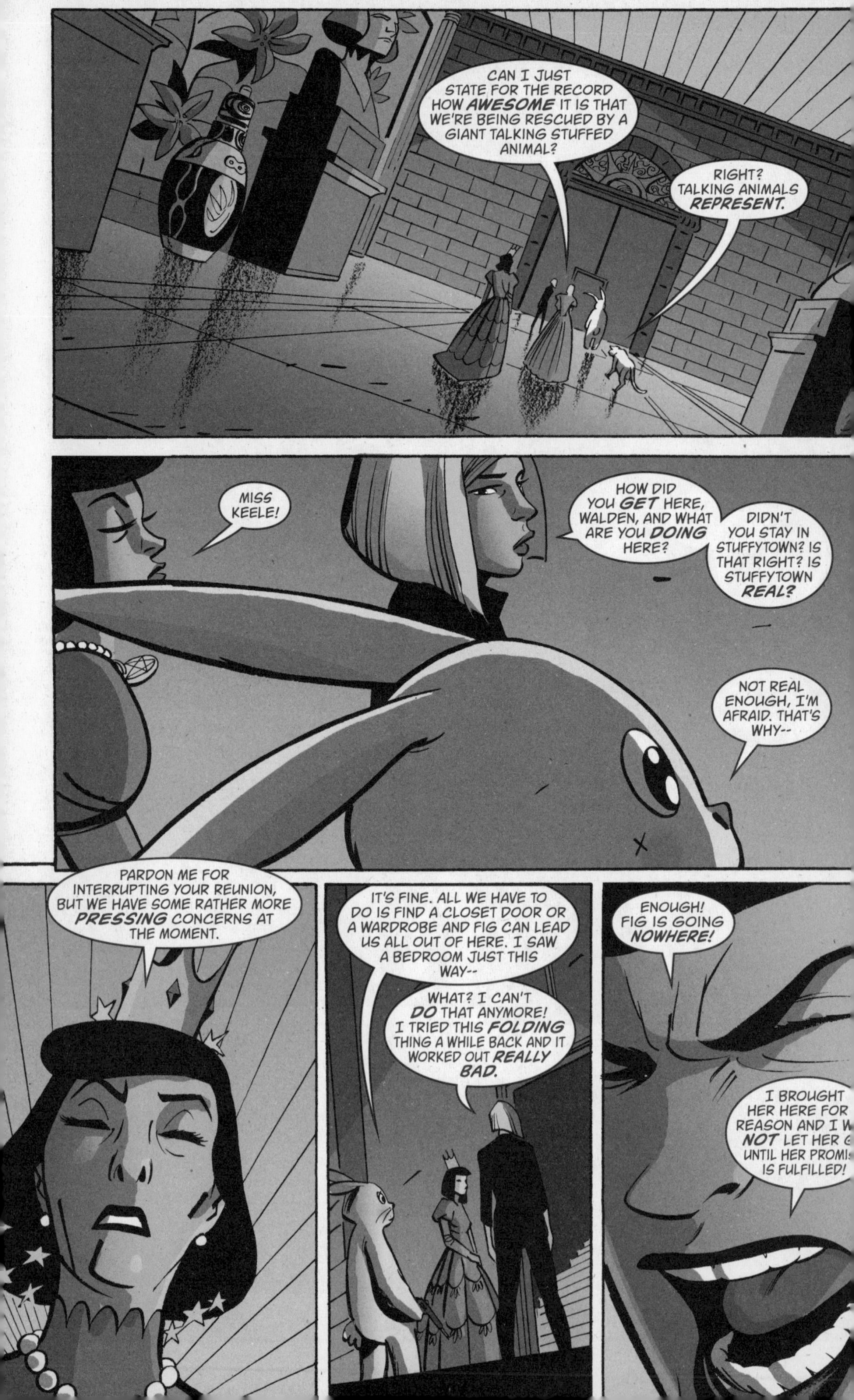
CAN I JUST STATE FOR THE RECORD HOW AWESOME IT IS THAT WE'RE BEING RESCUED BY A GIANT TALKING STUFFED ANIMAL?
RIGHT? TALKING ANIMALS REPRESENT.
MISS KEELE!
HOW DID YOU GET HERE, WALDEN, AND WHAT ARE YOU DOING HERE?
DIDN'T YOU STAY IN STUFFYTOWN? IS THAT RIGHT? IS STUFFYTOWN REAL?
NOT REAL ENOUGH, I'M AFRAID. THAT'S WHY--
PARDON ME FOR INTERRUPTING YOUR REUNION, BUT WE HAVE SOME RATHER MORE PRESSING CONCERNS AT THE MOMENT.
IT'S FINE. ALL WE HAVE TO DO IS FIND A CLOSET DOOR OR A WARDROBE AND FIG CAN LEAD US ALL OUT OF HERE. I SAW A BEDROOM JUST THIS WAY--
WHAT? I CAN'T DO THAT ANYMORE! I TRIED THIS FOLDING THING A WHILE BACK AND IT WORKED OUT REALLY BAD.
ENOUGH! FIG IS GOING NOWHERE!
I BROUGHT HER HERE FOR REASON AND I W NOT LET HER G UNTIL HER PROMI IS FULFILLED!

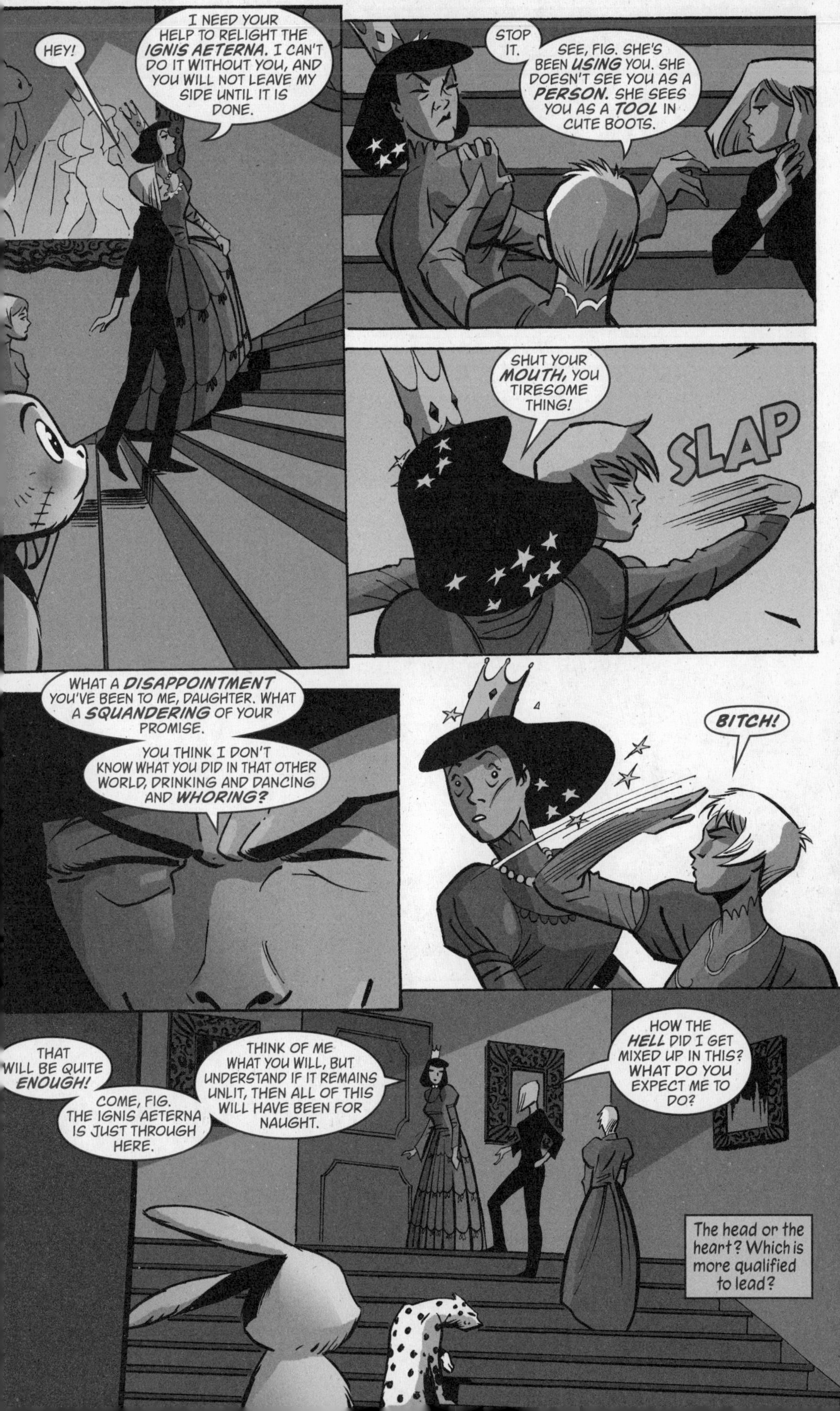
HEY!
I NEED YOUR HELP TO RELIGHT THE IGNIS AETERNA. I CAN'T DO IT WITHOUT YOU, AND YOU WILL NOT LEAVE MY SIDE UNTIL IT IS DONE.
STOP IT.
SEE, FIG. SHE'S BEEN USING YOU. SHE DOESN'T SEE YOU AS A PERSON. SHE SEES YOU AS A TOOL IN CUTE BOOTS.
SHUT YOUR MOUTH, YOU TIRESOME THING!
SLAP
WHAT A DISAPPOINTMENT YOU'VE BEEN TO ME, DAUGHTER. WHAT A SQUANDERING OF YOUR PROMISE.
YOU THINK I DON'T KNOW WHAT YOU DID IN THAT OTHER WORLD, DRINKING AND DANCING AND WHORING?
BITCH!
THAT WILL BE QUITE ENOUGH!
COME, FIG. THE IGNIS AETERNA IS JUST THROUGH HERE.
THINK OF ME WHAT YOU WILL, BUT UNDERSTAND IF IT REMAINS UNLIT, THEN ALL OF THIS WILL HAVE BEEN FOR NAUGHT.
HOW THE HELL DID I GET MIXED UP IN THIS? WHAT DO YOU EXPECT ME TO DO?
The head or the heart? Which is more qualified to lead?

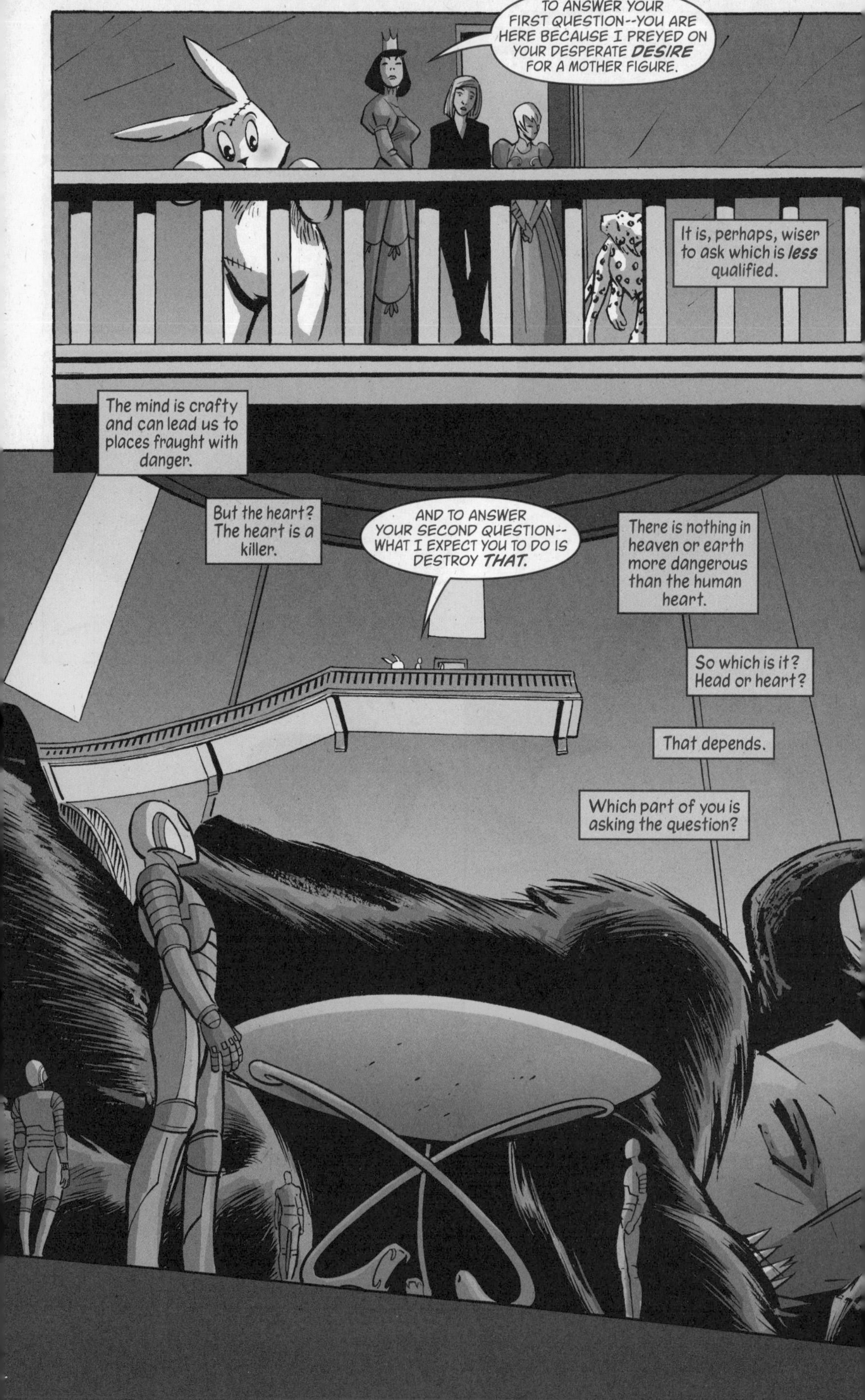
TO ANSWER YOUR FIRST QUESTION--YOU ARE HERE BECAUSE I PREYED ON YOUR DESPERATE *DESIRE* FOR A MOTHER FIGURE.
It is, perhaps, wiser to ask which is *less* qualified.
The mind is crafty and can lead us to places fraught with danger.
But the heart? The heart is a killer.
AND TO ANSWER YOUR SECOND QUESTION--WHAT I EXPECT YOU TO DO IS DESTROY *THAT.*
There is nothing in heaven or earth more dangerous than the human heart.
So which is it? Head or heart?
That depends.
Which part of you is asking the question?

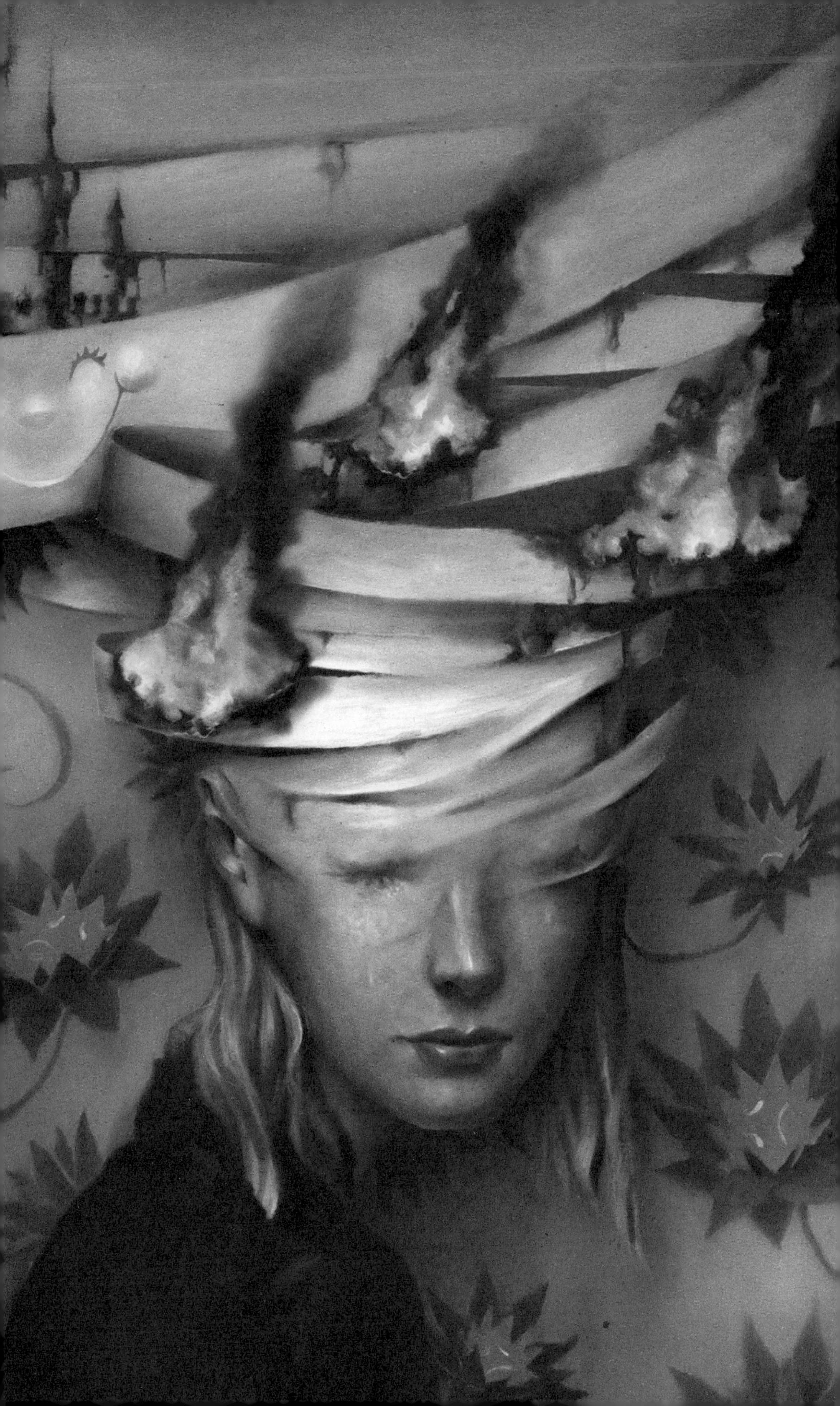

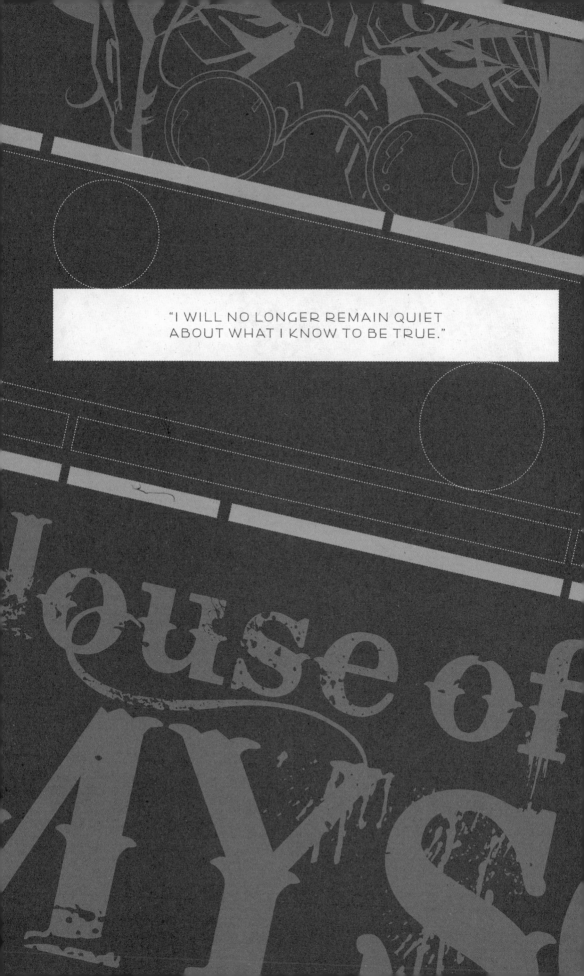

"I WILL NO LONGER REMAIN QUIET ABOUT WHAT I KNOW TO BE TRUE."

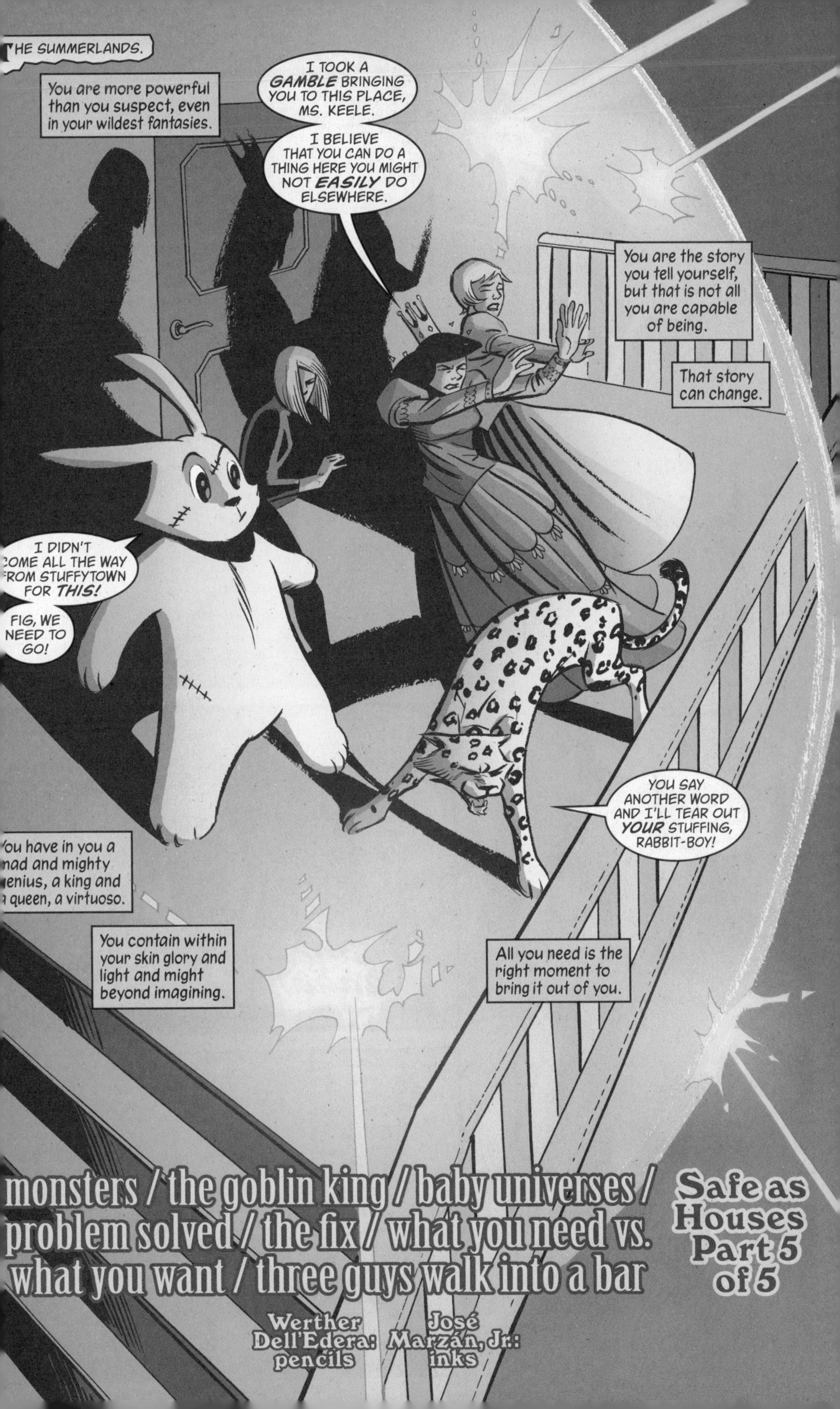

THE SUMMERLANDS.
You are more powerful than you suspect, even in your wildest fantasies.
I TOOK A GAMBLE BRINGING YOU TO THIS PLACE, MS. KEELE.
I BELIEVE THAT YOU CAN DO A THING HERE YOU MIGHT NOT EASILY DO ELSEWHERE.
You are the story you tell yourself, but that is not all you are capable of being.
That story can change.
I DIDN'T COME ALL THE WAY FROM STUFFYTOWN FOR THIS!
FIG, WE NEED TO GO!
YOU SAY ANOTHER WORD AND I'LL TEAR OUT YOUR STUFFING, RABBIT-BOY!
You have in you a mad and mighty genius, a king and a queen, a virtuoso.
You contain within your skin glory and light and might beyond imagining.
All you need is the right moment to bring it out of you.
monsters / the goblin king / baby universes / problem solved / the fix / what you need vs. what you want / three guys walk into a bar
Safe as Houses Part 5 of 5
Werther Dell'Edera: pencils
José Marzán, Jr.: inks

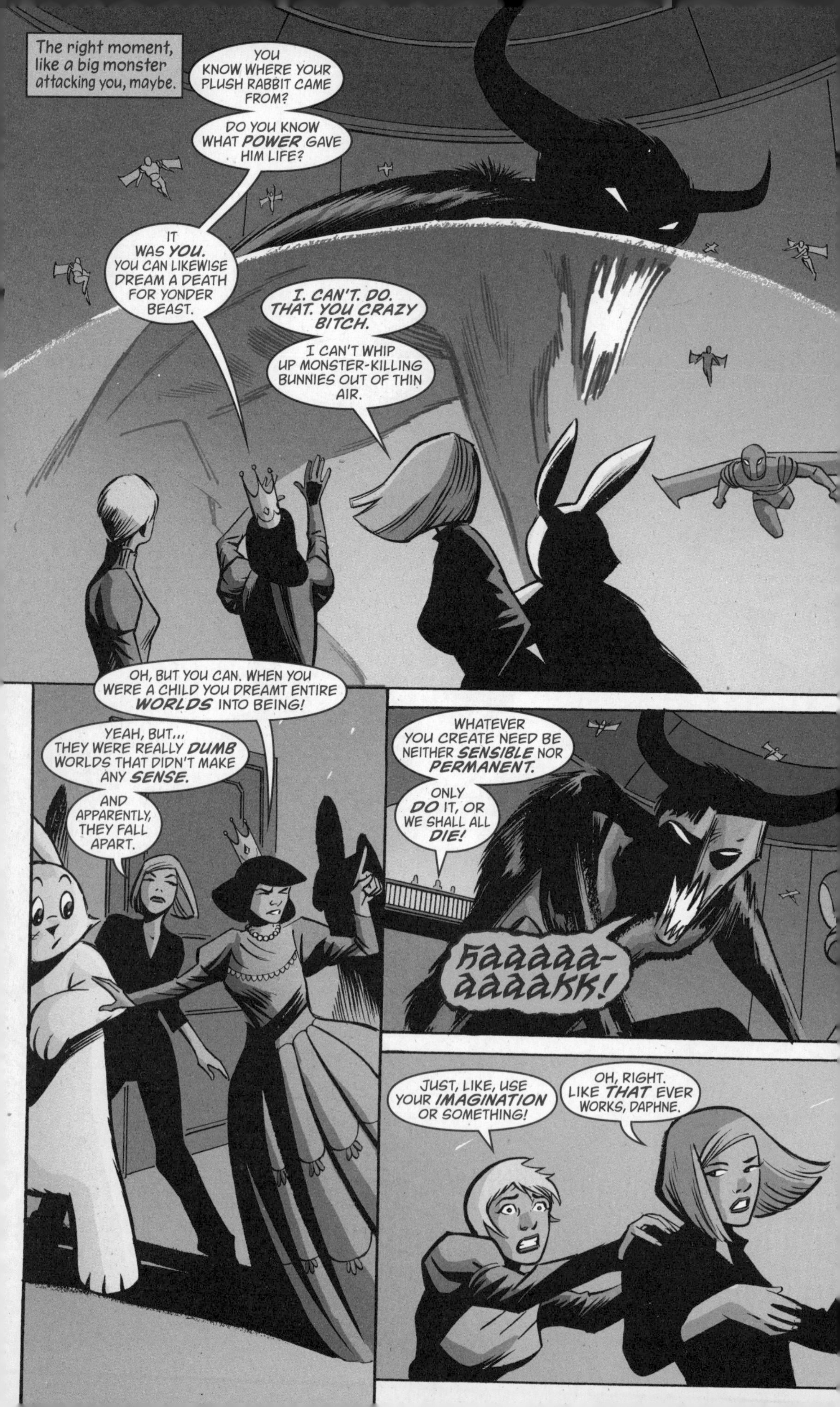
The right moment, like a big monster attacking you, maybe.
YOU KNOW WHERE YOUR PLUSH RABBIT CAME FROM?
DO YOU KNOW WHAT POWER GAVE HIM LIFE?
IT WAS YOU. YOU CAN LIKEWISE DREAM A DEATH FOR YONDER BEAST.
I. CAN'T. DO. THAT. YOU CRAZY BITCH.
I CAN'T WHIP UP MONSTER-KILLING BUNNIES OUT OF THIN AIR.
OH, BUT YOU CAN. WHEN YOU WERE A CHILD YOU DREAMT ENTIRE WORLDS INTO BEING!
YEAH, BUT... THEY WERE REALLY DUMB WORLDS THAT DIDN'T MAKE ANY SENSE.
AND APPARENTLY, THEY FALL APART.
WHATEVER YOU CREATE NEED BE NEITHER SENSIBLE NOR PERMANENT.
ONLY DO IT, OR WE SHALL ALL DIE!
HAAAAA-AAAAKK!
JUST, LIKE, USE YOUR IMAGINATION OR SOMETHING!
OH, RIGHT. LIKE THAT EVER WORKS, DAPHNE.

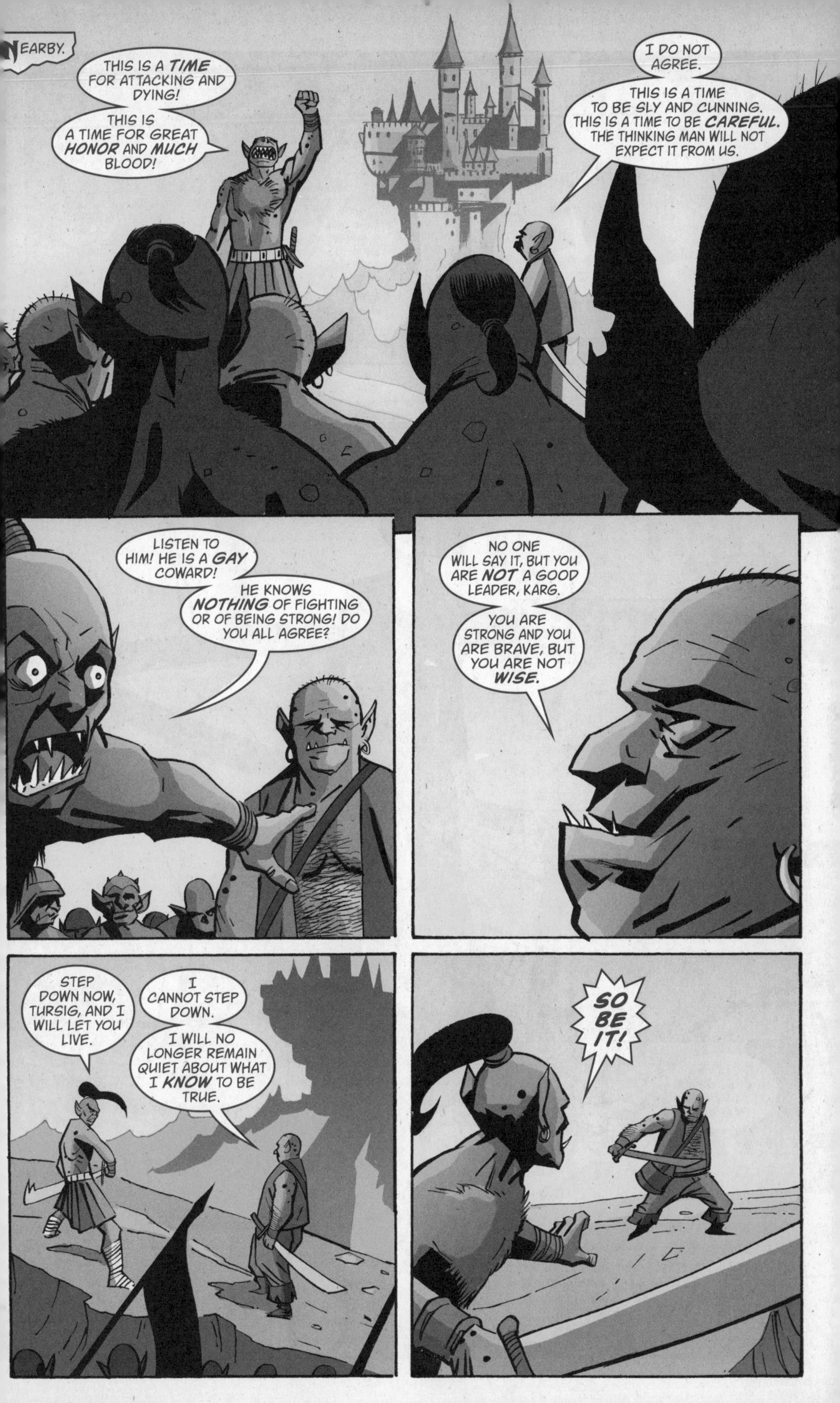
NEARBY.
THIS IS A TIME FOR ATTACKING AND DYING!
THIS IS A TIME FOR GREAT HONOR AND MUCH BLOOD!
I DO NOT AGREE.
THIS IS A TIME TO BE SLY AND CUNNING. THIS IS A TIME TO BE CAREFUL. THE THINKING MAN WILL NOT EXPECT IT FROM US.
LISTEN TO HIM! HE IS A GAY COWARD!
HE KNOWS NOTHING OF FIGHTING OR OF BEING STRONG! DO YOU ALL AGREE?
NO ONE WILL SAY IT, BUT YOU ARE NOT A GOOD LEADER, KARG.
YOU ARE STRONG AND YOU ARE BRAVE, BUT YOU ARE NOT WISE.
STEP DOWN NOW, TURSIG, AND I WILL LET YOU LIVE.
I CANNOT STEP DOWN.
I WILL NO LONGER REMAIN QUIET ABOUT WHAT I KNOW TO BE TRUE.
SO BE IT!

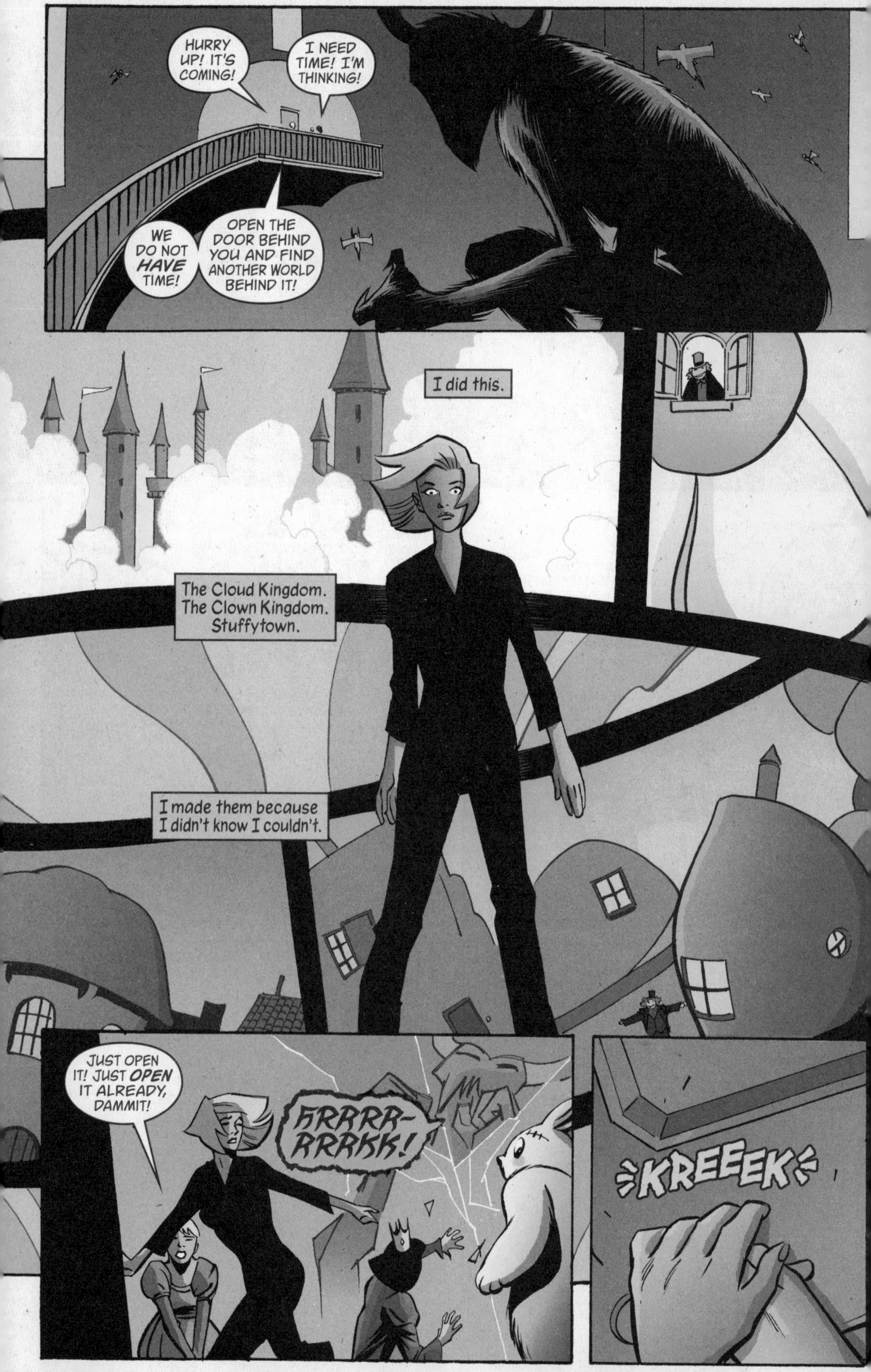
HURRY UP! IT'S COMING!
I NEED TIME! I'M THINKING!
WE DO NOT HAVE TIME!
OPEN THE DOOR BEHIND YOU AND FIND ANOTHER WORLD BEHIND IT!
I did this.
The Cloud Kingdom. The Clown Kingdom. Stuffytown.
I made them because I didn't know I couldn't.
JUST OPEN IT! JUST OPEN IT ALREADY, DAMMIT!
HRRRR-RRRKK!
KREEEK

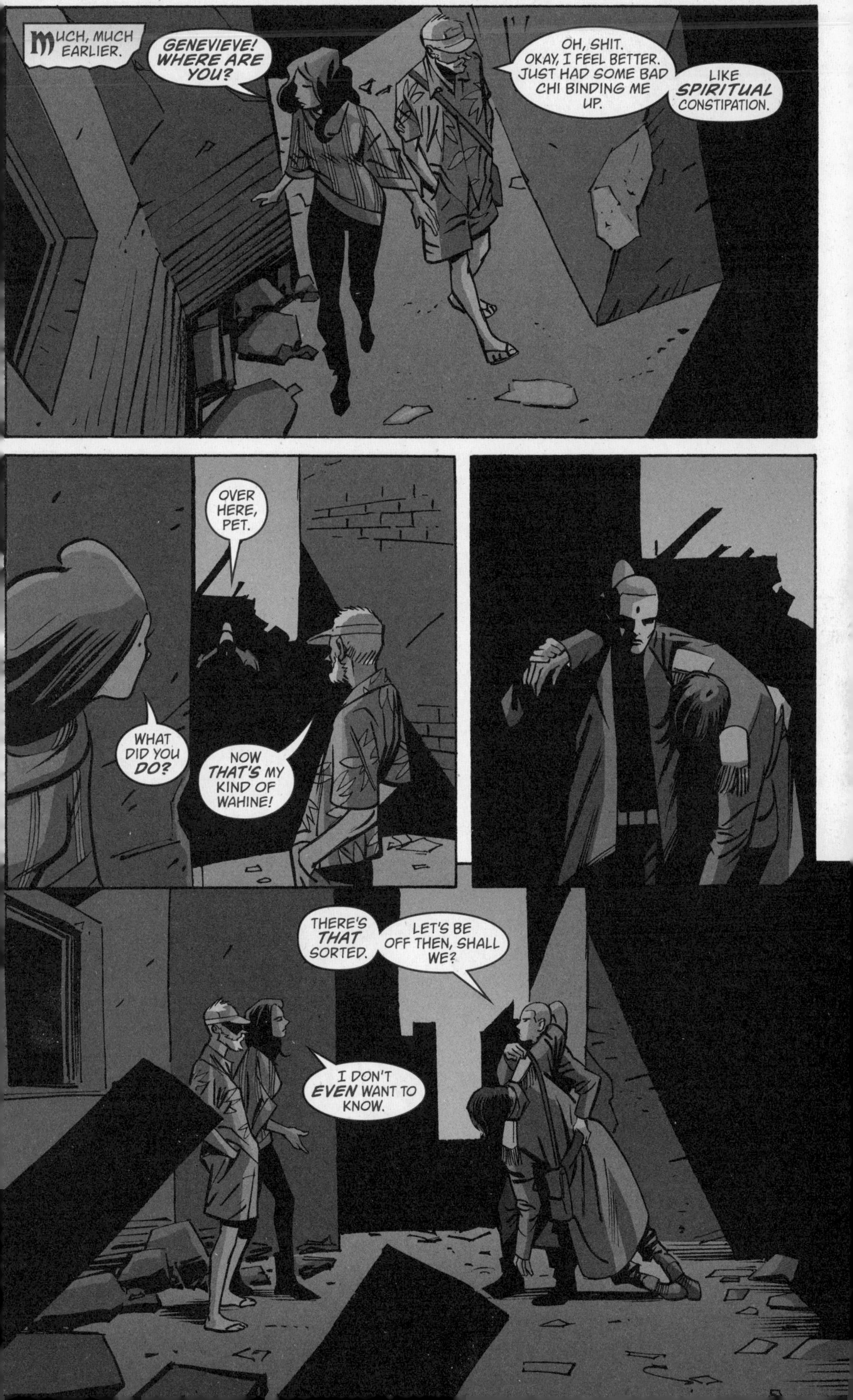
MUCH, MUCH EARLIER.
GENEVIEVE! WHERE ARE YOU?
OH, SHIT. OKAY, I FEEL BETTER. JUST HAD SOME BAD CHI BINDING ME UP.
LIKE SPIRITUAL CONSTIPATION.
OVER HERE, PET.
WHAT DID YOU DO?
NOW THAT'S MY KIND OF WAHINE!
THERE'S THAT SORTED.
LET'S BE OFF THEN, SHALL WE?
I DON'T EVEN WANT TO KNOW.

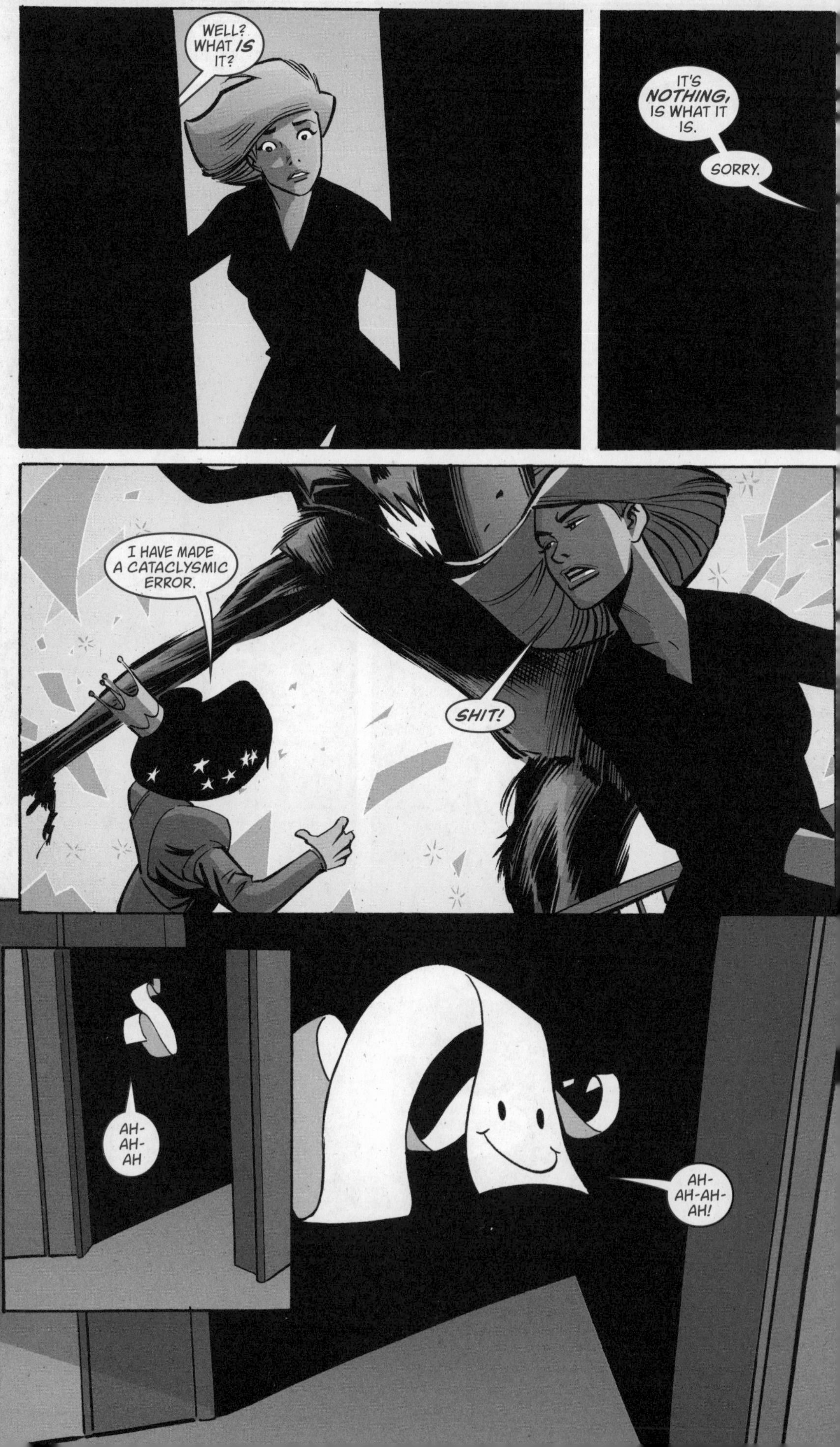
WELL? WHAT IS IT?
IT'S NOTHING, IS WHAT IT IS.
SORRY.
I HAVE MADE A CATACLYSMIC ERROR.
SHIT!
AH- AH- AH
AH- AH-AH- AH!

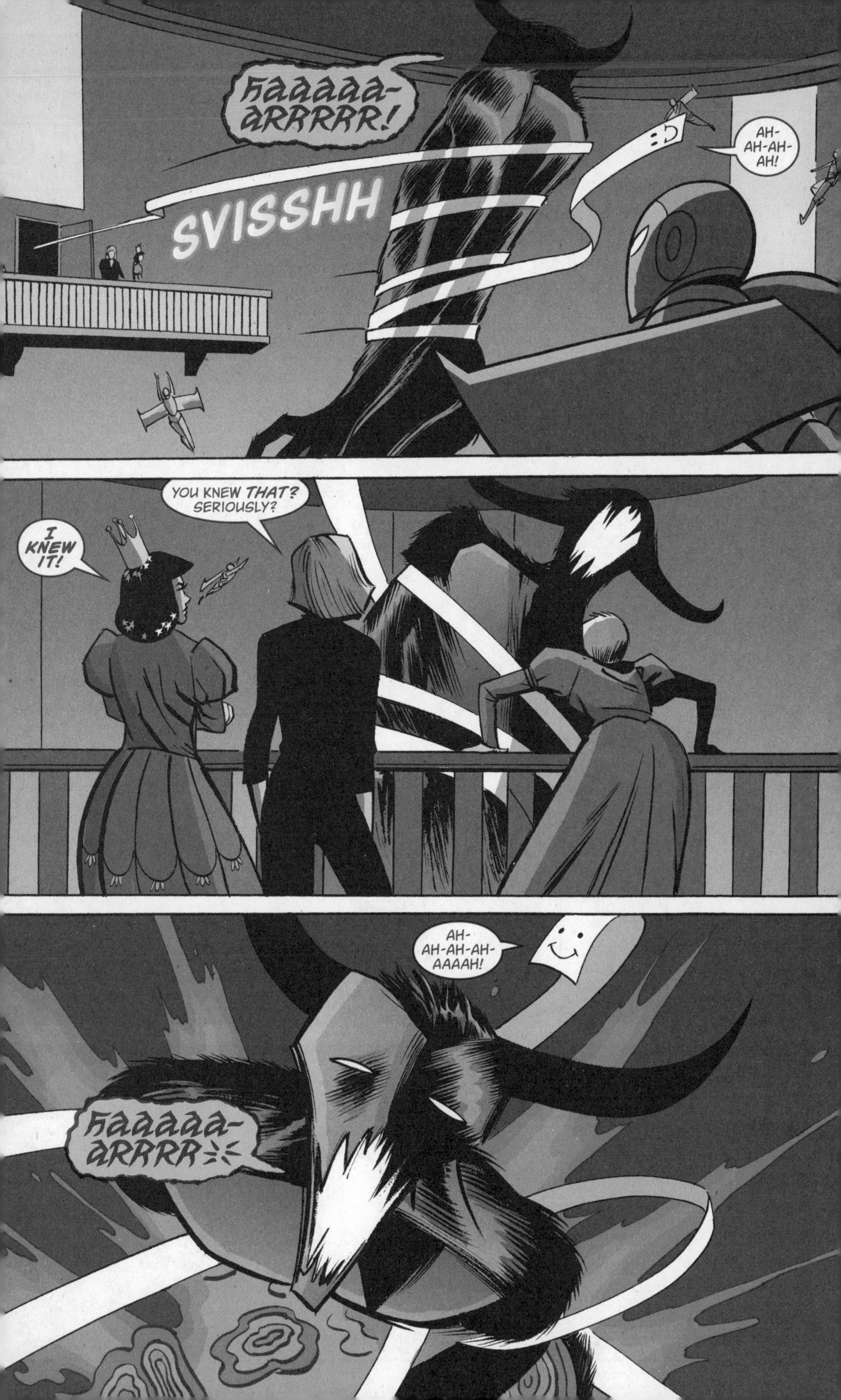
HAAAAA-ARRRRR!
SVISSHH
AH-AH-AH-AH!
I KNEW IT!
YOU KNEW THAT? SERIOUSLY?
AH-AH-AH-AH-AAAAH!
HAAAAA-ARRRR

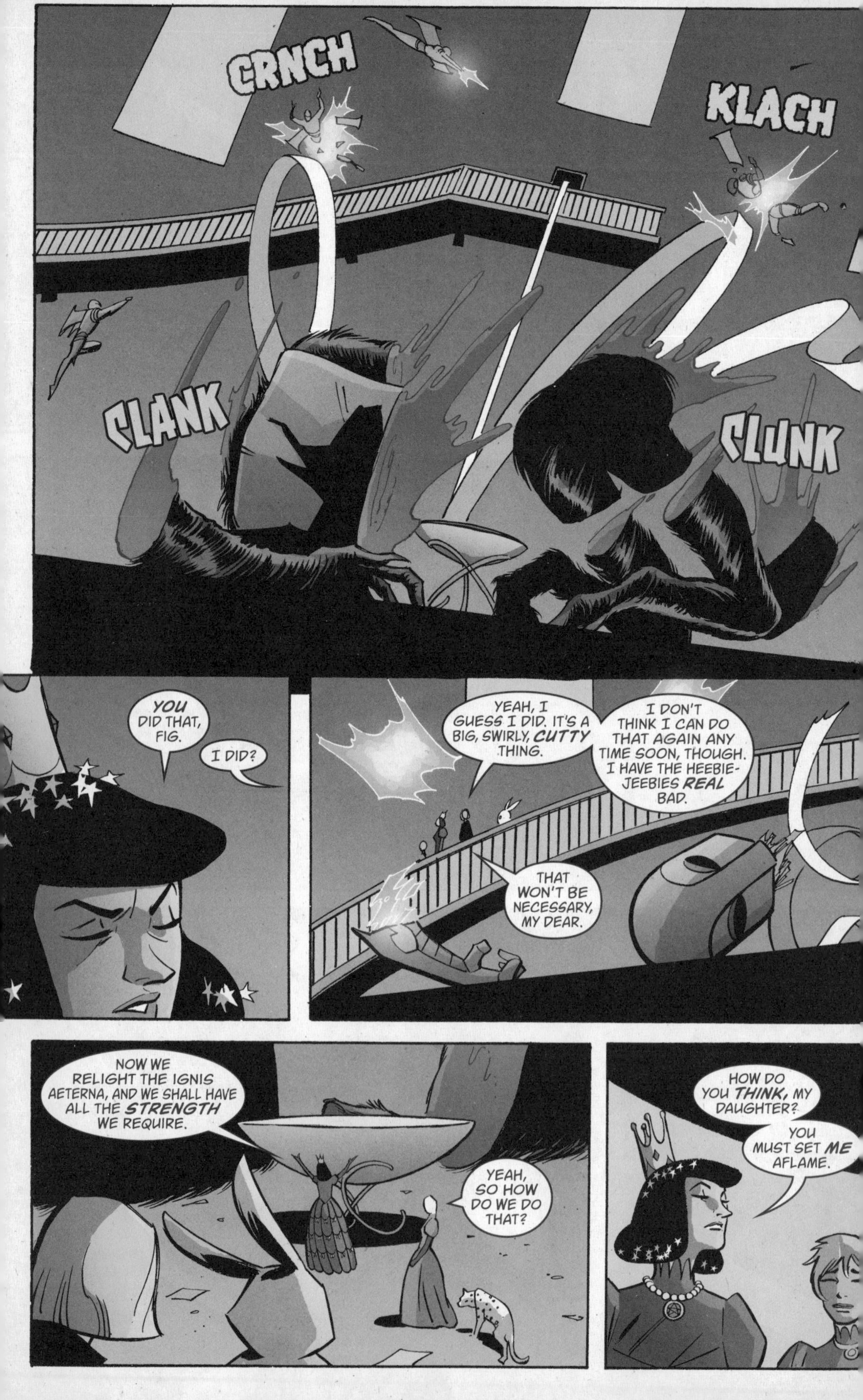
CRNCH
KLACH
CLANK
CLUNK
YOU DID THAT, FIG.
I DID?
YEAH, I GUESS I DID. IT'S A BIG, SWIRLY, CUTTY THING.
I DON'T THINK I CAN DO THAT AGAIN ANY TIME SOON, THOUGH. I HAVE THE HEEBIE-JEEBIES REAL BAD.
THAT WON'T BE NECESSARY, MY DEAR.
NOW WE RELIGHT THE IGNIS AETERNA, AND WE SHALL HAVE ALL THE STRENGTH WE REQUIRE.
YEAH, SO HOW DO WE DO THAT?
HOW DO YOU THINK, MY DAUGHTER?
YOU MUST SET ME AFLAME.

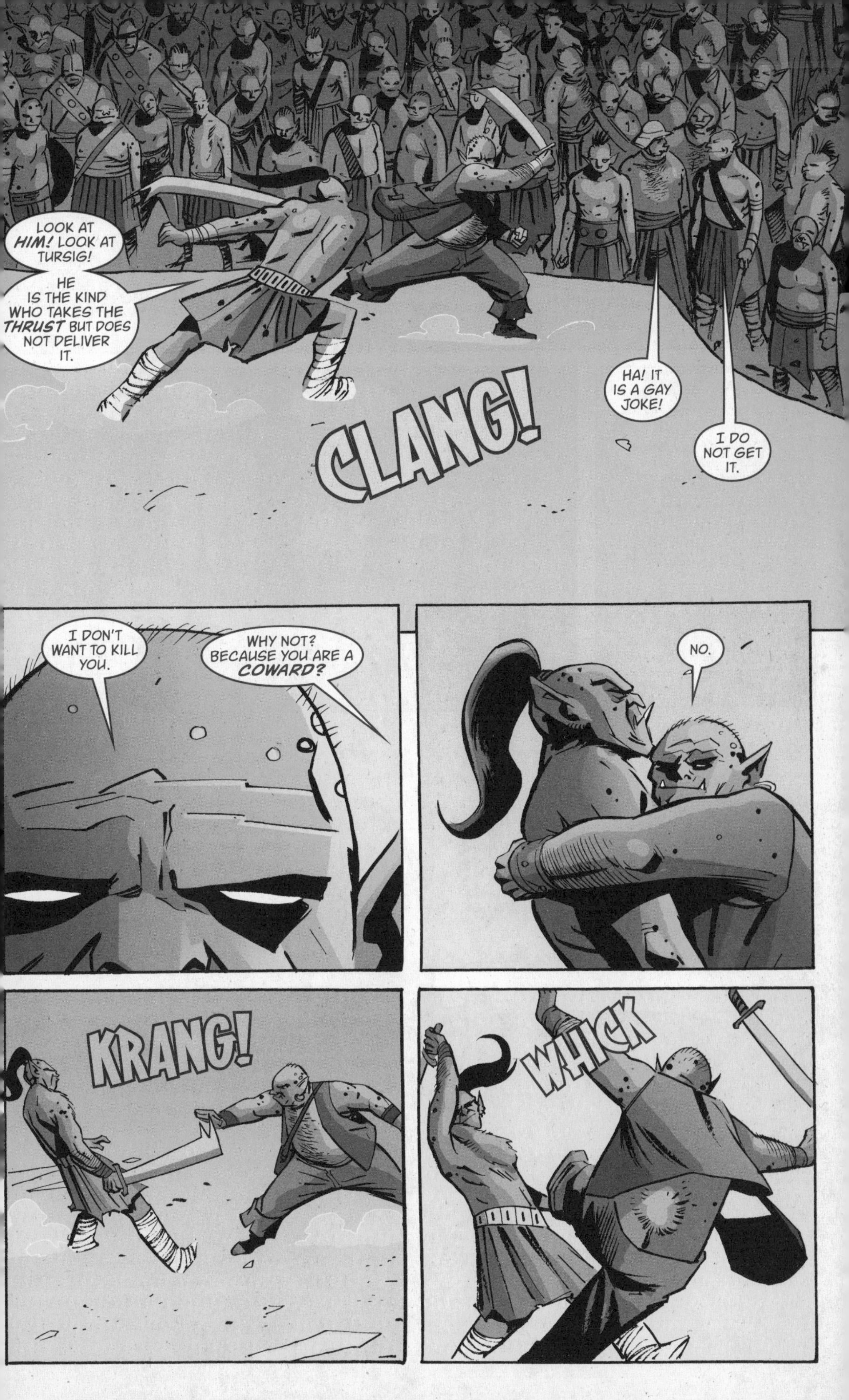
LOOK AT *HIM!* LOOK AT TURSIG!
HE IS THE KIND WHO TAKES THE *THRUST* BUT DOES NOT DELIVER IT.
HA! IT IS A GAY JOKE!
I DO NOT GET IT.
CLANG!
I DON'T WANT TO KILL YOU.
WHY NOT? BECAUSE YOU ARE A *COWARD?*
NO.
KRANG!
WHICK

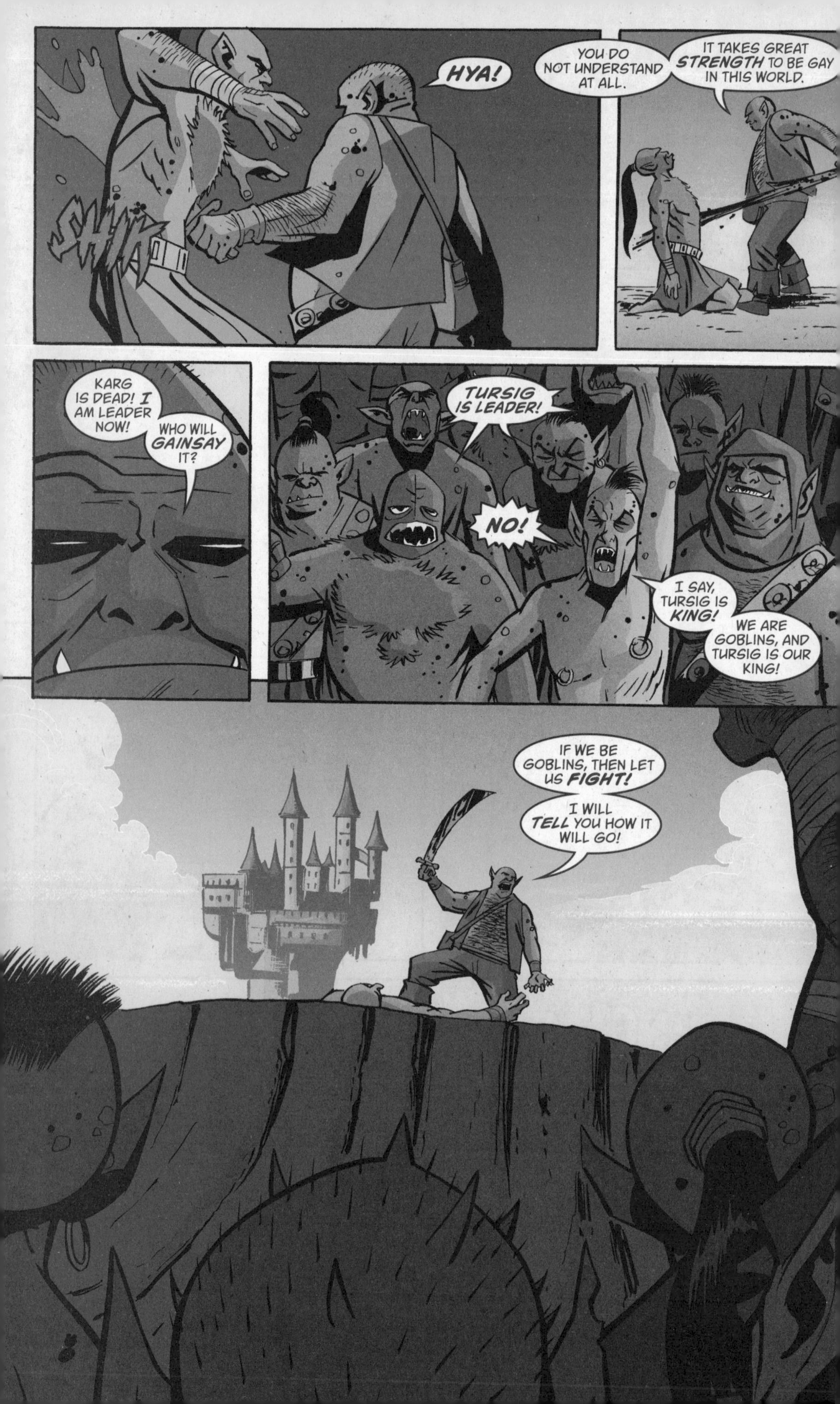

SHIK
HYA!
YOU DO NOT UNDERSTAND AT ALL.
IT TAKES GREAT STRENGTH TO BE GAY IN THIS WORLD.
KARG IS DEAD! I AM LEADER NOW!
WHO WILL GAINSAY IT?
TURSIG IS LEADER!
NO!
I SAY, TURSIG IS KING!
WE ARE GOBLINS, AND TURSIG IS OUR KING!
IF WE BE GOBLINS, THEN LET US FIGHT!
I WILL TELL YOU HOW IT WILL GO!

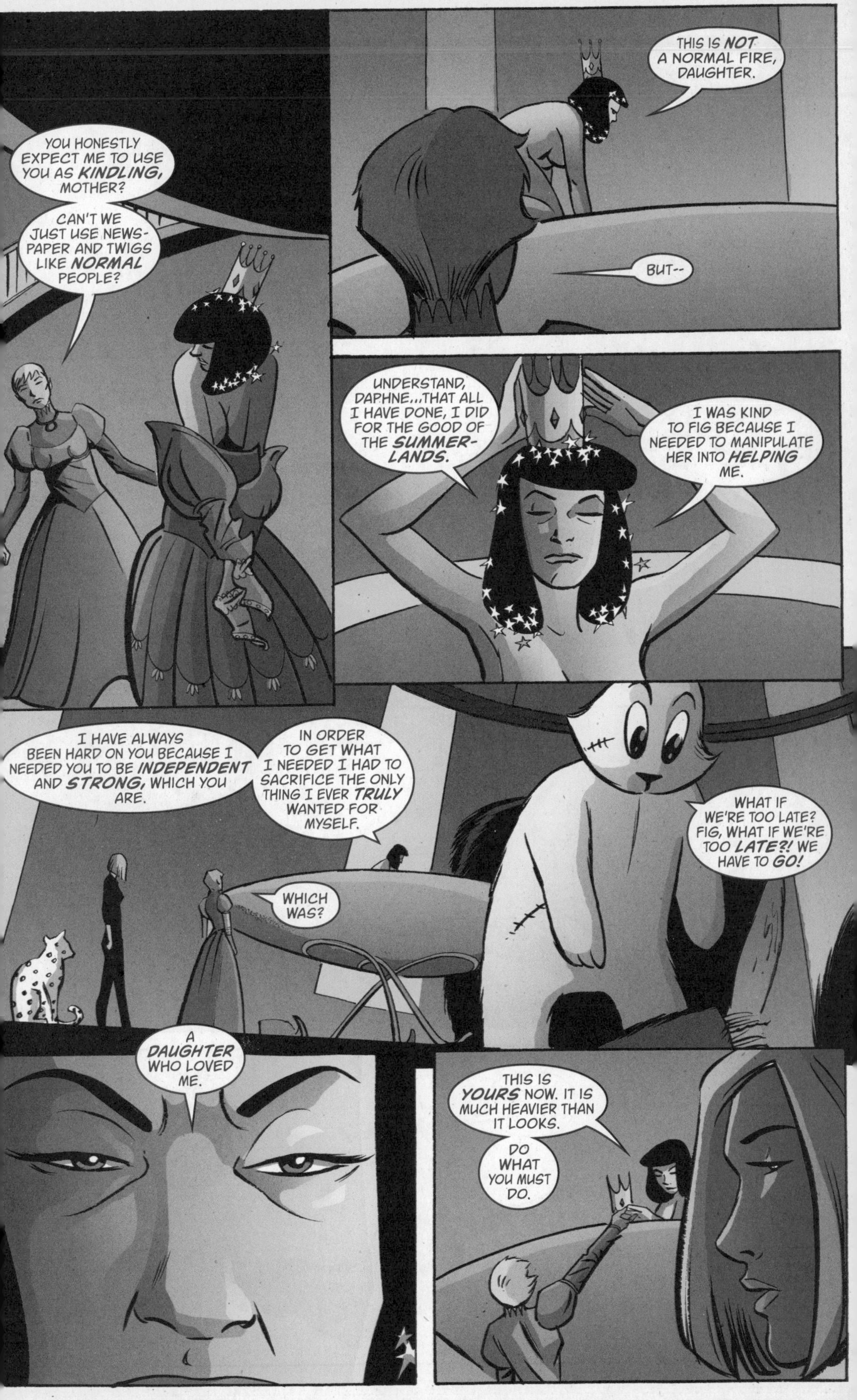
YOU HONESTLY EXPECT ME TO USE YOU AS KINDLING, MOTHER?
CAN'T WE JUST USE NEWS-PAPER AND TWIGS LIKE NORMAL PEOPLE?
THIS IS NOT A NORMAL FIRE, DAUGHTER.
BUT--
UNDERSTAND, DAPHNE...THAT ALL I HAVE DONE, I DID FOR THE GOOD OF THE SUMMER-LANDS.
I WAS KIND TO FIG BECAUSE I NEEDED TO MANIPULATE HER INTO HELPING ME.
I HAVE ALWAYS BEEN HARD ON YOU BECAUSE I NEEDED YOU TO BE INDEPENDENT AND STRONG, WHICH YOU ARE.
IN ORDER TO GET WHAT I NEEDED I HAD TO SACRIFICE THE ONLY THING I EVER TRULY WANTED FOR MYSELF.
WHICH WAS?
WHAT IF WE'RE TOO LATE? FIG, WHAT IF WE'RE TOO LATE?! WE HAVE TO GO!
A DAUGHTER WHO LOVED ME.
THIS IS YOURS NOW. IT IS MUCH HEAVIER THAN IT LOOKS.
DO WHAT YOU MUST DO.

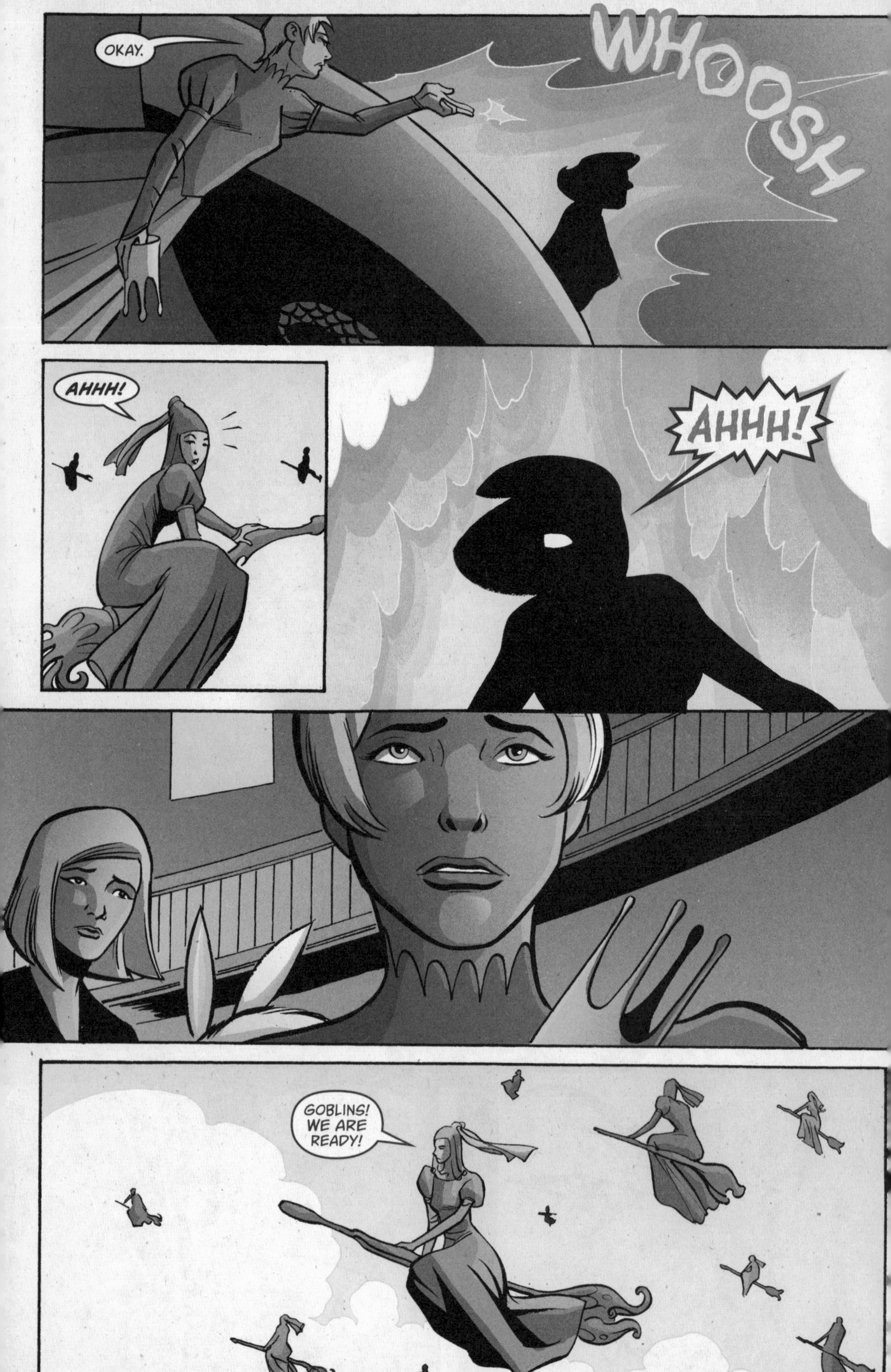
OKAY.
WHOOSH
AHHH!
AHHH!
GOBLINS! WE ARE READY!

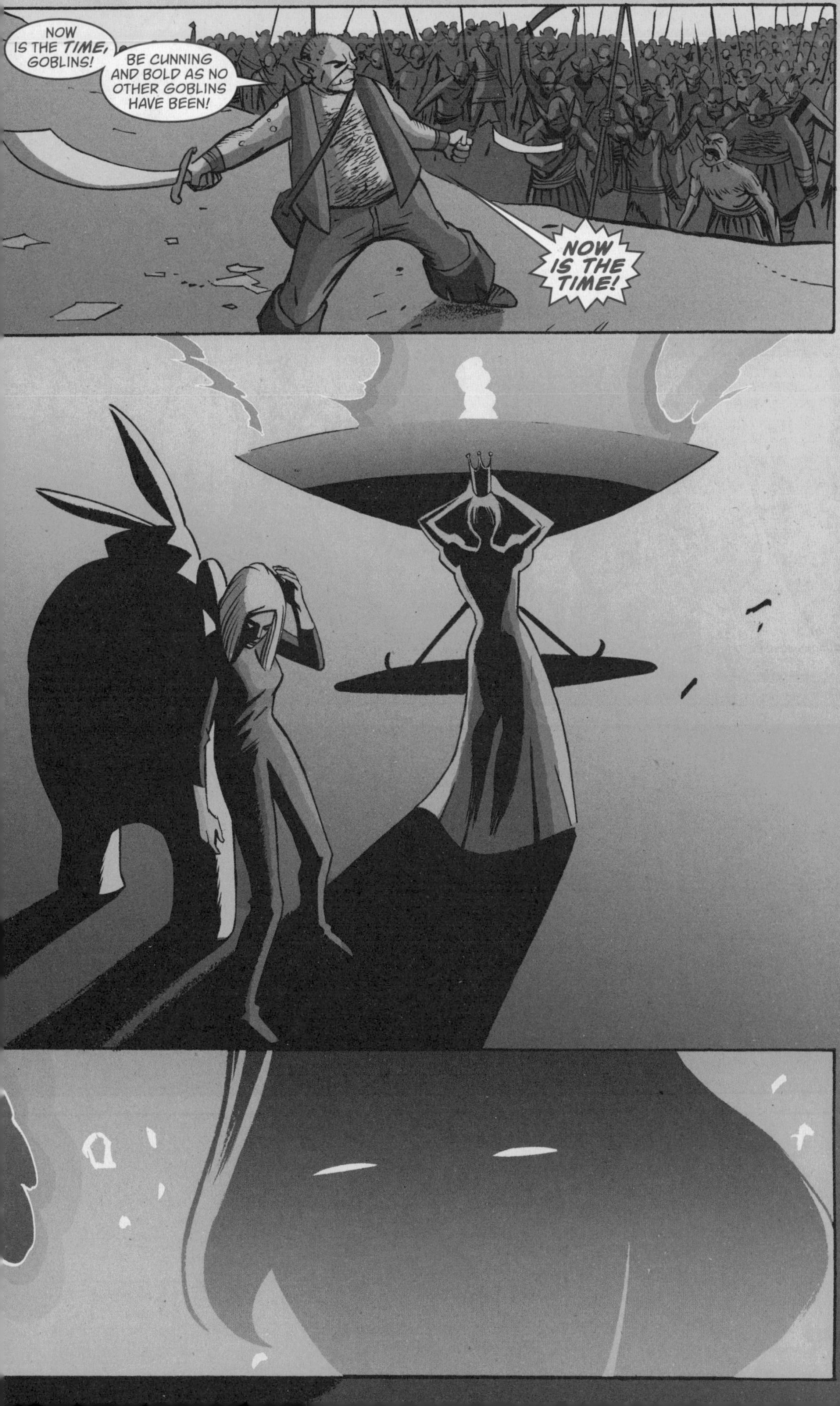
NOW IS THE *TIME,* GOBLINS!
BE CUNNING AND BOLD AS NO OTHER GOBLINS HAVE BEEN!
NOW IS THE TIME!

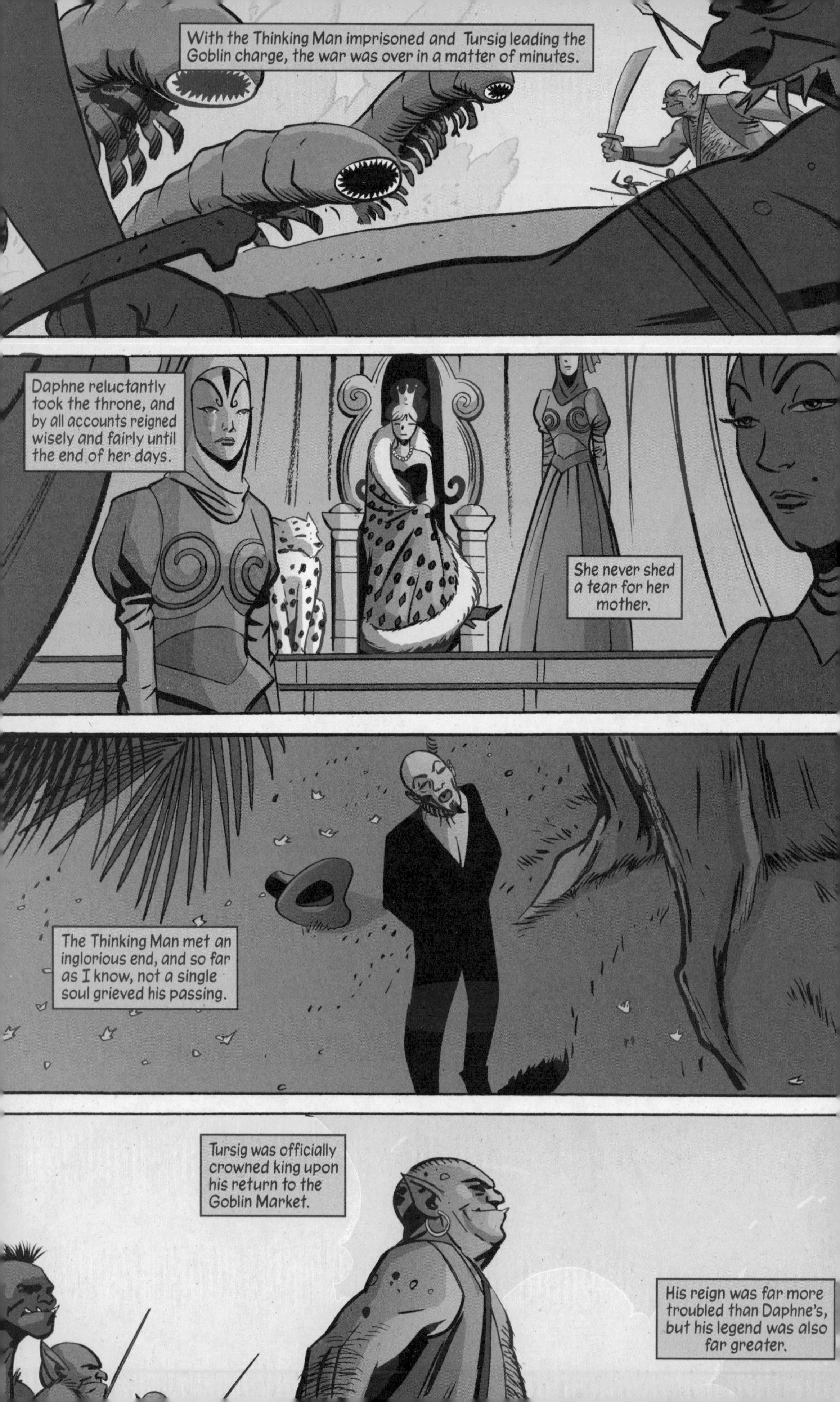

With the Thinking Man imprisoned and Tursig leading the Goblin charge, the war was over in a matter of minutes.
Daphne reluctantly took the throne, and by all accounts reigned wisely and fairly until the end of her days.
She never shed a tear for her mother.
The Thinking Man met an inglorious end, and so far as I know, not a single soul grieved his passing.
Tursig was officially crowned king upon his return to the Goblin Market.
His reign was far more troubled than Daphne's, but his legend was also far greater.

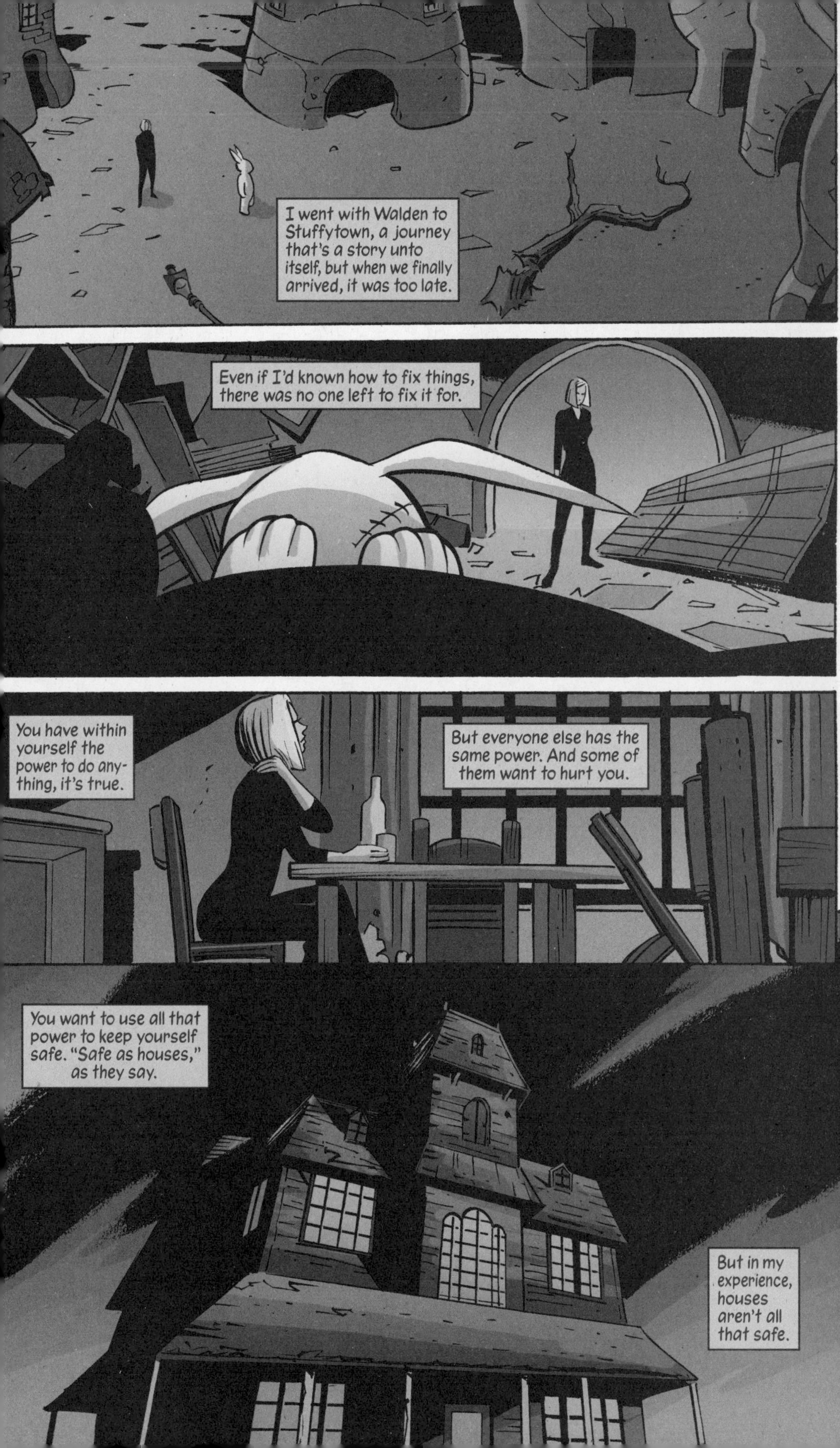
I went with Walden to Stuffytown, a journey that's a story unto itself, but when we finally arrived, it was too late.
Even if I'd known how to fix things, there was no one left to fix it for.
You have within yourself the power to do any-thing, it's true.
But everyone else has the same power. And some of them want to hurt you.
You want to use all that power to keep yourself safe. "Safe as houses," as they say.
But in my experience, houses aren't all that safe.

I believe that your name in large part determines who you are. If your name is Timothy, it means you're probably very tidy. If your middle name is Wayne, it means you are probably a serial killer. If your name is Nancy, it means you are kindly and bland. And if your name is Lotus Blossom Mackenzie, as mine is, it means you will die a virgin.

How I came to have my name is this: my parents publish a magazine that extols the virtues of hemp. That tells you everything you need to know about them; let us never speak of it again.

Some quick facts about me. My habitat: Costa Buena, California. My current predicament: High School. My grade: sophomore. The number of friends that I have: zero. I blame my lack of friends on the low quality of public education. A more enlightened system would give me the attention that I deserve. It would also base my grades on the content of my mind, not the quality of my assignments.

The attention intended for me has, erroneously, been lavished on a girl named Heather Webb. If your name is Heather it generally means that you are an evil bitch who deserves to die. So why is Heather popular and not me? This is one of the great unanswered questions in life. It may have something to do with her breasts. In addition to her breasts (perhaps, one assumes, because of them), Heather also has Austin Porter.

I am not in love with Austin Porter. I have no interest whatsoever in seeing him shirtless, running my fingers through his wavy hair, or biting his shoulder. These rumors are utter fabrications and should be summarily ignored. Though I will add without comment that if your name is Austin, it means that you are a Greek god with piercing blue eyes.

Now I am in Algebra class. Algebra is an excellent metaphor for life in that it is both pointless and uninteresting, and in that I am unsuccessful at it. At the end of life you don't die, you simply solve for x. I am sitting in Algebra class, back straight, pen out, doodling in the margin of my notebook. Around me are not other teenagers, but little squirrels. Little chattery squirrels with cell phones in their little hands, texting as though their lives depend on it. Text text text. Their tiny minds are so empty; I have no idea what they could possibly have to text about so much. Today the squirrels are texting even more than normal. I can hear the rit-tit-tit of fingers scrabbling over tiny keyboards from every direction.

My own cell phone surprises me by making the tiny blippy noise it presumably makes when I receive a text.

I reach slowly into my purse, as though reading a text is the most natural thing on earth for me. A brief fantasy in which I have received clever and amorous message from Austin Porter plays out in feverish double time in my mind, spinning off in several unspeakable variations before my hand closes on the phone. I pick up the phone. I open it. Time stops. It's a photo of me.

Well, sort of. The image has clearly been Photoshopped within an inch of its life. It contains a number of clear factual errors. For one thing, the girl has a tattoo on her neck, which I clearly do not have. She also has breasts, which I very clearly do not have. Trust me when I say there is nothing going on down there. If I could swap my grade average for my cup size, half of my problems would be solved. There is also a horse in the image. Let us walk no further down that road.

I close my phone and replace it in my purse, the epitome of poise. I try to look straight ahead, but some kind of malignant magnetism drags my gaze backward, over my classmates, all of whom are either looking at me or pretending not to. It grows hot, here in the place where Algebra is done. The skin on my face is prickling. My eyes find their target in the back row. Heather Webb is smiling at me. She blows me a kiss. Next to her, Austin Porter is shrugging at me, suppressing a smile.

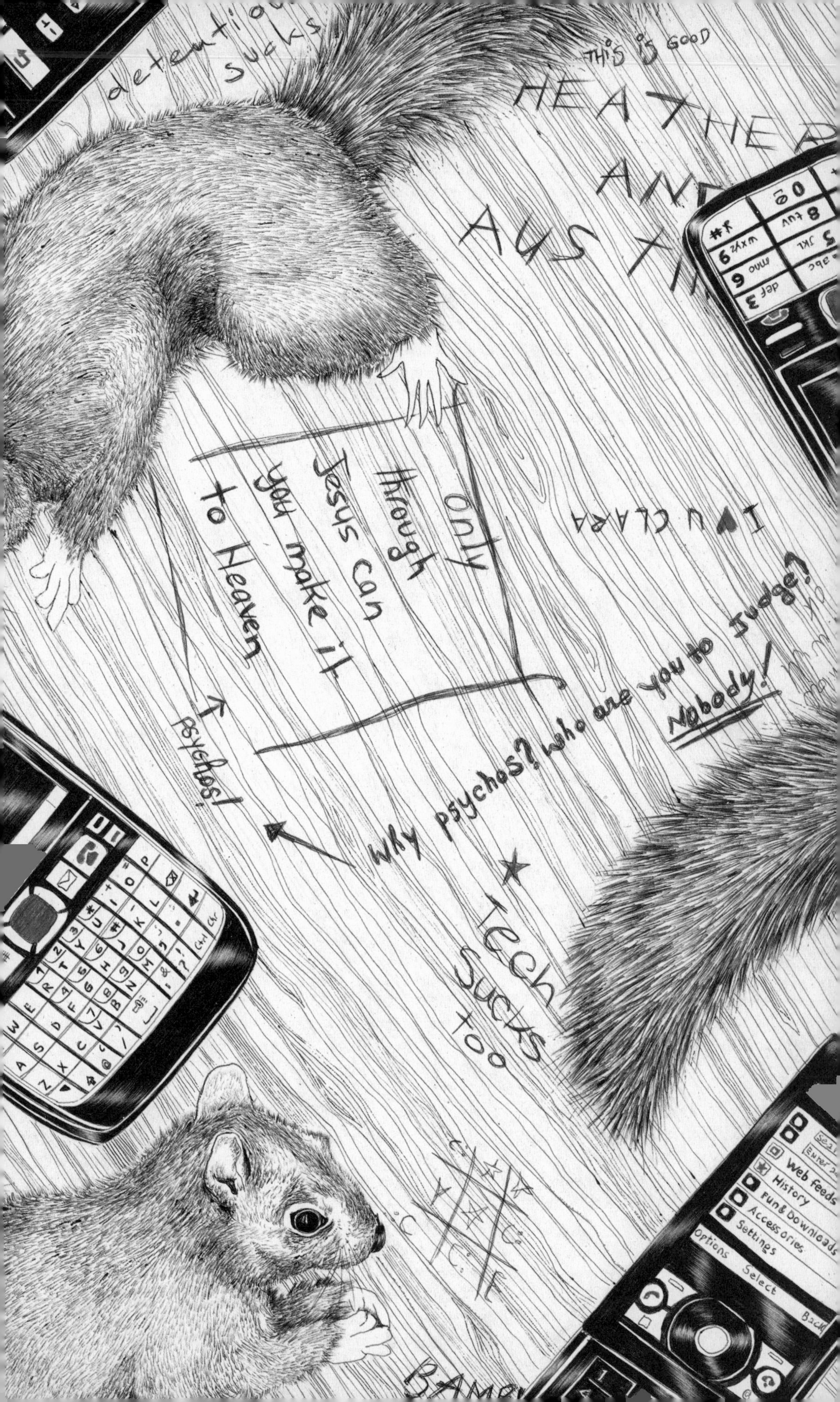

detention sucks
THIS IS GOOD
only through Jesus can you make it to Heaven
psychos!
Why psychos? who are you to judge?
Nobody!
TECH SUCKS too
Web feeds
History
Fun & Downloads
Accessories
Settings
Options
Select
Back

Heather mouths the words, "It sucks to be you." I dearly want to solve Heather Webb for x.

That evening I walk out to the beach, where my grandfather lives in an old RV. A 1967 Winnebago F-19 motor home, to be precise. My grandfather, Mack, is perversely proud of it. It has green shag carpet and matching vinyl interior. It smells musty. The cabinets are full of strange, wonderful, secret things. I love it.

Mack, I should mention, is a sorcerer. He's not the robe-wearing, pointy-hat kind. He says those guys are pretentious dickheads, and who can argue. When I poke my head in the Winnebago, Mack's wearing Bermuda shorts, a wife-beater, and a gimme cap that reads FUCK REAGAN.

"What's the word, bird?" says Mack, after releasing a hit from the largest bong that has surely ever been created by mankind.

"I need a spell," I say. "A spell that will murder everyone in my entire school in hideous, graphic, and painful ways that I will describe for you now."

Mack smiles in a kindly, grandfatherly way. "Something happen at school?"

I relay the events of the day, using any number of choice expletives, any of which would earn me an hour of mandatory meditation at home.

"Shit," says Mack, after a moment. "That Heather girl sounds like a real piece of work."

"She's just so fucking perfect," I say. "Everyone thinks she hung the moon."

"Nah," says Mack. "I know the guy that hung the moon. His name is Steve."

He takes a meditative bong hit, then jumps up. "I know!" he says. He starts rummaging through his cabinets, laying down foul-smelling ingredients on the tiny kitchenette counter. "You ever see that movie 'Freaky Friday'? With Barbara Harris? Man, that woman was a hot piece of ass."

"You want me to change bodies with my mother? Are you trying to get me to commit suicide?"

"Not your mom," he says. "This Heather Webb girl." He finds a mortar and pestle and starts grinding his ingredients with a vengeance. "You spend a day in her body, she spends a day in yours, and then you switch back and you've both learned a valuable lesson and all that happy crap."

He pauses. "That's a good idea, right? I don't just think it's a good idea because I'm baked?"

"Whuh," I say. "How does one go about doing such a thing?"

"Names," he says. "You just file the true names off and switch 'em around a little."

"Here," says Mack, once he's done. He hands me a little clay pot, full of some of the foulest-smelling shit you've ever encountered. "You get Heather Webb's true name, put it in here, and then go to sleep. When you wake up, you'll be switched. Then, twenty-four hours later, you smash the pot."

I reach for it, but he snatches it back. "No more than twenty-four hours, though," he says. "If you wait any longer than that, you'll start to forget you're you."

I take the pot and sniff it. "How do I get Heather's true name?" I say.

"Ah," says Mack. "For that you're going to need one more little ingredient."

The one more ingredient turns out to be one that only Heather Webb can provide. It takes me two days to get it. It's a body fluid, and not the good one. Get over it. The spell finally ready, I call my mother into my room before bed in order to prime the pump.

"What's wrong, little flower?" says Mom. My mom LOOKS like patchouli smells.

"It's Heather Webb," I say, fighting back alligator tears. "This girl from school. I can't stop thinking about her. Sometimes I want to be her so badly I can't stand it."

My mom's head almost explodes at the opportunity to give me some sound advice that I ignore. When she's done babbling I tell her that I'm tired and want to go to bed early. She kisses my forehead and finally gets the hell out of my room.

Once I'm sure she's gone and isn't coming back, I take the magic pot (which I have sealed in a trash bag) from under my bed and climb out my window. I walk to Heather Webb's house and peek in her bedroom window. She's there, brushing her hair, her expression blank. I watch her for longer than is healthy, and then when she turns out her light, I leave. I walk through the grabby cold air to the marina and hurl the pot into the ocean. Then I go home and get in bed, to wait. Sleep is dreamless.

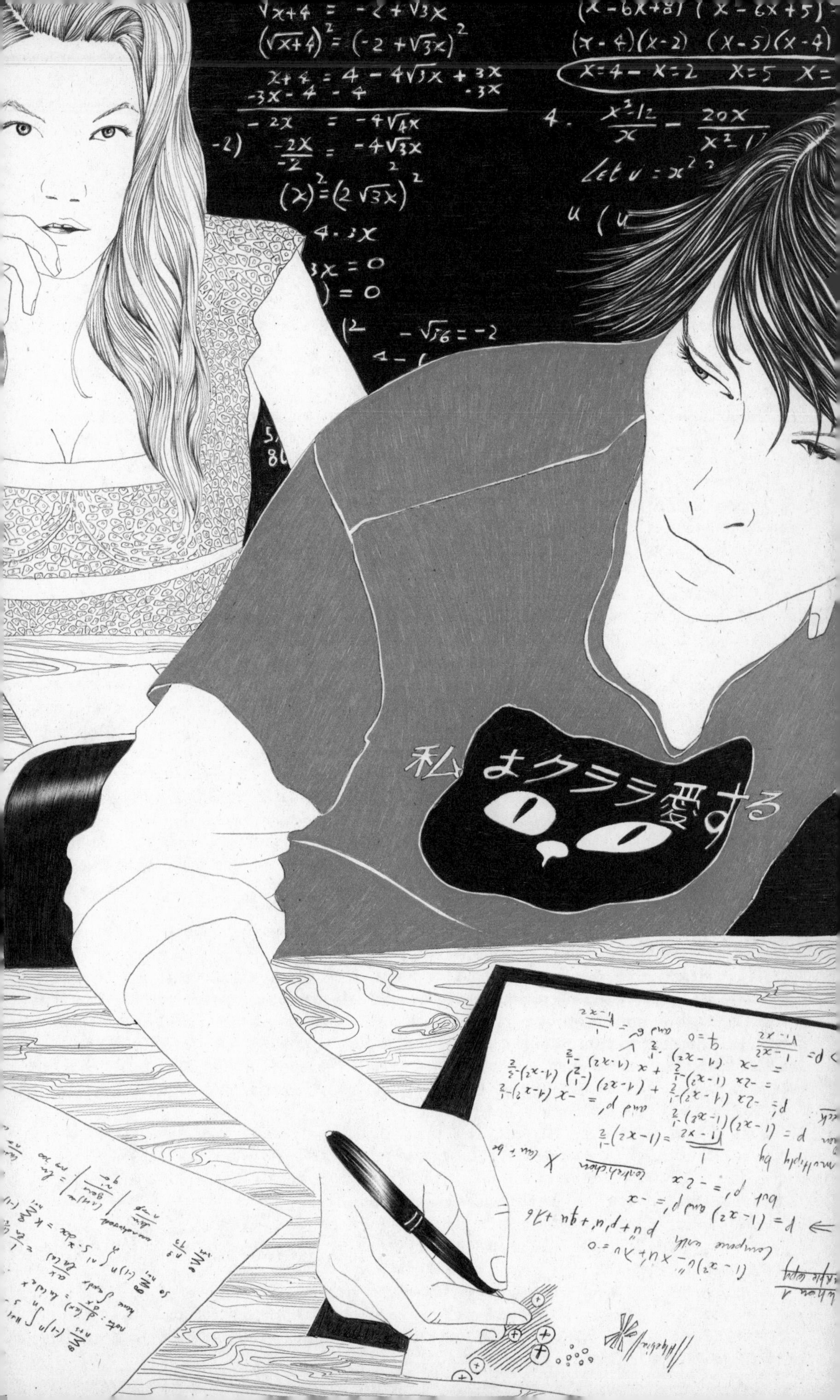

$(\sqrt{x+4})^2 = (-2+\sqrt{3x})^2$
$x+4 = 4 - 4\sqrt{3x} + 3x$
$(x-4)(x-2) \quad (x-5)(x-4)$
$x=4 \quad x=2 \quad x=5$
Let $u = x^2$
私 よクララ愛する

When I open my eyes my first thought is that I've fallen asleep with my contacts in, but the truth is that Heather Webb has perfect vision to go along with her perfect breasts. I pop out of bed and stand at Heather's (my) vanity mirror. Yup, I'm her all right. I'm pretty and normal. There's something in my eyes, though, that Heather doesn't have. A sharpness. No amount of squinting or deep breathing will make it go away.

Now I am Heather Webb. Now I have breasts, and friends, and Austin Porter.

While I am pondering the implications of this, my new cell phone rings. It's Cheyenne Hamish. If your name is Cheyenne, it means you're a vapid blonde girl who never stops chewing gum.

"Oh, my God," says Cheyenne. "I was just walking past Loser Blossom Mackenzie's house and there was a total scene."

"A scene?" I say, shocking myself with my new voice.

"I swear to fucking god they were dragging her out of her house on a stretcher. She was SCREAMING. It was some shit."

The appropriate Heather Webb's response to that? "What a drama queen," I deadpan.

Violent waves of Schadenfreude and satisfaction pulse through me. My mom, losing her shit. Heather, losing her shit. Everyone losing their collective shit over at my old house, and me at my new house laughing it up with good ol' Cheyenne Hamish

The doorbell rings. I end Cheyenne and trot to the door, noting that I'm alone in the house, which is good because I have no interest in encountering either of the elder Webbs. It's Austin, looking at me with lust in his eyes. I sense that he is interested in more than walking me to school. I am very okay with this. His tongue is already halfway down my throat before I realize the cataclysmic depths of the error I have made. This is my first kiss, but it isn't his. It isn't even his first kiss with me. It's not romantic, or even sexy. It's lewd. I want him far way. But the kissing is better than when the kissing stops because I realize I have no idea what to say to Austin Porter, or what he expects of me. I don't know him at all.

He, however, either doesn't notice or doesn't care, because we walk to school together without him batting an eye. He walks me all the way to my first period classroom and grabs my ass on the way out.

Everyone looks at Heather Webb. Nobody ever looked at Lotus Blossom Mackenzie. It's creepy. What's even creepier is how easy it is to become Heather Webb. Over the past few days I have studied her schedule, the way she walks and talks. I fall right into her rhythms without a single misstep. Cheyenne and Tamika and Naia don't notice a thing. I am she. I thought it would be harder. I thought I'd have to convince them, that they would be suspicious. It stings in an odd way that they aren't.

By lunch, the news of Lotus Blossom's breakdown has flooded the school. Better her than me, is all I can think. I feel vindicated.

Two days go by and none of the things I feared happening happen. Nobody at school sees through me. When I leave school, I go home to the right place. And all day long I am text text texting just like all the little squirrels around me. I have conquered Heather Webb's life in a totally bloodless coup.

On Friday I take the bus to Santa Clara, to pay Lotus Blossom Mackenzie a visit. I am a concerned schoolmate. I don't give my name as Heather Webb, of course, because it's common knowledge now that the poor girl has had a psychotic break and now has delusions that she's me. So that would be awkward. I say I'm Cheyenne Hamish and nobody asks for ID.

When I'm admitted to see her, it's in a bland, sprawling day room. She's sitting at a table watching daytime TV. I barely recognize her. When she sees me, her eyes widen, but she doesn't start screaming or throwing chairs. She mutters something. "Can't" or maybe "cunt." Either is acceptable.

I stare at her for a little bit. "It sucks to be you," I finally say.

Outside, there's a 1967 Winnebago F-19 parked near the bus stop. An old guy is leaning against the side, his arms crossed over his chest.

"What's the word, bird?" he says to me.

"I'm sorry," I say. "Have we met?" I walk past him to the bus stop.

He gives me a long look. Then he gets in the Winnebago and drives away without another word, and I wait for my bus.

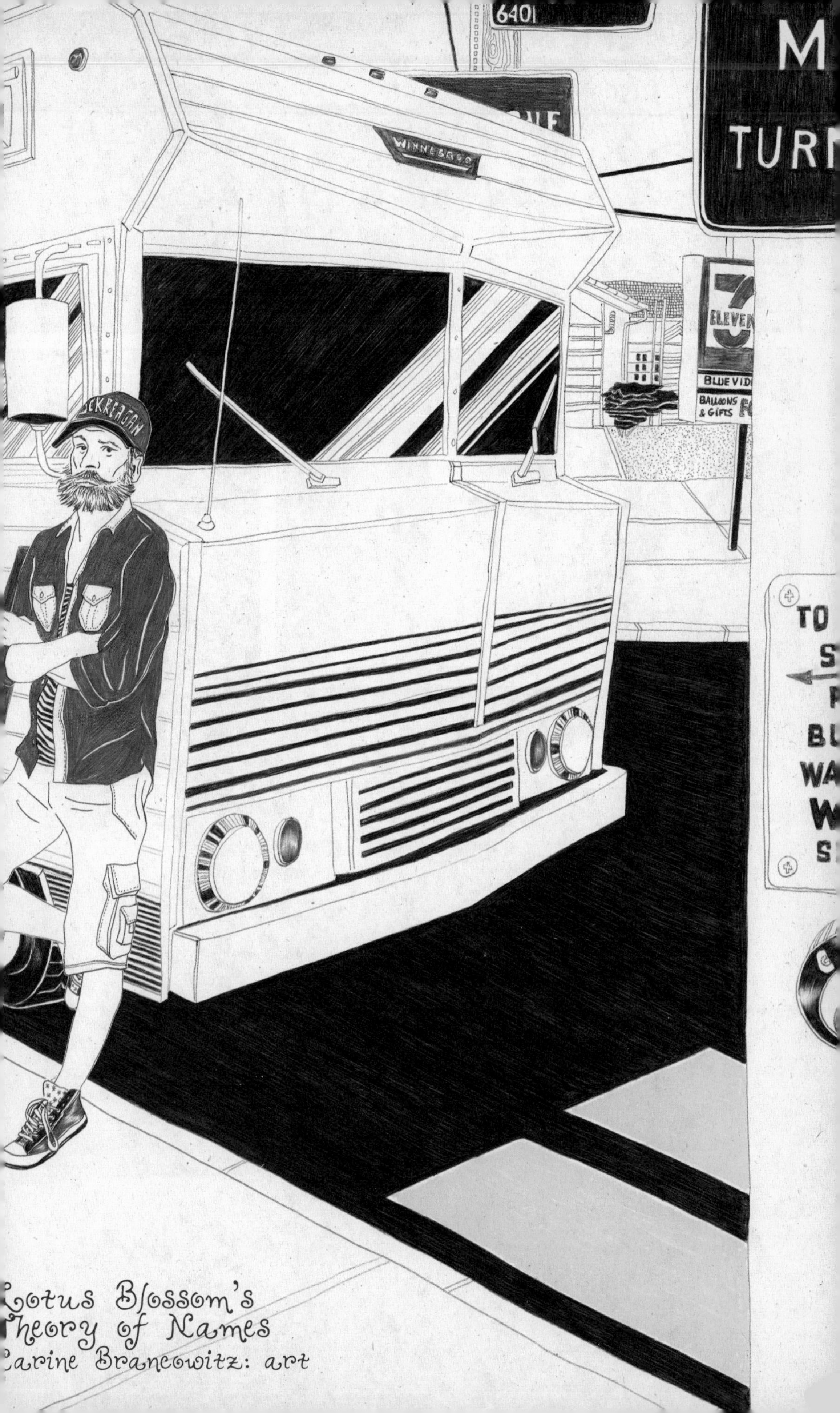
6401
WINNEBAGO
ELEVEN
BALLOONS & GIFTS
TO
Lotus Blossom's
Theory of Names
Carine Brancowitz: art

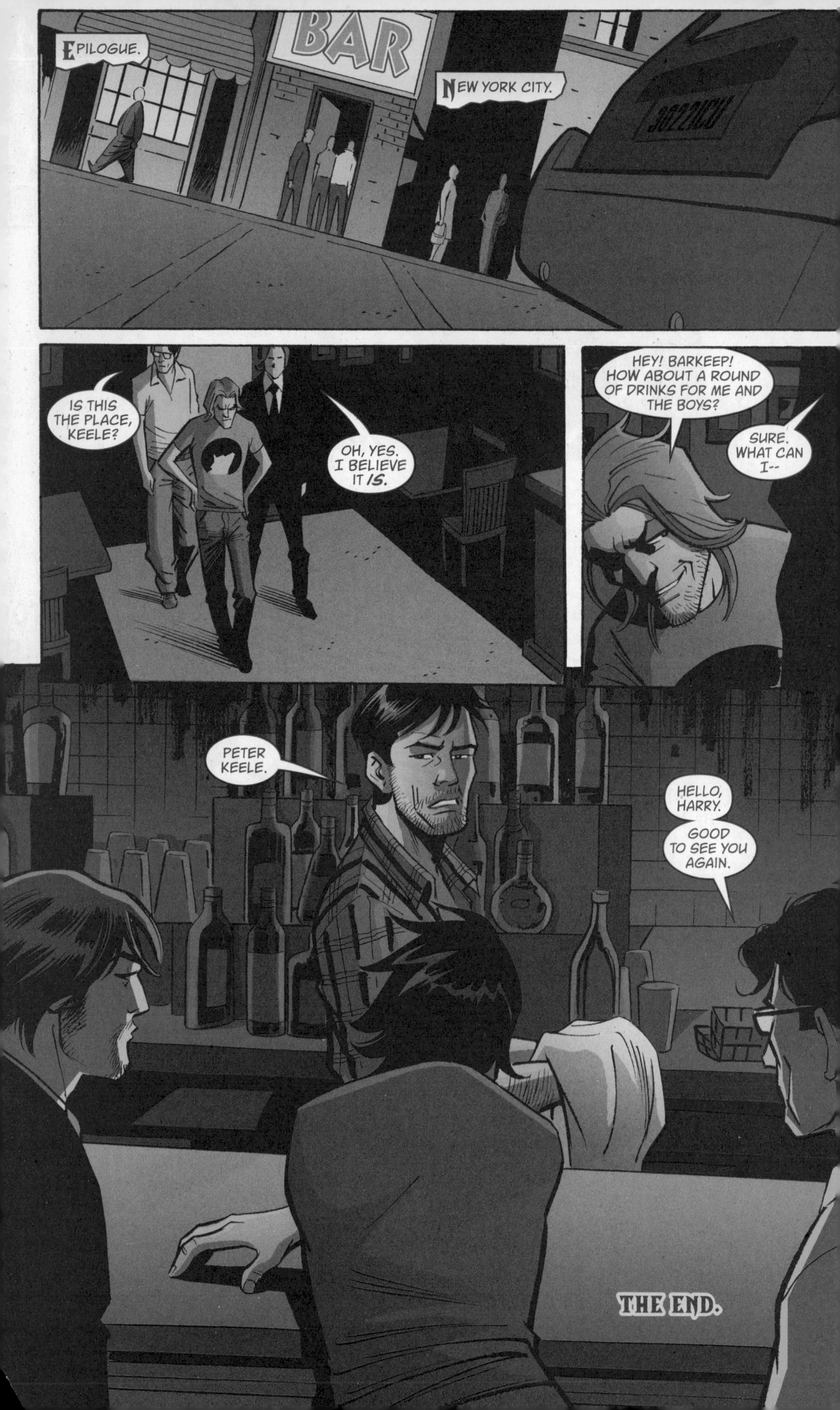
EPILOGUE.
BAR
NEW YORK CITY.
IS THIS THE PLACE, KEELE?
OH, YES. I BELIEVE IT IS.
HEY! BARKEEP! HOW ABOUT A ROUND OF DRINKS FOR ME AND THE BOYS?
SURE. WHAT CAN I--
PETER KEELE.
HELLO, HARRY.
GOOD TO SEE YOU AGAIN.
THE END.

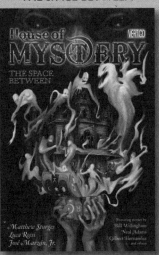

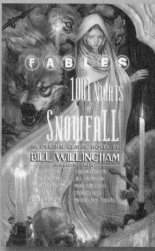